Lecture Notes in Economics and Mathematical Systems

Managing Editors: M. Beckmann and H. P. Künzi

147

Resource Allocation and Division of Space

Proceedings of an International Symposium
Held at Toba Near Nagoya, Japan
14–17 December, 1975

Edited by T. Fujii and R. Sato

Springer-Verlag
Berlin Heidelberg New York 1977

Library of Congress Cataloging in Publication Data
Main entry under title:

Resource allocation and division of space.

   (Lecture notes in economics and mathematical
systems ; 147)
   Bibliography: p.
   Includes index.
   1. Economics--Congresses. 2. Space in economics--
Congresses. I. Fujii, Takashi, 1929-(May)-
II. Satō, Ryūzō, 1931-   III. Series.
HB21.R42   330   77-14525

AMS Subject Classifications (1970): 90 A 15, 90 A 99

ISBN 3-540-08352-9 Springer-Verlag Berlin Heidelberg New York
ISBN 0-387-08352-9 Springer-Verlag New York Heidelberg Berlin

Printing and binding: Beltz Offsetdruck, Hemsbach/Bergstr.
2142/3140-543210

CONTENTS

RESOURCE ALLOCATION AND DIVISION OF SPACE

Edited by

Ryuzo Sato

Takashi Fujii

Page

PREFACE

This volume on the proceedings of a symposium on *Resource Allocation and Division of Space* represents a revised interest in the old problem of allocation and a fresh attack on the increasingly vital problem of space management. The symposium was held at the Toba International Hotel, near Nagoya, Japan in December, 1975.

Although the contributions included in this volume are all broadly concerned with either resource allocation or spatial problems, the editors have selected papers essentially on the basis of scientific merits and orginality rather than on the basis of narrowly focused topics and titles. The result is that all of the papers included, ranging from growth, index number, space density function, factor mobility, concentration and accumulation between sectors and spaces, distributions, relationship between spatial structure and organizational structure to the application of Lie group to production functions, are of the highest quality. It is the intention and belief of the editors that this collection of wide ranging but highly original papers is a major contribution to the advancement of economic science. The editors feel that a symposium of this kind is worthwhile and should be held at regular intervals.

The list of contributions can be divided into two parts. Part I, consisting of papers 1 through 9, deals in general with allocation. Papers 10 through 13 compose Part II, which is primarily concerned with spatial problems.

Sato opens this volume with a contribution dealing with the application of Lie group to the analysis of production functions. Using the concept of differential invariants of the Lie group theory, he presents the most satisfactory classification scheme for the non-homothetic general type of CES functions. It is shown that the general class of CES functions is completely described by the "projective" holothetic family, special cases of which are the well-known types of homothetic and almost-homothetic functions. Kimura's paper which follows is an extension of R. Sato's earlier work on dynamic stability. His contribution deals with finding sufficient conditions for the stochastic local stability of an economy which contains some gross complimentary goods.

General equilibrium theory has not succeeded so far in dealing effectively with some problems, i.e., the failure to provide an integration of Walrasian microeconomics with Keynesian macroeconomics and to take account of transactions cost. Negishi's paper introduces marketing costs into the Walrasian model of perfect competition and proves the existence of an equilibrium with Keynesian unemployment. Minagawa, on the other hand, investigates the problem of monopolistic equilibrium using a two-sector model. He assumes that pure monopoly prevails in either or each of the two sectors and derives the condition which assures the existence of equilibrium prices and outputs.

The contribution by Kurabayashi and Yatsuka deals with the analysis of income distribution among members of a society. They formulate a measure of income inequality associated with the value judgement on social justice that a society deems desirable. Their formulation serves not only to elucidate the problem, but also to serve as policy rules for income transfer among members of the society.

In the tradition of Inada, Kurz, and Shell and Stiglitz, Hori employs a two-sector model to treat the problem of allocating newly produced investment goods between the sectors through the rental rate. He first determines momentary equilibrium, then considers investment allocation between the two sectors. He ends by studying the growth path and possible oscillatory behaviors. Okuguchi's paper also deals with a two-sector model. However, his concern is with a more up-to-date problem. The model he describes is such that intersectoral reallocation of labour and capital occurs by intersectoral factor price differentials caused by exogenous changes in the prices of internationally traded goods.

Takayama extends the two countries trade problem treated in his former paper with Anderson to a many commodity world. His contribution makes clear the conditions under which devaluation sustains the stability of the steady state and its uniqueness. His model is notable for its treatment of multi-commodity flow and the flow of two currencies, assumed to be marketable assets, between two countries. One of the major characteristics of his paper is the separability assumption on the utility function. Contrasting with Takayama's commodity and money flow model, Umeshita's two space model focuses on capital movements, especially the functional combinations of concentration and accumulation of capital. This concentrated accumulation approach is one of the major tools for analyzing the urban-rural and the North-South problems. This approach is extended in Fujii's paper to the problem of sectorial movements of capital and is also reflected in Hori's paper.

Beckmann's paper starts off Part II. He applies his spatial equilibrium model to the analysis of urban structure and design of the typical American city. He examines in particular the density in residential areas with a single central business district in which all jobs and all shopping facilities are concentrated. Although the assumptions he introduces are simple, the results are plausible and consistent with results based on more complicated assumptions. Kojima's analysis varies from Beckmann's in that he deals with two closely located cities, one being the city where management service activity is concentrated and the other being the city where physical production activity is concentrated, with both cities surrounded with a residential zone. He might have had in mind Nagoya, the third largest city in Japan, in relation to Toyota City, renowned for its Toyota car, which is located 30 km. east of Nagoya. One of Kojima's results is consistent with the fact that Toyota's expansion become Nagoya's urban growth but the reverse has not been true.

Fukuchi's paper is a consolidation of the two types of approaches appearing in the papers by Beckmann, Kojima and Umeshita. These two approaches are the land use approach and the capital movement approach. He attempts to introduce these approaches simultaneously in his model to analyse urban structure formation in a growing city.

In the final paper, Fujii introduces the new concepts of unit of space and unit of management. Concentrated accumulation of factors forms urban growth and its structure and growth of social organization within this structure. The aim of the paper is to construct a series of simple models to depict the relationship between these two types of structural change in the course of autonomous growth of urban areas and organizations and to cover the series of problems one encounters during the transition process from industrial to post industrial society.

In the last paragraph of his paper, Fujii states that, "these models and analytical devices are sometimes such that certain new results are deduced very carefully and sometimes such that new ideas are audaciously prompted." This sentiment, is perhaps the most appropriate characterization of the temper of the papers included in this volume. Furthermore, while each paper has its own special interest and its own original contributions, the editors feel that in its entirety this volume of papers represents some keen insights into the problems which modern society confronts.

The editors would like to acknowledge a grant from the Japan Science Promotion Society which made the symposium financially possible and also the donation from the Volunteer Society. We are grateful to the participants of the Conference and especially to the contributors of papers. Particular reference should be made of the faculty members of

Nagoya University for their cordial support of this Conference. And we also wish to thank Mr. Isao Imagawa of Nanzan Seihan for his help with the editorial and typographical work of this volume.

February, 1977

Providence, R.I., U.S.A. Ryuzo Sato
and Nagoya, Japan Takashi Fujii

ANALYSIS OF PRODUCTION FUNCTIONS BY LIE THEORY
OF TRANSFORMATION GROUPS:
CLASSIFICATION OF GENERAL CES FUNCTIONS

by

Ryuzo Sato*

I.   Introduction

In my earlier papers [6, 7], the class of the most general types of constant-elasticity of substitution (CES) functions was derived as a general solution of a second-order partial differential equation which defines the elasticity of factor substitution. It is shown that this class of CES (nonhomothetic) functions has more meaningful economic applicability than the ordinary type of homothetic CES functions. However, one disadvantage of the general family is that it contains a large number of different types, actually an infinite number, and that the production functions are, in general, not expressible in explicit forms. Thus, those who are accustomed to thinking of the production function as an explicit relationship between inputs and outputs, may consider the general family of nonhomothetic CES functions to be very strange. Of course, this implicitness aspect presents no serious problems both in theory and in estimation, for the concept of the production function is simply the relationship, explicit or implicit, between the inputs and the maximum level of output resulting from them.

As the general family of nonhomothetic CES functions contains a large number of different types, it is only natural to ask if it is possible to devise a meaningful classification scheme. While in practice the family has been categorized in several respects, for example, separable vs. nonseparable, explicit vs. implicit, etc., these classification schemes are not entirely satisfactory. In most cases the existing classifications result in one type containing a majority of the functions with the other containing only a few, thereby reducing the effectiveness of these classifications.

The purpose of this paper is to present the most satisfactory classification scheme for nonhomothetic CES functions. We use the Lie theory of transformation groups. This approach is very powerful and also operational both from the mathematical and economic points of view. Lie group theory is considered as the most mathematically efficient way of identifying

* The author wishes to acknowledge financial aids from the National Science Foundation and the Guggenheim Foundation. Helpful comments by Professors Takayuki Nono and Taro Yamane are greatly appreciated.

the invariant properties of a function. Thus this method will enable us to classify the family of functions according to the types of invariants. From the economic perspective these invariants are nothing but economic magnitudes which often present themselves as indices of optimal economic behaviors, such as the marginal rate of substitution, the factor income ratio and so on. Since the family of nonhomothetic CES functions is, as was previously stated, the solution of a differential equation, we shall apply the Lie theory in order to investigate the differential equation according to its invariance properties under given groups. It will be shown that the general class of CES functions belongs to the "projective" holothetic family of production functions, special cases of which are the well-known types of homothetic and almost-homothetic functions.

II. The General Class of CES Functions

     The elasticity of substitution between factors (or commodities) K (capital) and L (labor) is defined as:

$$(1) \qquad \sigma = \frac{Kf_K + Lf_L}{KL\left(\dfrac{-f_K f_{LL}}{f_L} + 2f_{KL} - \dfrac{f_L f_{KK}}{f_K}\right)} = \frac{K + L\omega}{KL\left(\dfrac{\partial \omega}{\partial K} - \dfrac{\partial \omega}{\partial L}\omega^{-1}\right)}$$

where $\omega = f_L/f_K$ is the marginal rate of substitution between K and L. Rewriting (1) as

$$\sigma\, KL\left(\frac{\partial \omega}{\partial K}\right) - \sigma\, KL\, \omega^{-1}\left(\frac{\partial \omega}{\partial L}\right) - K - L\omega = 0$$

and letting $\omega = e^u$, equation (1) may be expressed as:

$$(1') \qquad e^u \frac{\partial u}{\partial K} - \frac{\partial u}{\partial L} = \frac{1}{\sigma L} + \frac{e^u}{\sigma K}, \qquad \sigma = \sigma(K, L, f).$$

If the elasticity of substitution σ is constant, equation (1') reduces to a rather simple partial differential equation whose solution is

$$(2) \qquad \omega = \left(\frac{K}{L}\right)^{1/\sigma} \cdot C(f)$$

This is *the general expression for the marginal rate of substitution corresponding to the class of CES (homothetic and non-homothetic functions)* (see [6]).

     To obtain the general family from (2) we need to solve (2) by setting $\omega = f_L/f_K$, i.e.,

$$(2') \qquad K^{1/\sigma} C(f) \frac{\partial f}{\partial K} - L^{1/\sigma} \frac{\partial f}{\partial L} = 0, \qquad \sigma = \text{const}, \qquad \infty > \sigma > 0.$$

The general solution to the above partial differential equation is found to be

$$(3) \quad \begin{cases} \text{(i)} \quad F(K, L, f) = C_1(f)K^{-\rho} + C_2(f)L^{-\rho} = 1, \quad \rho = \dfrac{1}{\sigma} - 1, \sigma \neq 1 \\[2ex] \text{(ii)} \quad F(K, L, f) = C_1(f)\log K + C_2(f)\log L = 1, \quad \rho = 0, \sigma = 1. \end{cases}$$

Thus, *the general class of nonhomothetic CES functions $F(K, L, f)$ is, in general, the implicit relationship between K, L and f defined by (3).*

An obvious classification of the general family of CES functions is to divide it into two basic types of CES functions: homothetic (or ordinary) CES including Cobb-Douglas, and nonhomothetic CES including nonhomothetic Cobb-Douglas functions, depending upon the relationship between C_1 and C_2 in (3). When $C_1 = aC_2$, a = constant, we obtain the ordinary CES and Cobb-Douglas family, while when $C_1 \neq aC_2$, we have the nonhomothetic CES and nonhomothetic Cobb-Douglas family. Thus, the general family is classified as:

$$\text{Homothetic} \begin{cases} \text{(i)} \quad aC(f)K^{-\rho} + C(f)L^{-\rho} = 1, \quad \text{Ordinary CES } (\sigma \neq 1) \\[2ex] \text{(ii)} \quad aC(f)\log K + C(f)\log L = 1, \quad \text{Ordinary Cobb-Douglas } (\sigma = 1), \end{cases}$$

and

$$\text{Nonhomothetic} \begin{cases} \text{(i)} \quad C_1(f)K^{-\rho} + C_2(f)L^{-\rho} = 1, \ C_1 \neq aC_2, \quad \text{nonhomothetic CES } (\sigma \neq 1) \\[2ex] \text{(ii)} \quad C_1(f)\log K + C_2(f)\log L = 1, C_1 \neq aC_2, \end{cases}$$

$$\text{nonhomothetic Cobb-Douglas (C-D) } (\sigma=1).$$

The problem with this classification scheme, however, is that the class of nonhomothetic CES (or C-D) contains an infinite number of different types again depending upon the relationship between C_1 and C_2 ($C_1 = aC_2$), while the homothetic class contains only one type consisting of the ordinary CES and the Cobb-Douglas functions. It seems only natural to try and devise a more meaningful classification scheme which enables one to divide the nonhomothetic family into different subclasses corresponding to different economic situations.[1]   To accomplish this we now present an alternative expression for the fundamental differential equation for the general CES family.

---

1) The nonhomothetic family has been divided into separable and nonseparable classes and also into "almost-homothetic" and "non-almost homothetic" classes (see Sato [8]).

III. Alternative Formulation of the Differential Equation Defining the Constancy of the Elasticity of Substitution

The elasticity of substitution between K and L can be alternatively expressed as

$$\sigma = \frac{d \log (K/L)}{d \log \omega} \quad , \quad \omega = f_L/f_K = -\frac{dK}{dL}\Big|_{f = \text{const.}}$$

Hence equation (1) can be written as

(1) $\quad \sigma = \dfrac{\dfrac{dK}{dL}}{KL} \cdot \dfrac{K - L\dfrac{dK}{dL}}{-\dfrac{d^2 K}{dL^2}} \quad , \quad -\dfrac{d^2 K}{dL^2} = \dfrac{d\omega}{dL} = \dfrac{\partial \omega}{\partial L} - \omega \dfrac{\partial \omega}{\partial K}.$

Assuming that σ is constant subject to $0 < \sigma < \infty$, the above is equal to

(4') $\quad \sigma\, KL\dfrac{d^2 K}{dL^2} + \dfrac{dK}{dL}(K - L\dfrac{dK}{dL}) = 0.$

The second order partial differential equation defined by (1) is now converted into the ordinary differential equation of the same order.

We now make the following important transformations:

(5) $\quad \begin{cases} \text{(i)} \quad L^{-\rho} = u,\ K^{-\rho} = v \quad \text{for } \rho = \dfrac{1}{\sigma} - 1,\ \text{i.e., } \sigma \neq 1, \\[2em] \text{(ii)} \quad \log L = u, \quad \log K = v \text{ for } \rho = 0,\ \text{i.e., } \sigma = 1. \end{cases}$

Then we have $\dfrac{dv}{du} = (\dfrac{K}{L})^{-\rho - 1} \cdot \dfrac{dK}{dL}$ for $\sigma \neq 1$ and $\dfrac{dv}{du} = (\dfrac{K}{L})^{-1} \cdot \dfrac{dK}{dL}$ for $\sigma = 1$. The second

derivative $\dfrac{d^2 v}{du^2}$ may be expressed as:

(6) $\quad \begin{cases} \text{(i)} \quad \dfrac{d^2 v}{du^2} = \dfrac{\sigma K^{-\rho - 2}}{-\rho L^{-2\rho - 1}}[\sigma KL\dfrac{d^2 K}{dL^2} + \dfrac{dK}{dL}(K - L\dfrac{dK}{dL})] \quad \text{for } \sigma \neq 1 \text{ or } \rho \neq 0 \\[2em] \text{(ii)} \quad \dfrac{d^2 v}{du^2} = \dfrac{L}{K^2}[KL\dfrac{d^2 K}{dL^2} + \dfrac{dK}{dL}(K - L\dfrac{dK}{dL})] \quad \text{for } \sigma = 1 \text{ or } \rho = 0. \end{cases}$

But the expression in the bracket in (6) is nothing but the differential equation which defines the constancy of the elasticity of substitution in (4'). Hence, for positive values of K and L, $\dfrac{d^2 v}{du^2}$ will be zero if and only if (4') is satisfied, i.e.,

(7) $\quad \dfrac{d^2 v}{du^2} = 0.$

In retrospect, the family of nonhomothetic CES functions could have been easily derived from (7) simply as,

$$v = a(f)u + b(f), \quad v - a(f)u = b(f)$$

or $\quad \dfrac{1}{b(f)}v - \dfrac{a(f)}{b(f)}u = 1 = C_1(f)v + C_2(f)u,$

where $u = L^{-\rho}$ for $\rho \neq 0$ or $u = \log L$ for $\rho = 0$ and $v = K^{-\rho}$ for $\rho \neq 0$ or $v = \log K$ for $\rho = 0$. From the standpoint of the Lie theory of transformation grounps, equation (7) represents one of the most remarkable transformations which can be used to classify the resulting solutions.

We summarize the results in the following:

Theorem 1:   *For positive values of K and L, the second order differential equation (4'), which defines the general class of CES functions will be satisfied if and only if equation (7) is met, i.e.,*

$$(7) \quad \frac{d^2 v}{du^2} = 0 \quad \Leftrightarrow \quad (4') \quad \sigma KL \frac{d^2 v}{du^2} + \frac{dK}{dL}\left(K - L\frac{dK}{dL}\right) = 0 \,,$$

where $u = L^{-\rho}$, $v = K^{-\rho}$ for $\rho \neq 0$, i.e., $\sigma \neq 1$; or $u = \log L$, $v = \log K$ for $\rho = 0$, i.e., $\sigma = 1$.

IV.   Classification by the Basic Projective Groups

We shall first prove a most important lemma[2] which will serve as the basis for using the Lie group theory in the classification of the different types of production functions.

Lemma: *For any given Lie group, there exists one and only one family of production function invariant under that group. The form of the family is completely described by the group.*

Proof: Let the Lie group be represented by the infinitesimal transformation

$$U = \xi(K, L) \frac{\partial}{\partial K} + \eta(K, L) \frac{\partial}{\partial L} \,;.$$ Then the invariant family of production functions

is derived from the partial differential equation $\xi(K, L) \frac{\partial f}{\partial K} + \eta(K, L) \frac{\partial f}{\partial L} = H(f) \neq 0$.
To obtain the solution, passing to the corresponding system of ordinary differential equations, we have [1, 2]:

$$\frac{dK}{\xi(K,L)} = \frac{dL}{\eta(K,L)} = \frac{df}{H(f)} = 0 \,.$$

We derive one of the canonical variables from the path curve $G(K, L) = C$. The general type of invariant differential equation for the isoquant map is $G' = Q(G)$. Hence, the general family of production functions invariant under the group U can be uniquely expressed as

$$Y = F[f(K, L)] = F[H(K, L) + G(K, L)] \,,$$

---

2) A slightly different version of this lemma was first proved by Sato [8] as Theorem 2.

where H and G are canonical variables. Q.E.D.

This lemma shows that the type of isoquant maps, and therefore, the type of production functions, may be classified according to the type of the group $U = \xi(K, L)\frac{\partial}{\partial K} + \eta(K, L)\frac{\partial}{\partial L}$, which leaves the isoquant map invariant. However, it is often more convenient to classify the family according to its extended groups [1, 2], such as U' and U'', where U' is the once-extended group, $U' = \xi(K, L)\frac{\partial}{\partial K} + \eta(K, L)\frac{\partial}{\partial L} + \eta'\frac{\partial}{\partial p}$, and U'', the twice-extended group,

$$U'' = \xi(K, L)\frac{\partial}{\partial K} + \eta(K, L)\frac{\partial}{\partial L} + \eta'\frac{\partial}{\partial p} + \eta''\frac{\partial}{\partial p'}, \quad p=\frac{dK}{dL}, \quad p'=\frac{dp}{dL}, \quad \eta'=\frac{dp}{dt}, \quad \eta''=\frac{dp'}{dt}.$$

From the point of view of the present analysis, we shall depend on the well-known property of the twice-extended group, that the second order differential equation which defines the isoquant map is invariant under U if and only if $U''f = 0$, whenever $f(K, L, \frac{dK}{dL}, \frac{d^2K}{dL^2}) = 0$ [1, 2]. Thus, what one must do is to find the types of group that leave the differential equation of the second order (7) invariant.

Our next task, therefore, is to identify the types of group which leaves invariant the differential equation that defines the general CES family. It is known that a differential equation of the second order is left unaltered by at most eight independent group [1]. The differential equation (7), $\frac{d^2v}{du^2} = 0$, is an equation that is left unaltered by the maximum number (eight) of independent groups. These independent groups belong to the general "projective" group:

$$(8) \quad G \begin{cases} u_1 = \dfrac{a_1 u + a_2 v + a_3}{a_7 u + a_8 v + 1} \\[2ex] v_1 = \dfrac{a_4 u + a_5 v + a_6}{a_7 u + a_8 v + 1}, \end{cases}$$

corresponding to,

$$(7) \quad \frac{d^2v}{du^2} = 0.$$

The set of linearly independent infinitesimal operators is

$$(9) \quad \begin{cases} U_1 = \dfrac{\partial}{\partial u}, \; U_2 = \dfrac{\partial}{\partial v}, \; U_3 = u\dfrac{\partial}{\partial u}, \; U_4 = v\dfrac{\partial}{\partial u}, \; U_5 = u\dfrac{\partial}{\partial v} \\[2ex] U_6 = v\dfrac{\partial}{\partial v}, \; U_7 = u^2\dfrac{\partial}{\partial u} + uv\dfrac{\partial}{\partial u}, \; U_8 = uv\dfrac{\partial}{\partial u} + v^2\dfrac{\partial}{\partial v}, \end{cases}$$

We are now in a position to employ these groups to make a distinction among the different types of general CES functions. We proceed by first determining the invariant family of functions which correspond to each of the eight basic one parameter groups.

1. *Additive Type I:* If the group is generated from $U_1 = \dfrac{\partial}{\partial u}$, the translation group, then the canonical variables are u and $g(v)$ and, thus, the invariant family must take the form:

   (10-1) $Y = F[f(u, v)] = F[u + g(v)]$.

2. *Additive Type II:* On the other hand, if the group is generated from $U_2 = \dfrac{\partial}{\partial v}$, the invariant family corresponding to this group must have the form:

   (10-2) $Y = F[f(u, v)] = F[v + g(u)]$.

3. *Log Additive I:* For the group $U_3 = u\dfrac{\partial}{\partial u}$, we have the invariant family

   (11-1) $Y = F[f(u, v)] = F[\log u + \log g(v)] = F[u{\cdot}g(v)]$.

4. *Log Additive II:* For the group $U_6 = v\dfrac{\partial}{\partial v}$, we have the form

   (11-2) $Y = F[f(u, v)] = F[\log v + \log g(u)] = F[v{\cdot}g(u)]$.

5. *Ratio Additive I:* If we have $U_4 = v\dfrac{\partial}{\partial u}$, the invariant family has the form

   (12-1) $Y = F[f(u, v)] = F[\dfrac{u}{v} + g(v)]$.

6. *Ratio Additive II:* On the other hand, for the infinitesimal transformation $U_5 = u\dfrac{\partial}{\partial v}$, we have the form

   (12-2) $Y = F[f(u, v)] = F[\dfrac{v}{u} + g(u)]$.

7. *Ratio Additive III:* For the group $U_7 = u^2\dfrac{\partial}{\partial u} + uv\dfrac{\partial}{\partial v}$, we will have an invariant family of the form

   (12-3) $Y = F[f(u, v)] = F[u^{-1} + g(\dfrac{v}{u})]$.

8. *Ratio Additive IV:* Finally when we have $U_8 = uv\dfrac{\partial}{\partial u} + v^2\dfrac{\partial}{\partial v}$, we will have an invariant family whose form is

   (12-4) $Y = F[f(u, v)] = F[v^{-1} + g(\dfrac{u}{v})]$.

Using these eight basic invariant families of production function, we shall now present the basic classification of the CES functions which must satisfy equation (7). First for Additive Type I, the CES must have the form

$$u + g(v) = f.$$

But $\dfrac{d^2 v}{du^2}$ must identically vanish and $g(v)$ must, therefore, be equal to $av + c$, where a and c are some constants. Thus, the type of CES functions, which is generated from the infinitesimal transformation of the group U_1 must be simply *homothetic*, i.e.,

(13) $Y = F[\beta_1 u + \beta_2 v]$.

In the same way, the type of CES functions generated from the infinitesimal transformation U_2 must be also homothetic. On other hand, the type of CES functions generated from U_3, or Log Additive I, must be of the form

(14) $Y = F[\dfrac{u}{av + c}]$,

while the type generated by U_6, Log Additive II, must be

(15) $Y = F[\dfrac{v}{au + c}]$.

The CES function corresponding to Ratio Additive I or $U_4 = v\dfrac{\partial}{\partial u}$ may be obtained from

$$\frac{u}{v} + g(v) = f \quad \text{satisfying} \quad \frac{d^2 v}{du^2} = 0.$$

This implies that $u = v[f-g(v)]$, $u' = f - g(v) - vg'(v)$ and $u'' = -g'(v) - g'(v) - vg'' = 0$, i.e., $2g' = -vg''$. Solving this differential equation we immediately obtain

$$g(v) = c_1 v^{-1} + c_2 .$$

Hence f must take the form $\dfrac{u}{v} + \dfrac{c_1}{v} + c_2 = f$ or

$$Y = F[\frac{u + c}{v}] ,$$

which is identical with the case of U_6. In the same manner, for Ratio Additive II, $U_5 = u\dfrac{\partial}{\partial v}$, we will have

$$Y = F[\frac{v + c}{u}] , \qquad \text{which is the same form as Log Additive I,}$$

or U_3 . For the group U_7, we must have

$$f = \frac{1}{u} + g(\frac{v}{u}).$$

Thus $\dfrac{v}{u} = G[f - u^{-1}]$ or $v = uG[f - u^{-1}]$. In order that $\dfrac{d^2 v}{du^2} = 0$, we must have $G'' = 0$ or $G = a(f - u^{-1}) + b$, or $v = a(uf - 1) + bu$. From this we have,

$$Y = F[\frac{v + a}{au}] ,$$

which is again identical with the case of U_3 . In the same way the CES production function generated from the invariant relationship U_8 must be of the form

$$Y = F[\frac{u+a}{av}] \, ,$$

which is the same as the case of U_6 .

In summary we have,

Theorem 2:   *The types of CES production functions generated from the basic eight groups of projective transformations must have the forms:*

(13) $Y = F[\beta_1 u + \beta_2 v]$

(14) $Y = F[\dfrac{\beta_1 u}{\beta_2 v + \theta_2}]$

(15) $Y = F[\dfrac{\beta_2 v}{\beta_1 u + \theta_1}] \, ,$

   where $u = L^{-\rho}$, $v = K^{-\rho}$ for $\rho \neq 0$, i.e., $\sigma \neq 1$, or $u = \log L$, $v = \log K$ for $\rho = 0$, i.e., $\sigma = 1$. They all belong to the separable class of CES functions.

V.   Classification by the general one parameter subgroups

In view of a fundamental theorem in the Lie group theory [1, 2], the differential equation (7) will be invariant under the general one parameter subgroups. The special one will be obtained from a linear combination of the eight basic types such as

$$a_1 \frac{\partial f}{\partial u} + a_2 \frac{\partial f}{\partial v} = a_1 U_1 f + a_2 U_2 f, \quad \text{and} \quad a_1 \frac{\partial f}{\partial u} + a_3 u \frac{\partial f}{\partial u} = a_1 U_1 f + a_3 U_3 f \, ,$$

etc. They must, in general, come from,

(16) $$Uf = e_1 u \frac{\partial f}{\partial u} + e_2 v \frac{\partial f}{\partial u} + e_3 \frac{\partial f}{\partial u} + e_4 u \frac{\partial f}{\partial v} + e_5 v \frac{\partial f}{\partial v} + e_6 \frac{\partial f}{\partial v}$$
$$- e_7 (u^2 \frac{\partial f}{\partial u} + uv \frac{\partial f}{\partial v}) - e_8 (uv \frac{\partial f}{\partial u} + v^2 \frac{\partial f}{\partial v}) \, ,$$

where e_i ($i = 1, 2, ..., 8$) are constants.

We shall begin with,

1.   *Almost-Homogeneous Type:* $e_1 u \dfrac{\partial f}{\partial u} + e_5 v \dfrac{\partial f}{\partial v} = Uf.$

The production function generated by this group must be equal to

(17) $Y = F[u^{1/e_1} Q(v^{1/e_5}/u^{1/e_1})] = F[v^{1/e_5} P(u^{1/e_1}/v^{1/e_5})].$

Equation (17) is the class of almost-homothetic production functions (Sato [8]), which has the characteristic of $f(\lambda^{e_1} u, \lambda^{e_s} v) = \lambda^{\gamma} f(u, v)$, where $f = u^{1/e_1} q(v^{1/e_s}/u^{1/e_1})$ or $f = v^{1/e_s} p(u^{1/e_1}/v^{1/e_s})$. This is perhaps the most useful type of production functions in economic theory.

The family of CES functions that satisfies (17) must have the form

(18) $\beta_1 [C(Y)]^{e_1} L^{-\rho} + \beta_2 [C(Y)]^{e_s} K^{-\rho} = 1.$

Especially when $C(Y) = Y$, we have

(18') $\beta_1 Y^{e_1} L^{-\rho} + \beta_2 Y^{e_s} K^{-\rho} = 1.$

The above satisfies the condition of almost-homogeneity because of the condition:

$$\beta_1 (\lambda^{\rho} Y)^{e_1} (\lambda^{e_1} L)^{-\rho} + \beta_2 (\lambda^{\rho} Y)^{e_s} /(\lambda^{e_s} K)^{-\rho} =$$

$$\beta_1 \lambda^{\rho e_1 - \rho e_1} Y^{e_1} L^{-\rho} + \beta_2 \lambda^{\rho e_s - \rho e_s} Y^{e_s} K^{-\rho} =$$

$$\beta_1 Y^{e_1} L^{-\rho} + \beta_2 Y^{e_s} K^{-\rho} = 1.$$

This is the type of production function generated from the non-uniform magnification group $Uf = e_1 u \dfrac{\partial f}{\partial u} + e_s v \dfrac{\partial f}{\partial v}$. It should be noted that the three different types of CES functions derived from the basic groups (Theorem 2) are, in fact, special cases of this class, equation (18'). When $e_1 = e_s \neq 0$, we have the ordinary CES, equation (13), while when $e_1 = 0 \neq e_s$, we obtaine(15) and when $e_s = 0 \neq e_1$, we obtain (14).

It is interesting to see that the class of separable CES function [7] will be derived from $e_i \equiv 0$, except $i \neq 1, 3$, i.e., $e_1 = e^t$, $e_3 = \theta_1 (e^t - 1)$, or $u_1 = e^t u + \theta_1 (e^t - 1)$, $v_1 = v$, so that $f = \log (u + \theta_1) + \phi(v)$ and

(19) $Y = F[\dfrac{\beta_1 u + \theta_1}{\beta_2 v + \theta_2}].$

In summary, we have:

(a) $e_1 = e_s \neq 0$, homothetic CES,

(b) $e_1 \neq e_s$, $e_1 \neq 0$, $e_s \neq 0$, almost-homothetic CES,

(c) $e_1 = 0 \neq e_s$, capital-homothetic CES,

(d) $e_1 \neq 0 = e_s$, labor-homothetic CES,

(e) $e_1 \neq 0$, $e_3 \neq 0$, nonhomothetic (separable) CES.

2. *Projective-Holothetic (Homothetic) Type:*

Rather than presenting the remaining more general one parameter groups, we shall derive the general "projective-holothetic (projective-homothetic)" family of production functions, which includes all the general form of one parameter subgroups.

The general expression for the infinitesimal transformation for the projective group is given by equation (16). We are interested in deriving the invariant family of production functions generated from (16), and we must solve the partial differential equation defined by

(20) $\quad (e_1 u + e_2 v + e_3 - e_7 u^2 - e_8 uv) \dfrac{\partial f}{\partial u} + (e_4 u + e_5 v + e_6 - e_7 uv - e_8 v^2) \dfrac{\partial f}{\partial v}$

$\qquad = H(f).$

The invariants of the group will be derived from

$$\frac{du}{e_1 u + e_2 v + e_3 - e_7 u^2 - e_8 uv} = \frac{dv}{e_4 u + e_5 v + e_6 - e_7 uv - e_8 v^2} ,$$

which may be reduced to the Jacobi equation. Thus, the solution may be obtained from

(21) $\quad U^{\lambda_2 - \lambda_3} V^{\lambda_3 - \lambda_1} W^{\lambda_1 - \lambda_2} = \text{const},$

where $U = \alpha_1 u + \beta_1 v + \gamma_1$, $V = \alpha_2 u + \beta_2 v + \gamma_2$ and $W = \alpha_3 u + \beta_3 v + \gamma_3$, and λ_1, λ_2, λ_3 are the characteristic roots of

$$\begin{vmatrix} 0 - \lambda & e_3 & e_6 \\ e_7 & e_1 - \lambda & e_4 \\ e_8 & e_2 & e_5 - \lambda \end{vmatrix} = 0 .$$

Hence, one of the canonical variables is equal to

$\qquad \phi(U^{\lambda_2 - \lambda_3} V^{\lambda_3 - \lambda_1} W^{\lambda_1 - \lambda_2})$

and the other canonical variable may be obtained from (21) and the differential equation

$$\frac{dv}{e_4 u + e_5 v + e_6 - e_7 uv - e_8 v^2} = \frac{df}{H(f)} .$$

Let it be equal to $\psi(v)$, then the invariant family must be of the form:

(22) $\quad Y = F[\psi(u,v) + \phi(U^{\lambda_2 - \lambda_3} V^{\lambda_3 - \lambda_1} W^{\lambda_1 - \lambda_2})] .$

We shall call the above the *projective-holothetic (or projective-homothetic) family* of productions functions. This is the most general class of production functions invariant under all the transformations of the projective type (8), G.

For instance, if we have $e_1 \neq 0$, $e_2 = 0$, $e_3 = -1$, $e_4 = 0$, $e_5 = e_1$, $e_6 = 0$, $e_7 = 1$ and $e_8 = 0$, the Jacobi equation reduces to a simple form which yields:

$$(23) \quad Y = F(f), \quad f = -\frac{1}{2}\log(u^2 - e_1 u - e_3) + \frac{e_1}{\sqrt{B}}\tan^{-1}\left(\frac{2u - e_1}{\sqrt{B}}\right) + \log v, \quad B = 4 - e_1^2.$$

In summary we have

Theorem 3: *The most general class of production functions invariant under the general from of one parameter subgroups of the projective groups must be the projective-holothetic (or projective homothetic) family of*

$$(22) \quad Y = F[\psi(u,v) + \phi[(\alpha_1 u + \beta_1 v + \gamma_1)^{\lambda_2 - \lambda_3}(\alpha_2 u + \beta_2 v + \gamma_2)^{\lambda_3 - \lambda_1}(\alpha_3 u + \beta_3 v + \gamma_3)^{\lambda_1 - \lambda_2}]],$$

where α_1, α_2, ..., γ_3 are functions of $e_1, e_2, \ldots, e_8$. (We may assume that $\alpha_1 = 1$.)

Obviously equation (22) contains all the types of production functions that we have thus far discussed. For instance, if $\alpha_1 = \beta_2$, $\beta_1 = \gamma_1 = \alpha_2 = \gamma_2 = \alpha_3 = \beta_3 = 0$, $\gamma_3 \neq 0$ and $\lambda_2 = \lambda_1 = 0$, and $\psi(u,v) = \log v$, then we have $f = \log v + \phi[(\frac{\alpha_1 u}{\alpha_2 v})^{-\lambda_3}]$ which implies $vg(\frac{u}{v})$, the homothetic type. On the other hand, under the same conditions as the above with the exception $\lambda_3 \equiv 0$, we have $f = \log v + \phi(\frac{u_2 \lambda_2}{v\lambda_1})$, which implies the almost-homothetic type $\lambda_1 \neq \lambda_2$.

Up to this point we have subjected ourselves to the only one invariant condition of $\frac{d^2 v}{du^2} = 0$. If, in addition to this condition, the production function is invariant under $\frac{d^2 K}{dL^2} < 0$ (the usual law of diminishing marginal rate of substitution) and under $f_L/f_K = -\frac{dK}{dL} > 0$ (the positivity of marginal rate of substitution), together with the positivity of $K - L\frac{dK}{dL} > 0$, $\infty > K > 0$ and $\infty > L > 0$, then the diffantial equation $\frac{d^2 v}{du^2} = 0$ is invariant under only one family of one parameter Lie group i.e.,

$$(24) \quad U = e_1 u\frac{\partial}{\partial u} + e_5 v\frac{\partial}{\partial v}.$$

That is to say, the class of CES functions can only be generated from the almost-homothetic type under the non-uniform magnification group.

We may summarize the results in the following:[3]

Theorem 4: *The most general family of nonhomothetic CES production functions, invariant*

under the conditions of

$$\frac{d^2 K}{dL^2} < 0, \quad \frac{dK}{dL} < 0, \quad K - L\frac{dK}{dL} > 0, \quad +\infty > K > 0 \quad and \quad +\infty > L > 0,$$

must be of the almost-homothetic type, i.e.,

$$\beta_1 [C(Y)]^{e_1} L^{-\rho} + \beta_2 [C(Y)]^{e_2} K^{-\rho} = 1.$$

This class contains:

(a) *Homothetic Type:* $\qquad Y = [\beta_1 L^{-\rho} + \beta_2 K^{-\rho}]$

(b) *Capital-Homothetic Type:* $\quad Y = [\frac{\beta_1 L^{-\rho} + \theta_1}{\beta_2 K^{-\rho}}]$

(c) *Labor-Homothetic Type:* $\quad Y = [\frac{\beta_2 K^{-\rho} + \theta_2}{\beta_1 L^{-\rho}}]$

Needless to say that the above theorem applies to the case of nonhomothetic Cobb-Douglas functions with proper modifications whenever necessary.

---

3) The interested reader is asked to prove this assertion.

REFERENCES

[1]   Campbell, J.E., *Introductory Treatise on Lie's Theory of Continuous Transformation Groups*, (Reprint), 1966.

[2]   Eisenhart, L.P., *Continuous Groups of Transformations*, 1933.

[3]   Houthakker, H.S., "Additive Preferences," *Econometrica*, Vol. 28:2 (1960), pp. 244-257.

[4]   Lie, M.S., *Transformationsgruppen*, Vol. I, II, III.

[5]   Samuelson, P.A., " A Theory of Induced Innovations alongKennedy-Weizsäcker Lines," *Review of Economics and Statistics*, 1965, pp. 343-56.

[6]   Sato, R., "The Most General Class of CES Functions," *Econometrica*, September, 1975.

[7]   Sato, R., "On the Class of Separable Non-Homothetic CES Production Functions," *Economic Studies Quarterly*, April, 1974.

[8]   Sato, R., "The Impact of Technical Change under Homothetic and Holothetic Technology," presented at the Third World Congress of the Econometric Society, 1975, Toronto.

[9]   Sato, R. and M.J. Beckmann, "Neutral Inventions and Production Functions," *Review of Economic Studies*, 1968, pp. 57-65.

[10] Shephard, R.W., *Theory of Cost and Production Functions*, Princeton, 1970.

[11] Wolkowitz, B., "Homothetic Production Functions," Ph. D. Dissertation, Brown University, 1970.

[12] Aczél, J., *Lectures on Theory of Functional Equations and Their Applications*, Academic Press, 1966.

On Adjustment Speed,

Complementarity and Global Stability

Yoshio Kimura

1 Introduction

Recently Mukherji [5] and Okuguchi [6], specifying a particular commodity as the numéraire, have independently verified the global stability of the competitive equilibrium in an economy containing gross substitutes as well as gross complements. However, there is another way to the normalization of prices. Specifically, we can specify a composite commodity suitably compounded as the numéraire in stead of choosing a single numéraire. To elucidate the benefit obtained from selecting a composite numéraire, suppose that we have designated a particular commodity as the numéraire and that we are concerned with a tâtonnement process in which the price of any non-numéraire commodity rises if the corresponding excess demand is positive, falls if it is negative and remains constant otherwise. Assume further that the excess demand for the numéraire chosen is negative. Then, by virtue of Walras law, there exists a non-numéraire commodity, say the commodity α, with the corresponding excess demand positive. Consequently, in the next moment, the price of the commodity α (price α for short) is bidden up and hence the purchasing power of the numéraire in terms of the commodity α declines. Therefore the commodity α may become more preferable and the numéraire less preferable. As a natural consequence, the same situation as assumed above (excess demand for the commodity α and excess supply for the numéraire) will last for some periods during which thr price α (in terms of the numéraire) continue to rise. Hence, if either the positive excess demand for the commodity α lasts sufficiently long or the speed of the rise in price α is enough large, price α (in terms of numéraire) may become almost infinite, and hence the numéraire may eventually fail in filling its function.[1] Though this is not necessarily the case, we must emphasize that it is impossible to exclude the difficult situation described above. On the other hand, if we choose a composite commodity consisting of one unit of all commodities under consideration as the numéraire, we are able to be fairly free of the above difficulty since then there are included rising prices in the sum of all non-normalized prices which is, by definition, the price of the composite numéraire.

As is well known, a tâtonnement process in which all prices add up to unity because of the normalization of prices stated so far is one depicted by the Brown-von Neumann differential equations introduced into this field of research by Nikaido [7, 9]. However, the systems proposed there, were

---

[1] This kind of phenomenon is often observed in the foreign exchange market. For example, weak currency, say lira, is sold for strong currency, say mark.

based on a linear system in which the price of each commodity responded proportinately to its excess demand. The purpose of the present note is therefore to examine the global stability of a tâtonnement process given by the Brown-von Neumman differential equations associated with a non-linear price adjustment system in which the rate of change in price is a sign-preserving function of the corresponding excess demand and not only gross substitutability but gross complementarity prevails.[2]

2 Assumptions

We are here concerned with an economy with n commodities, labelled $1, 2, \ldots, n$. Let $p_i \geq 0$ be the price of the ith commodity and $p = (p_1, \ldots, p_n)$ be the price vector. If all entries of p add up to unity, p is said to be normalized, otherwise it is called non-normalized. By $E_i(p)$ denote the excess demand function for the ith commodity at prices p. Then excess demand functions are postulated to fulfill:

(A.1) $E_i(p), i = 1, \ldots, n$, are single valued continuous functions of $p \geq 0$[3] and are supposed to be twice continuously differentiable on the n-dimensional simplex $S = \left\{ x \geq 0: \sum_{i=1}^{n} x_i = 1 \right\}$.[4]

(A.2)   Each of the $E_i(p)$ is positively homogeneous of degree zero, symbolically, for all $\lambda > 0$ and for all $p \geq 0$

$$E_i(p) = E_i(\lambda p) \qquad i = 1, \ldots, n \tag{1}$$

The adjustment of p_i to the corresponding excess demand $E_i(p)$ may be thought of as a real valued function $H_i(E_i(p)) \equiv h_i(p)$, upon which we impose:

(A.3) $H_i(\cdot)$ is differentiable everywhere on its domain and possesses the following properties often called sign-preserving:

$$H_i(0) = 0 \tag{2.a}$$

$$\text{sign} \left(H_i(E_i(p)) \right) = \text{sign } E_i(p) \text{ for all } p \geq 0 \tag{2.b}$$

A tâtonnement mechanism which preserves the nonnegativity of prices throughout the whole adjustment process is

$$\dot{p}_i \equiv \frac{dp_i}{dt} = \max \left\{ H_i \left(E_i(p) \right), 0 \right\} \equiv \eta_i(p) \quad i = 1, \ldots, n \tag{3}$$

where t denotes the time.

Before proceeding further, we must observe that under assumptions (A.1), (A.2) and (A.3), every

---

2) Since the assumption (4) or (4') of Nikaido [7], which is the key assumption to the global stability asserted there, is irrelevant of the gross-substitutablity, we will claim no substantial progress in this respect.
3) $p \geq 0$ means that $p_i \geq 0$ for all i and that $p_j > 0$ for some j.
4) To meet the requirement that the Liapunov function has continuous partial derivatives, this kind of assumption seems to be indispensable. Moreover, by virtue of the assumed differentiability, every excess demand function is readily seen to fulfill the Lipschitz condition on S.

$\eta_i(p)$ is bounded on the non-negative orthant. This can be seen as follows: For any given $p \geq 0$,

define $x = (\sum\limits_{i=1}^{n} p_i)^{-1} \cdot p$. Then, clearly $x \in S$ and , by (A.2), $E_i(p) = E_i(x)$ for all i. Since $E_i(x)$ is

assumed to be continuous, it is surely bounded on a compact set S, which, together with (A.3), implies

that $H_i(E_i(p))$ is continuous on a closed interval. Hence $H_i(E_i(p))$ is again bounded. Taking into ac-

count of (3), $\eta_i(p)$ is also bounded as is desired. The implication of this observation is two fold. In

the first place, it is a key to the existence of a function $\alpha(t)$ which transforms any solution $p(t)$ of

(3), if it exists, to $x(t) = p(\alpha(t)) / \sum\limits_{i=1}^{n} p_i(\alpha(t))$ satisfying

$$\dot{x}_i(t) = \eta_i(x) - (\sum\limits_{i=1}^{n} \eta_i(x))x_i \quad ^{5)} \qquad i = 1, \ldots, n \qquad (4)$$

In the second place, from the observed boundedness of $\eta_i(x)$, it directly follows that $\eta_i(x) - (\sum\limits_{j=1}^{n} \eta_i(x))x_i$

is bounded on S. Since it is also continuous on S, in the light of the Cauchy-Peano existence theorem

[3: Theorem 2.1, p.10, 11], (4) evidently has a solution $x(t)$ starting from any given $x^0 \in S$ and being

defined on some time-interval. We can, in addition, see that $x(t)$ can be continued to $[0, \alpha)$ and that

it remains normalized over time,[6] which markes it meaningful to investigate the global stability of (4).

3   Some Preliminary Results

Throughout this section we are concerned with an $n \times n$ matrix with real entries a_{ij}. Following

Brauer [2], suppose that A is power positive, that is, there exists a positive integer k such that $A^k > 0$.

Then it turns out to assume that some power of A belongs to the class of indecomposable non-negative

matrices which are also primitive. There can be found, however, no reason why A^k is a member of this

special class of matrices. Moreover, any power of a decomposable matrix surely contains some zero

elements. It is therefore of some value to investigate the property of a matrix A with which there is associated

an integer $k > 0$ such that $A^k \geq 0$.

Lemma 1:   If there exists an integer $k > 0$ such that $A^k \geq 0$ and if A^k is indecomposable then the

eigen value of A of greatest magnitude[7] is real and simple, and the eigen vector of A corresponding

to that eigen value is positive.

Proof.   Denote the eigen values of A by $\lambda_j, j = 1, \ldots, n$. Let J be the Jordan canonical form of

A and let $P^{-1} AP = J$. Then $A^k = PJ^k P^{-1}$. A direct calculation of J^k therefore shows that the eigen

values of A^k are λ_j^k. Since A^k is non-negative and indecomposable the Forbenius root of A^k, say λ_1^k,

is positive and simple, and $\lambda_1^k \geq |\lambda_j^k|, j = 2, \ldots, n$. Hence we have

---

5)   By essentially the same procedure employed in Nikaido [7: p.658~659], we can easily prove the existence
     of $\alpha(t)$. Moreover, it is immediately seen that $\alpha(t)$ possesses the following properties:

   $$\alpha(0) = 0, \alpha(t) \geq 0, \dot{\alpha}(t) > 0, \text{ and } \lim_{t \to \infty} \alpha(t) = \infty.$$

6)   For the proof consult Nikaido [7: p.670].
7)   An eigen value with this property is often called the absolute greatest root of A.

$$|\lambda_1| \geqq |\lambda_j| \qquad j = 2, \ldots, n \tag{5}$$

If, in (5), the strict inequality holds for all j then λ_1 is obviously real and simple. Suppose that $|\lambda_1| = |\lambda_j|$ for some j. Then, without loss of generality, we can assume that $|\lambda_1| = |\lambda_2| = \ldots = |\lambda_p|$, where p is an integer not larger than n. As is well known,[8] $\lambda_j^k (j = 2, \ldots, p)$ can be expressed as

$$\lambda_j^k = \lambda_1^k \omega^{j-1}, \; j = 2, \ldots, p, \tag{6}$$

where ω is the primitive p-th root of 1.

Suppose that λ_1 is complex. Then there exists an index $j_0 \in \{2, \ldots, p\}$, for which

$$\overline{\lambda}_1 = \lambda_{j_0} \tag{7}$$

where $\overline{\lambda}_1$ signifies the conjugate of λ_1.

Noticing that $0 < \lambda_1^k = (\overline{\lambda}_1^k) = (\overline{\lambda_1})^k = \lambda_{j_0}^k$, (6) and (7) reduce to

$$\lambda_1^k = \lambda_1^k \omega^{j_0 - 1},$$

which is absurd since $j_0 - 1$ is less than p. Hence λ_1 must be real. To prove that λ_1 is simple, suppose the contrary then there again exists an index, say $j_1 \in \{2, \ldots, p\}$, such that

$$\lambda_1^k = \lambda_{j_1}^k = \lambda_1^k \omega^{j_1 - 1},$$

which again yields a contradiction, for $j_1 - 1 < p$. Thus λ_1 is real and simple. The proof of the second assertion is rather trivial and is omitted. Q.E.D.

A straightforward application of the lemma just shown yields:

Theorem 1: The absolute greatest root of a power-non-negative matrix is real.

Proof. Let A^k be non-negative. If A^k is indecomposable, there remains nothing to prove. It therefore suffices to verify the theorem when A^k is decomposable. Then, as is well known, we can find a permutation matrix Q such that

$$QA^kQ' = \begin{bmatrix} A_{11}^k & A_{12}^k & \cdots & A_{1m}^k \\ & \ddots & & \vdots \\ & & \ddots & \vdots \\ 0 & & & A_{mm}^k \end{bmatrix} \tag{8}$$

---

8) See Nikaido [8: especially p. 109~113].

where A_{ti}^k is indecomposable, $i = 1, \ldots, m$.

Recalling that $QA^k Q'$ is similar to A^k whose eigen values are $\lambda_1^k, \ldots, \lambda_n^k$, the conclusion immediately follows from Lemma 1 applied to each of $A_{11}^k, \ldots, A_{mm}^k$. This completes the proof.

4 The Global Stability

The main purpose of this section is to show that the power-positive transformation originally introduced by Sato [10, 11] well works to ensure the global stability of (4). Let N be the set of all indices, that is, $N = \{1, \ldots, n\}$. Associated with any given x of S, define a real valued function $V(x)$ and a subset J of N respectively by $V(x) = \dfrac{1}{2} \Sigma \, \eta_i^2 (x)$ and by $J = \{i \in N: E_i(x) > 0\}$. Then, from (A.3), we obviously have

$$J = \{i \in N: h_i(x)) > 0\} \tag{9}$$

which, in turn, implies that

$$V(x) = \frac{1}{2} \sum_{i \in J} H_i^2 \, (E_i(x))$$

Taking into account of (A.2), (4) and (9), the trajectory derivative of $V(x(t))$ is expressed as

$$V(x(t)) = \sum_{i,j \in J} H_i(E_i(x(t)) \, (H_i' \cdot \frac{\partial E_i}{\partial x_j}) \, H_j \, (E_j(x(t)) \tag{10}$$

where $x(t)$ is a solution of (4), H_i' is the speed of adjustment of the normalized price x_i evaluated at $E_i(x(t))$ and $\dfrac{\partial E_i}{\partial x_j}$ denotes the partial derivative of $E_i \, (x(t))$ with respect to x_j evaluated at $x(t)$. By H_J and A_J respectively denote a diagonal matrix with diagonal elements H_i', $i \in J$, and a matrix with entries $\dfrac{\partial E_i}{\partial x_j}$ $i,\, j \in J$.

In order to guarantee the global stability of (4), we postulate:

(A.4)   For H_J and A_J there exist a positive number ρ, an integer $k > 0$ and a non-singular matrix T of order $\#J$ such that $T(H_J A_J + \rho I)^k \, T^{-1} \geq 0$ and $B_J^k - \rho^k I$ is Hicksian, and furthermore there can be found a $\#J \times \#J$ non-singular matrix $G^{9)}$ with the following properties:

(i)   There exists an ϵ-neighbourhood $B_\epsilon(GH_J A_J)$ of $GH_J A_J$ such that

$$\nu^0 \, (X) = 0 \quad \text{for all square } X \text{ of } B_\epsilon \, (GH_J A_J)$$

---

9) As will be shown in the proof of Theorem 2, $H_j A_j$ is non-singular under the first half of (A.4). Unless G is non-singular, $GH_j A_j$ may be similar, in which case the condition (i) of (A.4) becomes false, since then 0 is an eigen value of $GH_j'A_j' \in B_\epsilon(GH_j A_j)$. The non-singularity of G is therefore indispensable. Moreover, it is needless to say that (A.4) is postulated to be true throughout the whole adjustment process, for the subset J of N clearly depends on the solution $x(t)$. In this context, we must notice that J is a proper subset of N over time, for the converse supposition that $J = N$ for some t, together with the ealier observation that any solution $x(t)$ of (4) always remains in S, would violate the Walras law. To clarify the implication of this observation, suppose the contrary. Then, by virtue of (A.2), $H_j A_j$ could never be non-singular for $J = N$, which is again inconsistent with the condition (i) of (A,4).

and

(ii) $\epsilon > ||GH_J A_J||$ [10)]

where $B_J = T(H_J A_J + \rho I)T^{-1}$, $\#J$ signifies the number of elements contained in the set J, $\nu^0(X)$ is the sum of the multiplicities of the eigen values of X of which real parts are zero and $|| \cdot ||$ denotes a matrix norm.[10)]

We can now state and verify our main result.

Theorem 2. Under assumptions (A.1) through (A.4), the dynamic system (4) is globally asymptotically stable, and hence so is the system (3).[11)]

Proof.   In view of the earlier observation concerning the existence of the transformation function $\alpha(t)$, the global stability of (3) is attributed to that property of (4). It therefore suffices to prove the theorem for the system (4).

By λ denote any eigen value of $H_J A_J$ and let μ be that of B_J. Then, by the definition of B_J, it is obvious that

$$\lambda = \mu - \rho \tag{11}$$

Since $B_J^k \geq 0$, Theorem 1 ensures that B_J has a real eigen value $\tilde{\mu}$ such that

$$|\tilde{\mu}| \geq |\mu| \tag{12}$$

---

10)   Following Lancaster [3: chap. 6], a real-valued function $||A||$ defined on all square matrices with complex elements is said to be a matrix norm if it satisfies the following axioms:

   (i) $||A|| \geq 0$ and $||A|| = 0$ if and only if $A = 0$

   (ii) $||cA|| = |c| \cdot ||A||$ for any complex number c

   (iii) $||A + B|| \leq ||A|| + ||B||$

   (iv) $||AB|| \leq ||A|| \cdot ||B||$

   Noticing that the axioms (i), (ii) and (iii) are completely analogous to those of a vector norm, the distance between two square matrices A and B of the same order can be defined by $||A - B||$. Thus an r-neighbourhood $B_r(A)$ is the family of all square matrices X such that $||A - X|| < r$. In view of the axiom (iv) above, the condition (ii) of (A.4) is likely to be true if $||G||$ is enough small.

11)   Sato [11: Theorem 2, p.758~759] shows that the Hicksian condition imposed on $B_J^k - \rho^k I$ mutatis mutandis is necessary and sufficient for the stability of the linear system therein investigated. On the other hand, we can dispense with postulating additional conditions ensuring that the absolute greatest root of B_J is positive, since our sole concern here is to find a sufficient condition under which the dynamic system (4) is globally asymptotically stable.

   The assumption (A.4) is thought of as a variant of that originally devised by Okuguchi [6] and it is an easy task to prove Theorem 2 with (A.4) replaced by (A.4'):

   (A.4')   For H_J and A_J there exist a $\rho > 0$, an integer $k > 0$ and a non-singular matrix T of order $\#J$ such that $T(H_J A_J + A'_J H_J + \rho I)^k T^{-1} \geq 0$ and $B_J^k - \rho^k I$ fulfills the Hicksian condition where $B_J = T(H_J A_J + A'_J H_J + \rho I)T^{-1}$.

   Conversely, it is readily seen that (A.4) mutatis mutandis also guarantees the global asymptotic stability of the system

   $$\dot{P}_i = H_i(E_i(p)) \qquad i = 1, \ldots, n - 1$$
   $$P_n = 1$$

   a non-linear version of the system investigated by Okuguchi [6] .

On the other hand, the Hicksian condition imposed on $B_j^k - \rho^k I$, which is a matrix with off-diagonal elements non-negative, implies that $\rho^k I - B_j^k$ fulfills so called Hawkins-Simon condition. Hence, in the light of the well known Frobeius theorem on non-negative matrices, it is readily seen that

$$\rho^k > (\widetilde{\mu})^k = |(\widetilde{\mu})^k| = |\widetilde{\mu}|^k \qquad (13)$$

Recalling that $\rho > 0$, from (14), (15) and (16) it follows that

$$0 > |\widetilde{\mu}| - \rho \geq |\mu| - \rho \geq Re(\mu) - \rho = Re(\lambda) \qquad (14)$$

Let δ be a positive number. Then from the properties of matrix norm, we obtain

$$\|GH_J A_J - \delta (H_J A_J + A_J' H_J)\| \leq \|GH_J A_J\| + \delta \|H_J A_J + A_J' H_J\|,$$

where A_J' is of course the transposed matrix of A_J. Since $\|GH_J A_J\| < \epsilon$ and $\|H_J A_J + A_J' H_J\|$ is a given constant, there can be chosen a $\delta_0 > 0$ so small that

$$\|GH_J A_J\| + \delta_0 \|H_J A_J + A_J' H_J\| < \epsilon$$

Hence, $C_J \equiv \delta_0 (H_J A_J + A_J' H_J)$ lies in $B_\epsilon (GH_J A_J)$. Similarly there exists a $\delta' > 0$ such that $\delta' H_J A_J \in B_\epsilon (GH_J A_J)$. Since $\delta' > 0$, (14) impries that $\delta' H_J A_J$ has no eigen value with non-negative real part. Noticing that $B_\epsilon (GH_J A_J)$ is convex and hence is connected, Corollary 4 of Arrow[1: p.193], together with the symmetry of C_J, guarantees that all eigen values of C_J are negative, which coupled with the fact that $\delta_0 > 0$, further implies that $H_J A_J$ is negative quasi-definite. Hence the global asymptotic stability of the system (4) follows directly from the well known Liapunov theorem.[12]

---

12) For example, see Hartman [3: Corollary 11.2, p.539].

References

[1] Arrow, K.J.,"Stability Independent of Adjustment Speed," in G. Horwich and P.A. Samuelson(eds.), *Trade, Stability, and Macroeconomics: Essays in Honour of Lloyd A. Metzler*, 181-202, N.Y. Academic Press, 1974.

[2] Brauer, A., "On the Characteristic Roots of Power-positive Matrices," *Duke Mathematical Journal*, vol.28 (1961), 439-445.

[3] Hartman, P., *Ordinary Differential Equations*, New York, John Wiley and Sons, 1964.

[4] Lancaster, P., *Theory of Matrices*, N.Y., Academic Press, 1969.

[5] Mukherji, A., "Stability in an Economy with Production," in G. Horwich and P.A. Samuelson(eds.), *Trade, Stability, and Macroeconomics: Essays in Honour of Lloyd A. Metzler*, 243-258, New York, Academic Press, 1974.

[6] Okuguchi, K., "Power-Positive Matrices and Global Stability of Competitive Equilibrium," *Keio Economic Studies*, vol.12 (1975), 37-40.

[7] Nikaido, H., "Stability of Equilibrium by the Brown-von Neumann Differential Equation," *Econometrica*, vol.27 (1959), 654-671.

[8] ——., *Linear Algebra for Economists (Keizai no tameno Senkei Sugaku)*, in Japanese, Tokyo, Baifukan, 1961.

 [9] ——., "Generalized Gross Substitutability and Extremization", in M. Dresher, S. Shapley and W. Tucker (eds.), *Advances in Game Theory*, Princeton, Princeton University Press, 1964.

[10] Sato, R., "The Stability of Competitive System which Contains Gross Complements, "*Review of Economic Studies*, vol.39 (1972), 495-499.

[11] ——., "On the Stability Properties of Dynamic Economic Systems," *International Economic Review*, vol.14 (1973), 753-764.

Marketing Costs and Unemployment Equilibrium *

T. Negishi

I.

There are three problems, as Arrow [1967] pointed out, that the general equilibrium theory has not succeeded in dealing with effectively, i.e.,the failures (1) to provide the integration of Walrasian microeconomics and Keynesian macroeconomics, (2) to incorporate imperfect competition properly and (3) to take account of the cost of making transactions. These three problems are, in our opinion, not independent but mutually related. Following the suggestion of Arrow [1959], we have already considered the problems (1) and (2) elsewhere.[1] The aim of this note is, therefore, to consider problems (1) and (3), i.e. the possibility of non-Walrasian, hopefully Keynesian, unemployment equilibrium due to the introduction of marketing costs into the Walrasian model of perfect competition.

After a brief survey of recent contributions incorporating transaction costs to general equilibrium theory and an old controvery on decreasing costs and marketing expenses, we conclude that the cost of marketing should be considered, for our purpose, as a function not only of the individual quantity of supply, but also of the state of market demand (Sections II and III). A recent paper of Varian [1975] on non-Walrasian equilibrium will also be briefly reviewed, since it suggests the possibility of explaining Keynesian unemployment equilibrium on the basis of costly transaction and disutility from searching for jobs (Section IV). Models of representative firms and households with transaction costs are presented in Section V. The final section is devoted to consider the existence of an equilibrium with Keynesian unemployment.

II.

To incorporate costs of transaction to the general equilibrium theory has been intensively studied by number of recent contributions, including those by Foley, Hahn and Kurz.[2]

The contributions are mainly formal and mathematical, with the result that precisely what are

*   This work was supported in part by National Science Foundation grant SOC74-11446 at the Institute for Mathematical Studies in the Social Sciences at Stanford University, and in part by the Japan Economic Research Foundation and the Tokyo Center for Economic Research.
1)   See Negishi [1974] and Negishi [1976].
2)   For a survey of these contributions, see Ulph and Ulph [1975].

included in transaction costs has not been much discussed. Foley [1970], one of the pioneering contributions, stated, however, he considered costs involved in marketing activities, i.e. the efforts required to inform buyers or sellers of the existence of a supply or demand for a commodity and its price, which, among others, include advertising and product certification. Ulph and Ulph [1975], on the other hand, surveyed these contributions and pointed out that they are mainly concerned with the costs of actually arranging trades at the given equilibrium prices (e.g. consts of acquiring or disseminating information about the prices and characteristics of goods and searching for prospective trading partners) rather than the costs of setting up markets and establishing equilibrium prices. There are no explanations given against possible objections to include certain kinds of transaction costs when equilibrium prices are known and announced at the beginning in these models.[3]

Although many important insights, particularly from the point of view of the theory of money, have been gained from these contributions,[4] what is important for us is the fact that are exclusively concerned with a full employment equilibrium. This seems to be because transaction costs are assumed to be dependent only on dividual notional demands and supplies.

For example, in Foley's [1970] model, the producers are assumed to maximize profit

$$p^s y + (p^b - p^s) y^b$$

being subject to $(y, y^b) \in Y$, where p^s and p^b are given vectors of selling prices and of buying prices, y and y^b are vectors of total net transaction the producer makes and of purchases and sales subject to the premium buying prices, and Y is the feasible set of (y, y^b). Transaction costs are defined implicitly in terms of p^s, p^b, y and y^b. Transactions do not necessarily have to be carried out through intermediaries in Foley's [1970] model, since some "producers may do all their marketing in all markets hiring resources at the selling price and selling their output at the buying price."[5]

Hahn [1971], another pioneering contribution, on the other hand, specified that M^t is the set of market activities (m^t, m^{Ht}) that are technologically feasible at time t, where $m^{Ht} \leq 0$ is the vector of inputs of named goods (i.e. goods owned by agents, to be exchanged or to be consumed in transactions), m^t is the vector of net outputs of anonymous goods (i.e. goods bought by agents) and H is the set of agents.

Finally and most explicitly, Kurtz [1974] defined transaction activities as

$$(x^h, y^h, g^h) \in T^h$$

3) See Kahn [1932], Ulph and Ulph [1975] and Section III.
4) See Ulph and Ulph [1975].
5) Ulph and Ulph [1975] seem, however, to insist that all transactions are carried out through intermediaries in Foley's [1970] model.

where x^h, y^h and g^h are respectively vectors of purchases, of sales and of real resources used in exchange of y^h for x^h of consumer h, and T^h is the feasible set of transaction activities of consumer h.

With these specifications of transaction activities, transaction costs are functions of the desired level of individual supplies and there exists no possibility of involuntary undersupplies (discrepancies between notional or desired and actual or realized supplies) at the competitive equilibrium.

In the practical world of management, however, marketing is always considered by the management with respect to the situation in which the supply of goods is greater than market demand. If it is considered as overproduction of goods, the policy is to cut production and lay off workers. If, on the other hand, it is viewed as underproduction of markets, the policy is to obtain a balance between demand and supply—produce more markets, hire more salesmen, increase advertising budgets.[6] Costs of transaction should be, therefore, a function of the state of market demand as well as of the desired level of individual supplies.

III.

As a matter of fact, this point was well recognized by aprticipants of the controversy concerning decreasing costs in the 1930's.

Sraffa [1926] argued that the chief obstacle against which competitive businessmen have to contend when they want to increase production does not lie in the cost of production but in the difficulty of selling the larger quantity of goods without reducing the price, or without having to face increased marketing expenses in the form of advertising, commercial travellers and facilities to consumers. Harrod [1931] also argued that a firm whose product is not standardized or whose market is not organized may meet the difficulty of marketing increments of produce in two ways, i.e. by lowering price, or by increasing market expenses. While Sraffa [1926] considered the case in which the former method is adopted and the analysis can be assimilated to that of the case of a monopoly, Harrod [1931] considered the case in which the latter method is adopted, the price remains unchanged and marketing costs are functions not only of the quantity of output, but also of the state of demand.[7] Allen [1932] further specifies that marketing expenses, which appear neither on the supply side nor on the demand side but in relation between the two, are functions of the ratio of the firm's individual output to the total demand to the industry, assuming that any variation in demand is distributed uniformly over the whole market. It is assumed to be an increasing function, i.e. "any attempt to push

---

6) See Drury [1962].
7) Sraffa [1926] admitted that two methods are equivalent from the point of view of formal correctness. If the latter method is adopted, we have the case of an imperfect and competitive market. See Stigler [1957]. Incidentally, the demand curve considered by Sraffa should be kinked, since firms are "prevented by competition from exceeding" the current price.

out into the competitor's territory is attended with rising marketing costs per unit of sales and a surrender of territory to him would allow a reduction in them."

It is Kahn [1932] who criticized Harrod [1931] and Allen [1932] to the effect that the infinitely elastic demand curve for the individual firm is hard to reconcile with the existence of marketing costs.[8] "If a firm can increase its sales to any desired extent by an infinitesimal reduction of its price, why should it go to the expense of incurring Mr. Harrod's marketing costs? " It is certainly true that the existence of marketing costs cannot be explained if a firm facing an infinitely elastic demand curve is selling the optimal amount of output, i.e. the marginal cost of production is currently equalized to the price. In the case of demand deficiency, however, current level of sales is lower than the optimal level and it is impossible to "increase its sales to any desired extent by an infinitesimal reduction of its price." It is necessary either to have a finitely small reduction of the price or to have a finitely small increase in marketing expenses, to increase the level of sales. In other words, the effect of increasing market expenses is not very large, particularly when other firms are in the same situation. If the market expenses are reduced, on the other hand, the reduction of the sales is very large. This suggests that the marketing costs curve is kinked at the point of current sales and only the extra transaction costs to increase sales of supplies facing demand deficiency does matter to consider the possibility of Keynesian unemployment equilibrium.

IV.

A recent paper of Varian [1975] on persistent disequilibrium is highly suggestive to consider the possibility of a Keynesian unemployment equilibrium from the point of view of the transaction costs which are functions of the state of market demand. Persistent disequilibrium is a stationary situation in which Walrasian excess demands exist but changes in prices are negligible. Such a stationary state, or a non-Walrasian equilibrium is possible if excess demands which affect price movements are effective excess demands which are different from Walrasian notional excess demands. Varian suggests that this difference comes from the agent's consideration of the likelihood of fulfilling his desired transactions when transactions are costly.

Varian considered a simple model of a market in which supply of the good is equal to 1. Demand for the good $C_D = (a/p)$ is derived from the maximizing utility.

(1) $\qquad a \log C + (1 - a) \log (1 - L)$

with respect to C (consumption) and L (labor supply), being subject to the budget constraint $pC = L$,

---

8) Allen excluded the advertising charges in a perfect market. Kahn stated, however, there is no difference between advertising charges and other marketing expenses.

where total available time is equal to 1, p is the price of a good in terms of labor service and a is a positive constant less than 1. Walrasian excess demand is easily calculated as $Z = (a/p) - 1$. Suppose there exists a positive excess demand for the current price. Consumers have disutility due to the disequilibrium, for example, due to the waiting time necessary for standing in line to obtain the good. Utility function is then modified to

(2) $a \log C + (1-a) \log (1 - L - 4pZC)$

and the demand for the good is changed to $C_D = a (p + 4pZ)$. Accumulated excess demand is

(3) $Z' = \dfrac{a}{p} + \dfrac{a}{p + 4a - 4p} - 2$

which gives non-Walrasian equilibrium price $p = 2a/3$ in addition to Walrasian $p = a$.

   Although this non-Walrasian equilibrium is not directly related to Keynesian equilibrium, Varian further suggests that unemployment equilibrium is possible if disutility of looking for work may encourage workers to lower their effective supply of labor so as to equate it with the effective demand for labor.

V.

   Let us consider the model of the competitive representative firm. Suppose the short-run production function and the marketing cost function are denoted respectively by $F(k)$ and $C(F(k)/D)pF(k)$, where k, D and p are respectively the level of unemployment, of current sales and the price of the output. Since D is assumed to be proportional to the aggregate effective demand, $F(k)$ should be equal to the given D when the short-term expectation is realized. The profit to be maximized with given p, w and D is

(4) $pF(k) - wk - C(\dfrac{F(k)}{D})pF(k)$

where w is the rate of wage. Conditions for the short-run equilibrium with short-term expectations realized are

(5) $F(k) = D$

(6) $p(1 - C'^{+} - C(1))F' - w \leq 0$

(7) $p(1 - C'^{-} - C(1))F' - w \geq 0$

where C'^{+} $(C'^{-}) = dC(1)/dk^{+}$ $(dC(1)/dk^{-})$ and $F' = dF/dk$. It is assumed that $C'^{+} > C'^{-} \cong 0$. There is no reason for the price (p) to change if these conditions are satisfied since effective supply $(F(k))$

is equilized to effective demand (D). If these conditions are satisfied with strict inequalities, further-more, small changes in D are absorbed in those in k and p remains unchanged.

Marketing costs $C(F/D)pF$ are defined so as to satisfy Harrod's [1932] requirement, i.e. average marketing costs are functions of the ratio of the firm's individual output to the aggregate demand, i.e. (F/D). For a firm in equilibrium, marketing costs are $C(1)pD$, i.e. its ratio to the total sale pD is constant $C(1)$, with whatever level of D and of p. It is a well known fact that firms really do seem to follow a rule of thumb to this effect with respect to advertising.[9] It has already been shown by Dorfman and Steiner [1954] and more generally by Nerlove and Arrow [1962] that optimal advertising can explain this fact by assuming that demand is a function of the level (or accumulated level) of advertising as well as of price. This explanation cannot be applied to our case, however, since such an optimal level of advertising is zero when the demand is infinitely elastic with respect to price.

Suppose the households of workers are identical and those who are employed (for the insti-tutionally given hours) and those who are unemployed are being chosen randomly, with the same probability and no serial correlation. Each worker perceives that his probability of employment k can be increased beyond the current level $\bar{k}$, which is assumed to be equal to the ratio of the employ-ment to the total working population, only with extra toils troubles to find a job, denoted by $h(\max (0, k - \bar{k}))$.[10]

If workers are assumed to have monetary or resaleable assets, the desired k is obtained by maximizing expected value of the utility of being employed U and of being unemployed $\bar{U}$, i.e.

$$(8) \qquad kU(\frac{w}{p}, h (\max (0, k - \bar{k})), p) + (1 - k)\bar{U} (0, h (\max (0, k - \bar{k})), p)$$

with respect to k, where (w/p) is the real wage, the marginal utility of (w/p), to be denoted by U_1 and $\bar{U}_1$, is positive and the marginal utility of h, to be denoted by U_2 and $\bar{U}_2$, is negative. At the equilibrium where short-term expectations are realized, i.e. $k = \bar{k}$, the conditions

$$(9) \qquad U(\frac{w}{p}, h(0), p) - \bar{U}(0, h(0), p) \geqq 0$$

$$(10) \qquad U(\frac{w}{p}, h(0), p) - \bar{U}(0, h(0), p) + kU_2 (\frac{w}{p}, h(0), p)h' + (1- k)\bar{U}_2 (0, h(0), p)h' \leqq 0$$

are satisfied, where $h' = dh(0)/d(\max (0, k - k))^+$ at $k = \bar{k}$ is positive. The rate of money wage w is kept unchanged with $k < 1$, if these conditions are satisfied for given p. Since these conditions are not violated by an increase in k, when the marginal utility of income is constant and that of leisure is diminishing, i.e. $U_2 ((w/p), h,p) - \bar{U}_2 (0, h, p) = U_2(w/p), h,p) - U_2(0, h,p) + U_2(0,h,p)$

---

9)   See Nerlove and Arrow [1962].
10)   The marketing cost to keep k at $\bar{k}$, i.e. $h(0)$, is not necessarily zero.

$- \bar{U}_2 (0, h, p) < 0$, the equality of effective demand and effective supply of labor is undisturbed by the increases in the effective demand which merely causes changes in the level of employment. The unemployment is therefore Keynesian involuntary unemployment, since the unemployed are willing to be employed at the current rate of wage .

VI.

Let us suppose that real saving s is a function of real national income and the level of price p, the latter being assumed to be arbitrarily fixed as given below. By taking the unit properly, we can make the amount of the total labor available to the representative firm equal to one. Then the level of employment k considered in (4) and the probability of employment k in (8) are identical.

The level of exogenous investment I^0 and real wage $(w/p)^0$ at the neoclassical full employment equilibrium can be obtained from the equality of real investment I and saving

(11) $\qquad s(F(1)) = 1$

and the equality form of (7), with $C'^- + C(1) = 0$, i.e. the neoclassical equality of marginal productivity of labor and real wage,

(12) $\qquad F'(1) = (\frac{w}{p})$.

Keynesian unemployment equilibrium can be possible only if $I < I^0$. Suppose $I^1 < I^0$ is given. Consider a solution of the equality of investment and saving

(13) $\qquad s(F(k)) = I^1$

and the equality form of (7),

(14) $\qquad (1 - C'^- - C(1)) F' (k) = (\frac{w}{p})$

which we denote as k^1 and $(w/p)^1$. We note that $(w/p)^1$ is not necessarily higher than $(w/p)^0$, since $C' + C(1) \geqq 0$, even if F' is strictly diminishing with respect to k, i.e. marginal productivity of labor is strictly diminishing. We also note that (6), i.e.

$$p(1 - C'^+ - C(1))F' - w \leqq 0$$

is satisfied with k^1 and $(w/p)^1$.

Let us assume that (9), i.e.

$$U(\frac{w}{p}, h(0)) - \bar{U}(0, h (0)) \geqq 0$$

is satisfied by $(w/p)^1$. This assumption means that the employment with the wage not less than some-thing like 95 percent of the full employment wage is preferred to the unemployment, since $C'^- \cong 0$ and $C(1)$, i.e. the ratio of marketing costs to total value of sales is something less than 5 percent.[11]

If $(w/p)^1$ happens to satisfy (10), i.e.

(15) $\qquad U((\frac{w}{p})^1, h(0)) - U(0, h(0)) + kU_2((\frac{w}{p})^1, h(0))h' + (1-k)\bar{U}_2(0, h(0))h' \leqq 0,$

then $(w/p)^1$ and k^1 are equilibrium real wage and equilibrium level of employment. If $(w/p)^1$ does not satisfy (10), i.e.

(16) $\qquad U((\frac{w}{p})^1, h(0)) - \bar{U}(0, h(0)) + kU_2((\frac{w}{p})^1, h'(0))h' + (1-k)U_2(0, h(0)) > 0,$

we have to assume further that

(17) $\qquad 1 - C'^+ - C(1) < 0$

which means that C'^+ is larger than something like 0.95, in view of the fact that $C(1)$ is something less than 0.05.[12] For sufficiently low $(\frac{w}{p})$, say $(\frac{w}{p})^2$, we have

(18) $\qquad U(\frac{w}{p}, h(0)) - \bar{U}(0, h(0)) < 0$.

Since U and $\bar{U}$ are continuous, there exists $(w/p)^3$ such that

(19) $\qquad (\frac{w}{p})^2 < (\frac{w}{p})^3 < (\frac{w}{p})^1$

(20) $\qquad U((\frac{w}{p})^3, h(0)) - \bar{U}(0, h(0)) > 0$

(21) $\qquad U(\frac{w}{p})^3, h(0)) - \bar{U}(0, h(0)) + kU_2((\frac{w}{p})^3, h(0))h' + (1-k)\bar{U}_2(0, h(0))h' = 0$

in view of (16) and (18). Because $(w/p)^3$ and k^1 satisfy (6) and (7), they are respectively the equili-brium real wage and equilibrium level of employment.

Since (4) can be rewritten as

$$(p - C(\frac{F(k)}{D})p)F(k) - wk = q(F(k), D, p)F(k) - wk$$

the model of the firm in the above, based on the second method of Sraffa [1926], is formally identical to the model considered in Negishi [1974] and Negishi [1976] which followed the first method of Sraffa, if $q = (p - Cp)$ is considered to be the net seller's price. Condition (17) is, therefore,

---

11) According to Doyle [1968], advertising as percentage of consumers' expenditure is 2.7 in the U.K. in the 60's and 3.7 in the U.S. for the past twenty years. For industrial differences in advertising outlays per dollar of sales, see Telser [1964].
12) See footnote 11.

identical to the condition imposed in Negishi [1976], i.e. the right hand side elasticity of demand with respect to price is smaller than one, since the latter implies

$$-(\frac{dq}{dF(k)})^+(\frac{F(k)}{q}) = C'^+ (\frac{p}{p-Cp})> 1$$

which is identical to (17). The model of households of workers in the above is, however, different from the model given in Negishi [1974] and Negishi [1976]. This is because transaction costs for workers are not given in terms of money and individual workers are not certain to be employed.

Let us finally emphasize that the equilibrium shown to exist here is not merely non-Walrasian but positively Keynesian, since an increase in effective demand, i.e. in I causes an increase in employment with unchanged rate of wage.[13]

---

13) Perhaps it should be mentioned that marketing costs of firms form a part of non-wage income, i.e. income of marketing specialists.

References

Allen, R.G.D. [1932], "Decreasing Costs: A Mathematical Note," *Economic Journal*, 42, 323-326.

Arrow, K.J. [1959], "Towards a Theory of Price Adjustment," *The Allocation of Economic Resources*, Stanford.

Arrow, K.J. [1967], "Samuelson Collected," *Journal of Political Economy*, 75, 730-737.

Dorfman, R. and P.O. Steiner [1954], "Optimal Advertising and Optimal Quality," *American Economic Review*, 44, 826-836.

Doyle, P. [1968], "Economic Aspects of Advertising: A Survery," *Economic Journal*, 78, 570-602.

Drury, J.G. [1962], "Is your Problem Overproduction or Underproduction of Markets? " *Managerial Marketing*, Laezer and Kelley (eds.), Irwin.

Foley, D.K. [1970], "Economic Equilibrium with Costly Marketing," *Journal of Economic Theory*, 2, 276-291.

Hahn, F.H. [1971], "Equilibrium with Transaction Costs" *Econometrica*, 39, 417-439.

Harrod, R.F. [1931], "The Law of Decreasing Costs," *Economic Journal*, 41, 566-576.

Kahn, R.F. [1932], "A Note on the Contributions of Mr. Harrod and Mr. Allen," *Economic Journal*, 42, 657-661.

Kurz, M. [1974], "Equilibrium with Transaction Cost and Money in a Single Market Exchange Economy," *Journal of Economic Theory*, 7, 418-452.

Negishi, T. [1974], "Involuntary Unemployment and Market Imperfection," *Economic Studies Quartery*, 25, 32-41.

Negishi, T. [1976], "Existence of an Underemployment Equilibrium," *Equilibrium and Disequilibrium in Economic Theory*, G. Schwödiauer (ed.), R. Reidel.

Nerlove, M. and K.J. Arrow [1962], "Optimal Advertising Policy under Dynamic Conditions," *Economica*, 29, 129-142.

Sraffa, P. [1926], "The Law of Returns under Competitive Conditions," *Economic Journal*, 36, 535-550.

Stigler, G.J. [1957], "Perfect Competition, Historically Contemplated," *Journal of Political Economy*, 65, 1-17.

Ulph, A.M. and D.T. Ulph [1975], "Transaction Costs in General Equilibrium Theory — A Survey" *Economica*, 42, 355-372.

Varian, H.R. [1975], "On Persistent Disequilibrium," *Journal of Economic Theory*, 10, 218-228.

MONOPOLY AND GENERAL EQUILIBRIUM

by

Tadashi Minagawa

Introduction

Competitive equilibrium, because of its economic and mathematical elegance, has been studied from all angles, and seemingly, there remains no more problem to be further explored. However, apart from the pioneering works by some economists, the attempt has been almost disregarded to ask the meaning of the basic conditions of competitive equilibrium, to consider the economic relevance of these conditions, and to clarify the overall working of the entire economy under more realistically relevant conditions.

Certainly, the assumptions: (1) peculiar mechanism defined by the term of "perfect competition," and (2) convexity of production possibility sets and preferences, have played an essential role to prove the existence and stability of competitive equilibrium. But the assumption (1), implying that no individual can control prices, is based on the supposed behaviour of auctioneer in a market, and therefore depicts a market rule not corresponding to the facts obtaining in almost all the markets. Moreover, setting aside their actual relevance, if we are to inquire the origin of "perfect competition" mechanism, we should be brought to analyzing some state of imperfect competition. On the other hand, the phenomenon of increasing returns to scale or decreasing marginal cost, which is not infrequently noticed in the current industrial production, is not compatible with the assumption (2). Not only that, it also contradicts the very premise of assumption (1) that firms are numerous, and that an individual entrepreneur can increase or reduce his output level without noticeably altering the market price.

Now, if the proper purpose of general equilibrium theory is to abstract the working of an entire national economy and to reveal its fundamental framework, it will be evidently required that assumption (1) or (2) should be replaced by some other assumption with more realistic pertinence.

I.   Demand Functions: Objective versus Subjective
1)

Nikaido [4] presents an equilibrium model with competitive and monopolistic sectors in which production technologies are of Leontief type. And he shows that for any given price vector, there exists a unique output vector which brings about the demand and supply equilibrium for every market. This relationship of correspondence is defined as the objective demand functions. Therefore, the objective demand functions mean the correspondence between price vector and output vector, which realizes both the demand-supply equilibrium in every market and the consistent circular flow of national income. An objective demand function is envisaged as covering an industry's demand function, commonly used by the orthodox industrial organization's approach about monopoly or oligopoly. But it is interesting to notice that the objective demand function does not necessarily represent the downward sloping curve with respect to the price of the good in question.

Within the more general framework, where a production possibility set for each firm is not always convex and contains joint production, FitzRoy [1] indicates that between activity vectors of monopolistic firms and price vector of all the goods and services, there exists the same relation as is pointed out by Nikaido, though the existence of this relation is not proved explicitly in his article.

It must be noted here that no assumption is given about the behaviour-rule of each firm in the said relationship of correspondence. It merely explains the relation between prices and outputs (or inputs) which brings about simultaneously equality of demand and supply for every market, satisfaction of the budget constraint by each household, and nonnegative profit for every firm. Therefore, a set of prices and outputs (or inputs) at a general equilibrium must satisfy the objective demand functions, whatever behaviour pattern each firm may choose. According to the different behaviours of firms, an equilibrium point to be determined on the functions will also vary.
2)

Negishi, in his important pioneering work [3], presents a general equilibrium model of monopolistic competition. His model is based on the assumption that each monopolistically competitive firm perceives subjective inverse demand (or supply) functions for his outputs (or inputs) under the given information of the actual state of the market, and strives for the maximization of his profit calculated in terms of these functions. Now, the given information of the actual state of the market means a set of current price and trade vectors. Therefore, this set of vectors must satisfy the above objective demand (or supply) functions. But the existence of general equilibrium, which is characterized by the simultaneous realization of the noncooperative profit maximizing behaviours of all firms and the equality of demand and supply for every good and service, is proved by defining independently each domain of current price and trade vectors. Consequently, this model does not take into consideration such correspondence as is supposed by the objective demand (or supply) functions. In order to define the domain of current price or trade vector, it will be clearly needed to take into account the budget constraint or nonnegativity of profit, even if the actual state of the economy involves market disequilibrium.

Though the subjective demand (or supply) function is a realistic conception, and it seems to play a very important role in the general disequilibrium theory, the objective demand (or supply) function should be a constant referrant, in so far as a general equilibrium situation is considered. Because the very notion of general equilibrium is objective in character.

II.   General Equilibrium with a Monopolistic Sector

There are two sectors of production: the capital good sector (sector 1) and the consumption good sector (sector 2). There exists monopolist in either or each of these sectors, who tries to maximize the monopoly profit calculated in terms of the objective demand function for his product. Monopoly is assumed in the product markets, in which there is no freedom of entry, but perfect competition in the factor markets.

In the following we inquire the conditions to assure the existence of equilibrium prices and outputs which bring about the equality of demand and supply for every market.

1)

First, we suppose the economy where a monopolistic sector and a competitive sector co-exist, and consumers are represented by a single representative household who supplies both labour and capital service. The household determines the quantity of each good demanded and that of labour and capital service supplied for any given prices. In view of the demand function for his product calculated from such determination, the monopolist on his part determines the quantity of his product supplied and that of each factor of production demanded so as to maximize the monopoly profit. The maximum monopoly profit thus realized is all distributed to the household. On the other hand, the production function of the competitive sector is homogeneous of degree one, and the demands for factors of production are determined so as to minimize the unit cost, which equals to the price of the product of this sector under the assumption of perfect competition.

Now, let us define the following variables,

x_i : output in the ith sector,

l_i : quantity of labour employed in the ith sector, i=1,2,

k_i : quantity of capital employed in the ith sector, i=1, 2,

L : total labour supply,

K : total quantity of available capital,

p_i : price of the ith good, i=1, 2,

w : wage rate,

q : rental of capital,

π_i : monopoly profit distributed to the household from the ith sector, i=1, 2.

Without loss of generality, we assume that sector 1 is perfectly competitive and sector 2 is mono-polistic.

Now, for given prices p_1, p_2, w, q, and monopoly profit π_2, the household determines the quantity of each good demanded x_1, x_2, and that of each factor of production supplied L, K respectively, so as to maximize his utility. We suppose that the demand functions and the supply functions satisfy the following assumption:

(Assumption 1) Each of the demand function for the ith good $x_i(p_1, p_2, w, q, \pi_2)$, i=1, 2, and the supply function of labour $L(p_1, p_2, w, q, \pi_2)$ is single-valued, continuous, nonnegative and homogeneous function of degree zero with respect to (p_1, p_2, w, q, π_2), where $(p_1, p_2) > 0$, $(w, q) \geq 0$ and $\pi_2 \geq 0$. For any nonnegative p_1, p_2, w, q, and π_2 such that $(p_1, p_2) > 0$ and $(w, q) \neq 0$, at least one component of (x_1, x_2) is strictly positive, and the supply function of capital service takes a constant value $K^* > 0$. [1]

Let us now consider the side of supply. As stated before, sector 1 determines the capital- and labour-input coefficients α_1, β_1, so as to minimize the average cost subject to the production function homogeneous of degree one. We assume that the capital- and labour-input coefficients in sector 1 satisfy the following assumption:

(Assumption 2)   Each of $\alpha_1(w, q)$ and $\beta_1(w, q)$ is single-valued, continuous, positive and homogeneous function of degree zero with respect to (w, q), where $(w, q) \geq 0$.

Under competitive situations, the minimum cost $q \cdot \alpha_1(w, q) + w \cdot \beta_1(w, q)$ must be equal to the price of the 1st good. Thus we obtain the following relation:

$$p_1 = q\,\alpha_1(w, q) + w\,\beta_1(w, q),$$

which implies by (Assumption 2) that p_1 is single-valued, continuous, positive and homogeneous function of degree one with respect to $(w, q) \geq 0$. We denote this function by

$$p_1 = p_1(w, q). \tag{1}$$

For given prices w, q, and output x_2, sector 2 determines the labour and capital inputs so as to minimize the total cost. Then, the demand function for each factor of production in sector 2 satisfies the following assumption:

(Assumption 3)   Each of the demand function for labour $l_2(x_2, w, q)$ and the demand function for capital service $k_2(x_2, w, q)$ is single-valued, continuous, and nonnegative function of x_2, w, and q, where $x_2 \geq 0$ and $(w, q) \geq 0$, and is homogeneous of degree zero with respect to $(w, q) \geq 0$. For any $x_2 > 0$ and $(w, q) \geq 0$, $l_2(x_2, w, q)$ and $k_2(x_2, w, q)$ are strictly positive. It should be noted that (Assumption 3) does not exclude the phenomenon of increasing returns to scale. We make the additional assumptions:

---

[1]   We follow the usual conventions for vector inequalities. $x \geq y$ means $x_i \geq y_i$ for all i; $x \geq y$ means $x \geq y$ and $x \neq y$; $x > y$ means $x_i > y_i$ for all i.

(Assumption 4) Sector 2 produces $x_2 \in X_2$, where X_2 is a compact real interval $[\underline{x}_2, \bar{x}_2]$ such that $0 < \underline{x}_2 < \bar{x}_2$.

(Assumption 5) There exists the inverse demand function for the 2nd good $p_2(x_2, p_1, w, q, \pi_2)$ such that $p_2(x_2, p_1, w, q, \pi_2)$ is single-valued, continuous and positive function of x_2, p_1, w, q, and π_2, where $x_2 \in X_2$, $p_1 > 0$, $(w, q) \geq 0$ and $\pi_2 \geq 0$, and is homogeneous of degree one with respect to $p_1 > 0$, $(w, q) \geq 0$, and $\pi_2 \geq 0$.

For given p_1, w, q, and π_2, the monopolist in sector 2 can, by selecting $x_2 \in X_2$, obtain the profit:

$$R_2(x_2, p_1, w, q, \pi_2) = x_2 \cdot p_2(x_2, p_1, w, q, \pi_2) - w \cdot l_2(x_2, w, q)$$
$$- q \cdot k_2(x_2, w, q).$$

Under (Assumption 3) - (Assumption 5), there exists a point $x_2(p_1, w, q, \pi_2) \in X_2$ which satisfies:

$$R_2(x_2(p_1, w, q, \pi_2); p_1, w, q, \pi_2) = \max R_2(x_2; p_1, w, q, \pi_2)$$
$$\text{over all } x_2 \in X_2.$$

Now, we make the following assumption:

(Assumption 6) For any nonnegative p_1, w, q, and π_2, such that $p_1 > 0$ and $(w, q) \neq 0$, $x_2(p_1, w, q, \pi_2)$ is unique and $R_2(x_2(p_1, w, q, \pi_2); p_1, w, q, \pi_2) > 0$.

By (1) and (Assumption 3) - (Assumption 6), x_2 is single-valued, continuous, positive and homogeneous function of degree zero with respect to $(w, q) \geq 0$ and $\pi_2 \geq 0$.[2] We write this function as

$$x_2 = x_2(w, q, \pi_2). \tag{2}$$

In view of (1) and (2), the demand function for labour in sector 1, $l_1(x_1, w, q)$ can be represented by:

$$x_1(p_1, p_2, w, q, \pi_2) \cdot \beta_1(w, q) = x_1(p_1(w, q), p_2(x_2(w, q, \pi_2),$$
$$p_1(w, q), w, q, \pi_2), w, q, \pi_2) \cdot \beta_1(w, q),$$

which implies that l_1 is a single-valued, continuous and nonnegative function of w, q, and π_2, where $(w, q) \geq 0$ and $\pi_2 \geq 0$. Similarly, we can show that each of the demand function for

---

2)   See Okuguchi [5, pp.7-12].

labour in sector 2, l_2, the supply function of labour, L, the demand function for capital service in the i-th sector, k_i, and the profit function, R_2, is a single-valued, continuous and nonnegative function of $(w, q) \geq 0$ and $\pi_2 \geq 0$. Therefore, we rewrite $l_i(i = 1, 2)$, L, $k_i(i = 1, 2)$, and R_2 as $\lambda_i(w, q, \pi_2)$, $\lambda(w, q, \pi_2)$, $\kappa_i(w, q, \pi_2)$ and $r_2(w, q, \pi_2)$, respectively. Then it will be clear that $\lambda_i(i = 1, 2)$, $\kappa_i(i = 1, 2)$, and λ are homogeneous of degree zero in w, q, and π_2, while r_2 is homogeneous of degree one in the same variables.

Thus we can normalize the price system so that $(w, q) \in Q$, where the set Q stands for the fundamental simplex in the 2-dimensional Euclidian space. Finally, we make the following assumptions:

(Assumption 7)   For any nonnegative p_1, p_2, w, q, and π_2 such that $(p_1, p_2) > 0$, and $(w, q) \neq 0$,

$$w \cdot \lambda(w, q, \pi_2) + q \cdot K^* + \pi_2 = p_1 \cdot x_1 (p_1, p_2, w, q, \pi_2) + p_2 \cdot x_2 (w, q, \pi_2)$$

holds.

(Assumption 8)   (a)   If $w = 0$, then $\lambda(w, q, \pi_2) = 0$. (b) For $(w, q) \in Q$, there exists a sufficiently large number $\bar{\pi}_2 > 0$ such that $\Sigma_{i=1}^2 \lambda_i(w, q, \bar{\pi}_2) - \lambda(w, q, \bar{\pi}_2) > 0$.[3]

(Assumption 7) is what we call the Walras law. From (Assumption 7) we obtain:

$$w \cdot x_1 (p_1, p_2, w, q, \pi_2) \cdot \beta_1 (w, q) + q \cdot x_1 (p_1, p_2, w, q, \pi_2) \cdot \alpha_1 (w, q) +$$
$$w \cdot \lambda_2 (w, q, \pi_2) + q \cdot \kappa_2 (w, q, \pi_2) + p_2 \cdot x_2 (w, q, \pi_2) - w \cdot \lambda_2 (w, q, \pi_2) -$$
$$q \cdot \kappa_2 (w, q, \pi_2) - w \cdot \lambda(w, q, \pi_2) - q \cdot K^* - \pi_2 = 0,$$

which, if rearranged, becomes

$$w \cdot (\Sigma_{i=1}^2 \lambda_i(w, q, \pi_2) - \lambda(w, q, \pi_2)) + q \cdot (\Sigma_{i=1}^2 \kappa_i(w, q, \pi_2) - K^*) +$$
$$r_2 (w, q, \pi_2) - \pi_2 = 0. \tag{3}$$

(Assumption 8)   (b)   implies that if sufficiently large profit as against the wage rate is distributed to the household, he loses his will to supply labour service, and consequently excess demand for labour arises at labour marcket.

From maximizing the additive logarithmic utility function $a_1 \text{ Log } x_1 + a_2 \text{ Log } x_2 + a_3 \text{ Log } (L_0 - L)$, where $L_0 - L$ is leisure, subject to the constraints $x_i > 0$ $(i = 1, 2)$, $L_0 > L \geq 0$,

---

3)   For $(w, q) \in Q$ and $\pi_2 = \bar{\pi}_2$, $\Sigma_{i=1}^2 \lambda_i(w, q, \pi_2)$ is strictly positive.

and $\Sigma_{i=1}^{2} p_i x_i = wL + qK^* + \pi_2$, we can derive the following supply function of labour:

$$w \cdot (L_0 - L) = \frac{a_3}{a_1 + a_2 + a_3} (wL_0 + qK^* + \pi_2),$$

$$L = 0 \quad \text{for} \quad w \cdot (L_0 - L) < \frac{a_3}{a_1 + a_2 + a_3} (wL_0 + qK^* + \pi_2),$$

which satisfies (Assumption 8).

We are now ready to prove the following theorem:

(Theorem) Under (Assumption 1) - (Assumption 8), there exists at least one triplet of (w^*, q^*, π_2^*) which satisfies:

$$\Sigma_{i=1}^{2} \lambda_i(w^*, q^*, \pi_2^*) = \lambda(w^*, q^*, \pi_2^*),$$

$$\Sigma_{i=1}^{2} \kappa_i(w^*, q^*, \pi_2^*) \leqq K^*,$$

$$r_2(w^*, q^*, \pi_2^*) = \pi_2^*.$$

(Proof)[4]

For any point $(w, q, \pi_2) \in Q \times \pi$, where $\pi = \{\pi_2 \mid 0 \leqq \pi_2 \leqq \bar{\pi}_2\}$, we shall define $\varphi_1(w, q, \pi_2)$, $\varphi_2(w, q, \pi_2)$, and $\varphi_3(w, q, \pi_2)$ as follows:

$$\varphi_1(w, q, \pi_2) = (\Sigma_{i=1}^{2} \lambda_i(w, q, \pi_2) - \lambda(w, q, \pi_2)) \cdot \pi_2,$$

$$\varphi_2(w, q, \pi_2) = (\Sigma_{i=1}^{2} \kappa_i(w, q, \pi_2) - K^*) \cdot \pi_2,$$

$$\varphi_3(w, q, \pi_2) = (r_2(w, q, \pi_2) - \pi_2).$$

Further we let:

$$\theta_i(w, q, \pi_2) = \max(\varphi_i(w, q, \pi_2), 0) \quad (i = 1, 2, 3).$$

In terms of these auxiliary variables, we shall construct single-valued and continuous mappings:

$$\psi_1(w, q, \pi_2) = \frac{1}{1 + \Sigma_{i=1}^{2} \theta_i(w, q, \pi_2)} \cdot (w + \theta_1(w, q, \pi_2)),$$

$$\psi_2(w, q, \pi_2) = \frac{1}{1 + \Sigma_{i=1}^{2} \theta_i(w, q, \pi_2)} \cdot (q + \theta_2(w, q, \pi_2)),$$

$$\psi_3(w, q, \pi_2) = \frac{\bar{\pi}_2}{\bar{\pi}_2 + \Sigma_{i=1}^{3} \theta_i(w, q, \pi_2)} \cdot (\pi_2 + \theta_3(w, q, \pi_2)).$$

_____

4) Our method of proof is a slight modification of Morishima [2].

It is clear that $(\psi_1(w, q, \pi_2), \psi_2(w, q, \pi_2), \psi_3(w, q, \pi_2)) \epsilon Q \times \Pi$. Thus the mapping:

$(w, q, \pi_2) \rightarrow (\psi_1(w, q, \pi_2), \psi_2(w, q, \pi_2), \psi_3(w, q, \pi_2))$ from $Q \times \Pi$ to $Q \times \Pi$ has a fixed point

$(w^*, q^*, \pi_2^*) \epsilon Q \times \Pi$ by virtue of Brouer's fixed point theorem.

After some manipulations, this point satisfies:

$$w^* \cdot \Sigma_{i=1}^2 \theta_i(w^*, q^*, \pi_2^*) = \theta_1(w^*, q^*, \pi_2^*),$$

$$q^* \cdot \Sigma_{i=1}^2 \theta_i(w^*, q^*, \pi_2^*) = \theta_2(w^*, q^*, \pi_2^*),$$

$$\pi_2^* \cdot \Sigma_{i=1}^3 \theta_i(w^*, q^*, \pi_2^*) = \bar{\pi}_2 \cdot \theta_3(w^*, q^*, \pi_2^*). \qquad (4)$$

Let us now prove that $\pi_2^* > 0$. Suppose $\pi_2^* = 0$; then we find by (Assumption 6) that $\varphi_3(w^*, q^*, \pi_2^*) = r_2(w^*, q^*, \pi_2^*) - 0 > 0$. Hence $\theta_3(w^*, q^*, \pi_2^*) > 0$, contradicting (4). Thus $\pi_2^* > 0$.

Next suppose $\Sigma_{i=1}^2 \theta_i(w^*, q^*, \pi_2^*) > 0$. Then,

$$w^* > 0 \quad \text{if and only if} \quad \theta_1(w^*, q^*, \pi_2^*) > 0,$$

$$q^* > 0 \quad \text{if and only if} \quad \theta_2(w^*, q^*, \pi_2^*) > 0,$$

$$\pi_2^* > 0 \quad \text{if and only if} \quad \theta_3(w^*, q^*, \pi_2^*) > 0.$$

Since $(w^*, q^*) \geq 0$ and $\pi_2^* > 0$, we obtain $w^* \cdot \varphi_1(w^*, q^*, \pi_2^*) + q^* \cdot \varphi_2(w^*, q^*, \pi_2^*) + \pi_2^* \cdot \varphi_3(w^*, q^*, \pi_2^*) > 0$, which yields $\pi_2^* \cdot \{ w^* \cdot (\Sigma_{i=1}^2 \lambda_i(w^*, q^*, \pi_2^*) - \lambda(w^*, q^*, \pi_2^*)) + q^* \cdot (\Sigma_{i=1}^2 \kappa_i(w^*, q^*, \pi_2^*) - K^*) + (r_2(w^*, q^*, \pi_2^*) - \pi_2^*) \} > 0$. This contradicts (3). Hence $\Sigma_{i=1}^2 \theta_i(w^*, q^*, \pi_2^*) = 0$, so that $\theta_i(w^*, q^*, \pi_2^*) = 0$ $(i = 1, 2)$.

If $\theta_3(w^*, q^*, \pi_2^*) > 0$, it follows from $\Sigma_{i=1}^2 \theta_i(w^*, q^*, \pi_2^*) = 0$ and (4) that $\pi_2^* = \bar{\pi}_2$. Therefore, from (Assumption 8) we obtain $\bar{\pi}_2 \cdot (\Sigma_{i=1}^2 \lambda_i(w^*, q^*, \pi_2^*) - \lambda(w^*, q^*, \pi_2^*)) > 0$, which implies $\varphi_i(w^*, q^*, \pi_2^*) = \theta_1(w^*, q^*, \pi_2^*) > 0$. This contradicts $\theta_1(w^*, q^*, \pi_2^*) = 0$. Hence $\theta_3(w^*, q^*, \pi_2^*) = 0$.

Thus there exists a fixed point (w^*, q^*, π_2^*) such that $\varphi_i(w^*, q^*, \pi_2^*) \leq 0$ $(i = 1, 2, 3)$.

Next we can prove that

$$w^* = 0 \quad \text{if} \quad \varphi_1(w^*, q^*, \pi_2^*) < 0,$$

$$q^* = 0 \quad \text{if} \quad \varphi_2(w^*, q^*, \pi_2^*) < 0,$$

$$\pi_2^* = 0 \quad \text{if} \quad \varphi_3(w^*, q^*, \pi_2^*) < 0.$$

Because if, for example, $w^* > 0$ when $\varphi_1(w^*, q^*, \pi_2^*) < 0$, we would have $\pi_2^* \cdot \{ w^* \cdot (\Sigma_{i=1}^2$

$\lambda_i(w^*, q^*, \pi_2^*) - \lambda(w^*, q^*, \pi_2^*)) + q^* \cdot (\Sigma_{i=1}^2 \kappa_i(w^*, q^*, \pi_2^*) - K^*) + (r_2(w^*, q^*, \pi_2^*) - \pi_2^*) \} < 0$,

which contradicts (3).

Now we shall show that $\varphi_1(w^*, q^*, \pi_2^*) = 0$. If we suppose that $\varphi_1(w^*, q^*, \pi_2^*) < 0$, then $w^* = 0$. Therefore we obtain by (Assumption 8) that $\lambda(w^*, q^*, \pi_2^*) = 0$. This leads to $\varphi_1(w^*, q^*, \pi_2^*) > 0$, because $\Sigma_{i=1}^2 \lambda_i(w^*, q^*, \pi_2^*) > 0$ for $(w^*, q^*) \epsilon Q$ and $\pi_2^* \epsilon \Pi$. Of course $\varphi_1(w^*, q^*, \pi_2^*) < 0$ contradicts $\varphi_1(w^*, q^*, \pi_2^*) > 0$. Hence $\varphi_1(w^*, q^*, \pi_2^*) = 0$.

Next suppose that $w^* = 0$; then $\varphi_1(w^*, q^*, \pi_2^*) > 0$, contradicting the above. So that $w^* > 0$.

Since $\pi_2^* > 0$, it is shown that $\varphi_3(w^*, q^*, \pi_2^*) = r_2(w^*, q^*, \pi_2^*) - \pi_2^* = 0$. Moreover, if $\pi_2^* = \bar{\pi}_2$, then it follows from (Assumption 8) that $\Sigma_{i=1}^2 \lambda_i(w^*, q^*, \pi_2^*) - \lambda(w^*, q^*, \pi_2^*) > 0$, which contradicts $\varphi_1(w^*, q^*, \pi_2^*) = 0$. Hence $\pi_2^* \neq \bar{\pi}_2$.

Thus we have proved that for $w^* > 0, q^* \geq 0$, and $\pi_2^*(\neq \bar{\pi}_2) > 0$, the following conditions are satisfied:

$$\Sigma_{i=1}^2 \lambda_i(w^*, q^*, \pi_2^*) = \lambda(w^*, q^*, \pi_2^*),$$

$$\Sigma_{i=1}^2 \kappa_i(w^*, q^*, \pi_2^*) \leq K^*,$$

$$r_2(w^*, q^*, \pi_2^*) = \pi_2^*.$$

$$\text{Q.E.D.}$$

2)

Now let us examine about the case in which both sector 1 and sector 2 are monopolistic. In the same way as in 1), considering the objective demand function for his product, each monopolist determines the quantity of his product supplied and that of each factor of production demanded so as to maximize the monopoly profit.

But unlike the case in 1), since the profit function for each sector has output of other sector as one of its arguments, an equilibrium will become an Cournot-Nash equilibrium.

The notation is the same as that in 1). We make the following assumptions:

(Assumption 1)   Each of the demand function for the ith good $x_i(p_1, p_2, w, q, \pi_1, \pi_2)$, $i = 1, 2$, and the supply function of labour $L(p_1, p_2, w, q, \pi_1, \pi_2)$ is single-valued, continuous, nonnegative and homogeneous function of degree zero with respect to $(p_1, p_2, w, q, \pi_1, \pi_2)$, where $(p_1, p_2) > 0, (w, q) \geq 0$ and $(\pi_1, \pi_2) \geq 0$. For any nonnegative p_1, p_2, w, q, π_1, and π_2 such that $(p_1, p_2) > 0$ and $(w, q) \neq 0$, at least one component of (x_1, x_2) is strictly positive, and the supply function of capital service takes a constant value $K^* > 0$.

(Assumption 2)   Each of the demand function for labour $l_i(x_i, w, q)$, $i = 1, 2$, and the demand function for capital service $k_i(x_i, w, q)$, $i = 1, 2$, is single-valued, continuous, and non-negative function of x_i, w, and q, where $x_i \geqq 0$ and $(w, q) \geqq 0$, and is homogeneous of degree zero with respect to $(w, q) \geqq 0$. For any $x_i > 0$ and $(w, q) \geqq 0$, $l_i(x_i, w, q)$ and $k_i(x_i, w, q)$ are strictly positive.

(Assumption 3)   Sector i $(i = 1,2)$ produces $x_i \in X_i$, where X_i is a compact real interval $[\underline{x}_i, \bar{x}_i]$ such that $0 < \underline{x}_i < \bar{x}_i$.

(Assumption 4)   There exists the inverse demand function for the ith good $p_i(x_1, x_2, w, q, \pi_1, \pi_2)$, $i = 1, 2$, such that $p_i(x_1, x_2, w, q, \pi_1, \pi_2)$ is single-valued, continuous and positive function of x_1, x_2, w, q, π_1, and π_2, where $x_1 \in X_1$, $x_2 \in X_2$, $(w, q) \geqq 0$ and $(\pi_1, \pi_2) \geqq 0$, and is homogeneous of degree one with respect to $(w, q) \geqq 0$, and $(\pi_1, \pi_2) \geqq 0$.

For given x_j, w, q, π_1, and π_2, the monopolist in sector $i(\neq j)$ can, by selecting $x_i \in X_i$, obtain the profit:

$$R_i(x_i; x_j, w, q, \pi_1, \pi_2) = x_i \cdot p_i(x_i, x_j, w, q, \pi_1, \pi_2)$$

$$- w \cdot l_i(x_i, w, q) - q \cdot k_i(x_i, w, q)$$

$$(i, j = 1, 2, i \neq j).$$

Under (Assumption 2) - (Assumption 4), there exists a point $x_i(x_j, w, q, \pi_1, \pi_2) \in X_i$ which satisfies:

$$R_i(x_i(x_j, w, q, \pi_1, \pi_2); x_j, w, q, \pi_1, \pi_2) = \max R_i(x_i; x_j, w, q, \pi_1, \pi_2)$$

$$\text{over all } x_i \in X_i.$$

(Assumption 5)   For any $x_j \in X_j$ $(j \neq i)$, $(w, q) \geqq 0$, and $(\pi_1, \pi_2) \geqq 0$, $x_i(x_j, w, q, \pi_1, \pi_2)$ is unique and $R_i(x_i(x_j, w, q, \pi_1, \pi_2); x_j, w, q, \pi_1, \pi_2) > 0$.

By (Assumption 2) - (Assumption 5), x_i is single-valued and continuous function of x_j, w, q, π_1, and π_2, where $x_j \in X_j$, $(w, q) \geqq 0$ and $(\pi_1, \pi_2) \geqq 0$, and is homogeneous of degree zero with respect to $(w, q) \geqq 0$ and $(\pi_1, \pi_2) \geqq 0$.

Now we can verify[5] that for any nonnegative w, q, π_1, and π_2, such that $(w, q) \neq 0$, there exists at least one pair of equilibrium outputs $(x_1(w, q, \pi_1, \pi_2), x_2(w, q, \pi_1, \pi_2)) \in \Delta$, $\Delta = \{(x_1, x_2)$ $| \underline{x}_i \leqq x_i \leqq \bar{x}_i$ $(i = 1, 2)\}$, which satisfies:

---

5)　For a proof, see Okuguchi [5, pp.7-12].

$$x_1 = x_1(x_2, w, q, \pi_1, \pi_2)$$

$$x_2 = x_2(x_1, w, q, \pi_1, \pi_2).$$

(Assumption 6)   For any nonnegative w, q, π_1, and π_2, such that $(w, q) \neq 0$, $x_i(w, q, \pi_1, \pi_2)$ $(i = 1, 2)$ is unique.

By virtue of (Assumption 6), $x_i(w, q, \pi_1, \pi_2)$ $(i = 1, 2)$ is single-valued, continuous and homogeneous function of degree zero with respect to $(w, q) \geq 0$, and $(\pi_1, \pi_2) \geq 0$. Therefore we can, similarly as in 1), rewrite l_i $(i = 1, 2)$, L, $k_i (i = 1, 2)$, and R_i $(i = 1, 2)$ as $\lambda_i(w, q, \pi_1, \pi_2)$, $\lambda(w, q, \pi_1, \pi_2)$, $\kappa_i(w, q, \pi_1, \pi_2)$ and $r_i(w, q, \pi_1, \pi_2)$, respectively. Each of these functions is single-valued and continuous function of $(w, q) \geq 0$ and $(\pi_1, \pi_2) \geq 0$. It will be clear that λ_i, κ_i, and λ are homogeneous of degree zero in w, q, π_1, and π_2, while r_i is homogeneous of degree one in the same variables.

Thus we can normalize the price system so that $(w, q) \epsilon Q$.

(Assumption 7)   For any nonnegative p_1, p_2, w, q, π_1, and π_2 such that $(p_1, p_2) > 0$, and $(w, q) \neq 0$,

$$w \cdot \lambda(w, q, \pi_1, \pi_2) + q \cdot K^* + \pi_1 + \pi_2 = \Sigma_{i=1}^2 p_i x_i(w, q, \pi_1, \pi_2)$$

holds.

(Assumption 8)   (a)   If $w = 0$, then $\lambda(w, q, \pi_1, \pi_2) = 0$.   (b)   For $(w, q) \epsilon Q$, there exists a sufficiently large number $\bar{\pi} > 0$ such that for any $(\pi_1, \pi_2) \geq 0$ which satisfies $\Sigma_{i=1}^2 \pi_i \geq \bar{\pi}$, $\Sigma_{i=1}^2 \lambda_i(w, q, \pi_1, \pi_2) - \lambda(w, q, \pi_1, \pi_2) > 0$.

From (Assumption 7) we obtain:

$$w \cdot (\Sigma_{i=1}^2 \lambda_i(w, q, \pi_1, \pi_2) - \lambda(w, q, \pi_1, \pi_2)) + q \cdot (\Sigma_{i=1}^2 \kappa_i(w, q, \pi_1, \pi_2) -$$

$$K^*) + (\Sigma_{i=1}^2 r_i(w, q, \pi_1, \pi_2) - \pi_1 - \pi_2) = 0.$$

With a proof practically identical to that of (Theorem) in 1), we now obtain the following result:

(Theorem)   Under (Assumption 1) - (Assumption 8), there exists at least one equilibrium $(w^*, q^*, \pi_1^*, \pi_2^*)$ which satisfies:

$$\Sigma_{i=1}^2 \lambda_i(w^*, q^*, \pi_1^*, \pi_2^*) = \lambda(w^*, q^*, \pi_1^*, \pi_2^*),$$

$$\Sigma_{i=1}^2 \kappa_i(w^*, q^*, \pi_1^*, \pi_2^*) \leq K^*,$$

$$r_1(w^*, q^*, \pi_1{}^*, \pi_2{}^*) = \pi_1{}^*,$$

$$r_2(w^*, q^*, \pi_1{}^*, \pi_2{}^*) = \pi_2{}^*.$$

We shall see immediately from the above models that some limitative assumptions, say (Assumption 6) in 1), and (Assumption 5) and (Assumption6) in 2), not familiar to us, must be posited so as to assure the continuity of the mapping necessary for the fixed point theorem. There is yet room for consideration about the economic implications of these assumptions or their deducibility from the other more pertinent ones.

III. On the Stability of Equilibrium

A general equilibrium can be obtained simply by solving a set of equations which represent the working of an entire national economy. But the analysis of its dynamic stability seems to require systematic investigation about the circular flow of national income and the decision-making of each economic unit under the condition of disequilibrium. So, it becomes necessary to make clear the relation of cause and effect underlying these equations and not to simply solve them.

Within the structure of exchange economy, the relevant activities are reversible, and adjust-ments towards an equilibrium seem to work immediately. But once production is thrown into the economy, the situation will become remarkably complicated whether the competition is perfect or not. The relation between input and output is irreversible, intervening the flow of time between them. Accordingly, if the flow of input-output-consumption per unit of time is chosen as the subject of the study, a deviation — at the time of input — from the (notional) relation which is made necessary from general equilibrium view point, will exert an influence upon the output and the consumption. We can not say anything definite about whether the "short side principle" will operate and whether prices will display an effective function in the demand and supply adjustment. If an economy can be represented by perfect competition system, further discussion will be needed about the question, i.e., which adjustment process is more rele-vant, at the same time, asking who adjusts a price. If imperfect competition mechanism works, for example, in the case where a producer is faced with the excess demand for labour, the pro-ducer will judge on the profitability of the following alternatives: keeping the wage rate constant and reducing his production plan so as to adapt his labour demand to the labour supply or raising the wage rate for the purpose of increasing the labour supply. Therefore, an adjustment process should not be framed in arbitrary forms from individual point of view, but in the form representing the rational action of producers. Moreover, the operative process of adjustment should be sought not only in relation to the adjustment in a definite unit of time, but that extending over some units of time. It may be possible that disequilibrium, as defined by the general equilibrium theory, will be realized in a stable manner.

REFERENCES

[1] FitzRoy, F.R., "Monopolistic Equilibrium, Non-convexity and Inverse Demand," *Journal of Economic Theory*, 7 (1974), 1-16.

[2] Morishima, M., "Existence of Solution to the Walrasian System of Capital Formation and Credit," *Zeitschrift für Nationalökonomie*, xx (1960), 238-243.

[3] Negishi, T., "Monopolistic Competition and General Equilibrium," *Review of Economic Studies*, 28 (1961), 196-201.

[4] Nikaido, H., *Monopolistic Competition and Effective Demand*, Princeton University Press, Princeton, 1975.

[5] Okuguchi, K., *Kasen no Riron* (The Theory of Oligopoly), Sobunsha, 1971.

REDISTRIBUTION OF INCOME AND MEASURES OF

INCOME INEQUALITY

by Yoshimasa Kurabayashi and Atsuo Yatsuka

1. Postulate and Measure of Income Inequality.

   Suppose a society constituted of n members. A state of the distribution of income in the society is given by a vector of members' income, which is expressed by y

$$y = (y_i), i = 1, 2, \ldots, n; \tag{1.1}$$

where y_i stands for the income of i-th member of the society. A measure of income inequality is a function of y and is expressed by $I[y]$. It is assumed that the measure of income inequality is comparable in the sense that for any pair of income distribution (y, y') one of the following alternatives is conceivable

$$\begin{array}{lll} \text{(i)} & I[y] < I[y'] & \\ \text{(ii)} & I[y] = I[y'] & \tag{1.2} \\ \text{(iii)} & I[y] > I[y'] & \end{array}$$

In the alternatives of (1.2), y is called greater in equality than y' for (i), equal to y' for (ii) and less than y' for (iii) respectively. Any formulation of the measure of income inequality is necessarily associated with the value judgement on social justice that a society considers desirable. The point is left untouched in this article for further consideration, but it is reasonable to assume for our purpose that $I[y]$ is satisfied by the following postulates.

Postulate 1   Suppose the transfer of income from i-th member to j-th member preserving the order of income size by members in a given distribution of income y. Let $y^T (i, j)$ stand for the state of income distribution after the transfer of income. Then, the following relation is fulfilled.

$$I[y^T(i, j)] < I[y] \quad \text{for any } y \tag{1.3}$$

where

$$y^T(i, j) = (y_{i'}^T), \quad y = (y_{i'}), y_i > y_j \; .$$
$$y_i^T = y_i - d$$
$$y_j^T = y_j + d, \quad d \in (0, \frac{y_i - y_j}{2} \,];$$
$$y_{i'}^T = y_{i'} \quad \text{any } i' \neq i, j$$

Postulate 1 is termed the Daltonian principle of income transfer.[1]

Postulate 1'   Under the situation of income transfer in postulate 1, the following relation is fullfilled.

---

1) See, in particular, H. Dalton (3), p. 351.

$$I[y^T(i, j)] \leqq I[y] \tag{1.4}$$

Postulate 1' is called the weak Daltonian principle of income transfer.

Postulate 2   Suppose the income of all members changes proportionately. Then, the measure of income inequality is left unchanged, *i.e.*

$$I[\lambda y] = I[y] \text{ for any } \lambda > 0 \text{ and } y > 0 \tag{1.5}$$

Postulate 2'   Under the situation of proportionate change in income of members in Postulate 2, the following relations are maintained for any $y > 0$.

$$I[\lambda y] < I[y] \text{ for any } \lambda > 1$$
$$I[\lambda y] > I[y] \text{ for any } \lambda < 1 \tag{1.6}$$

Postulate 2' is called the Daltonian principle of proportionate additions to incomes.[2] It is also noted that Postulate 2 states that $I[y]$ is homogeneous of 0-th degree with respect to y.

Postulate 3   Suppose the income of all members is changed by equal amounts. Then, the measure of income inequality decreases (or increases) according to the increase (or decrease) of income by equal amounts. Hence, the following relations are maintained.

$$I[y + te] < I[y] \text{ for any } t > 0$$
$$I[y + te] > I[y] \text{ for any } t < 0 \tag{1.7}$$

where

$$y + te > 0, e = (1, 1, \ldots, 1)$$

Postulate 3 is termed the Daltonian principle of equal additions to incomes.[3]

Postulate 4   No special importance is attached to whom in particular the income is distributed in the formulation of income inequality. Putting it in another words, a state of income distribution is anonymous in the sense that $I[y]$ is symmetric with respect to y. Accordingly, the following relation is satisfied.

$$I[Py] = I[y] \text{ for any } y > 0, \tag{1.8}$$

where P stands for any permutation matrix.

Postulate 5   The measure of income inequality assumes zero if and only if the income of all members is equaly distributed. Hence,

(i) $I[y] \geqq 0$ for any $y > 0$,

(ii) $I[y] = 0$ if and only if $y = \mu e$ \hfill (1.9)

where

$$\mu = (1/n) \sum_{i=1}^{n} y_i$$

Suppose a state of income distribution y' is generated by a finite sequence of the income transfer for any pairs of members. Let y stand for the initial state of income distribution in the sequence of income transfer. The relation between the generated state of income distribution by

---

2) H. Dalton (3), p. 355.
3) H. Dalton (3), p. 356.

the sequence of income transfer and the initial state is expressed by

$$y' \geq_{DT} y \tag{1.10}$$

A set of the state of income distribution with a given level of total income of a society is defined by S_Y as indicated below:

$$S_Y = \{ y \mid \Sigma y_i = Y, y \in R_+^n \}, \quad Y \in (0, +\infty).$$

Following properties are readily seen as for the relation generated by the sequence of income transfer.

(i) $\mu e \geq_{DT} y$, for any $y \in S_Y$, where $\mu = (1/n)Y$.

(ii) $\alpha y + (1 - \alpha)\mu e \geq_{DT} y$, for any $y \in S_Y$ and $\alpha \in [0, 1]$.

(iii)   If an arbitrary permutation is made possible by the sequence of income transfer, then (1.10) is equivalent to say that there exists a bistochastic matrix such that $\quad y' = Py$[4]

Property (i) states that the state of equal distribution of income is generated by a finite sequence of income transfer, whereas Property (ii) claims that a linear combination of the initial state and the state of equal distribution is also generated by the sequence of income transfer, which is expressed in terms of a bistochastic matrix P by Property (iii). These properties are found useful for guaranteeing Theorem 1 in the sequence of income transfer.

(Theorem 1)   (i) A function $I[y]$ satisfies Postulates 1, 2, 3, 4 and 5 if and only if (a), (b) and (c) are satisfied:[5]

(a) $I[y]$ is strictly S-convex in $R_+^n - \{0\}$

(b) $I[y]$ is homogeneous of degree zero with respect to y,

(c) $I[\mu y] = 0$, for any $\mu \in (0, +\infty)$.

(ii) $I[y]$ satisfies Postulates 1, 2', 3, 4 and 5 if and only if (a), (c) and (b') in place of (b) are fullfilled:

(b') For any $y > 0$,

$$I[\lambda y] < I[y], \text{ for any } \lambda > 1,$$

$$I[\lambda y] > I[y], \text{ for any } \lambda \in (0, 1).$$

(iii) (b') is satisfied if $I[y]$ is a negatively super-homogeneous function of y or its strictly increasing transformation. A function $H(y)$ is called negatively super-homogeneous with respect to y if for any $\lambda \in [1, +\infty)$

---

4) A bistochastic matrix is a square matrix, whose elements are non-negative and the sum of each rows and columns is equal to unity. For the properties of bistochastic matrix, see, in particular, C. Berge (2), p. 180 et seq. (iii) owes to a Theorem by Hardy, Littlewood and Polya which is referred by P. Dasgupta, A. Sen and D. Starrett (4) in their Lemma 2.

5) $I[y]$ is called a strictly S-convex function on D, if
(i) for all y in D and all bistochastic matrices P
$\qquad I[Py] \leq I[y]$, and
(ii) whenever Py is not a permutation of y
$\qquad I[Py] < I[y]$.
It is noted that $I[y]$ is strictly S-convex if $I[y]$ is strictly quasi-convex and symmetric with respect to y. For the definition of S-convexity, see C. Berge (2), p. 219.

$$H(\lambda y) \leqq (1/\lambda)H(y) \text{ and } H\left[(1/\lambda)y\right] \geqq \lambda H(y).$$

(Proof)   It is ready to show Theorem 1 noting that the following propositions are made.

(i)   Postulate 1 necessarily leads the relation:

$I[y] \geqq I[\mu e]$, for any $y > 0$ with strict inequality for $y \neq \mu e$.

(ii)   Postulate 3 is satisfied if Postulate 1 and 2 (or 2') are satisfied.

(iii)   Postulates 1 and 4 are satisfied if and only if $I[y]$ is strictly S-convex.

(iv)   Postulate 5 follows from (a) and (c).

Following corollaries immediately result from Theorem 1.

(Corollary)   For any function of y, $\psi[y]$, which satisfies (a) of Theorem 1, a function defined by a strictly increasing or fixed valued function F mapping R into R:

$$I[y] = F(\psi\left[(1/\mu)y\right]) - F(\psi[e]), \tag{1.11}$$

satisfies Postulates 1, 2, 3, 4 and 5.

(Corollary)   For any function of y, $\psi[y]$, which is strictly S-concave, a function defined by a strictly decreasing function F mapping R into R:[6]

$$I[y] = F(\psi\left[(1/\mu)y\right]) - F(\psi[e]), \tag{1.11'}$$

satisfies Postulates 1, 2, 3, 4 and 5.

In particualr, putting $F(t) = -t$ into (1.11), $I[y]$ is expressed by

$$I[y] = \psi[e] - \psi\left[(1/\mu)y\right]$$

2. Admissible Inequality Set and Attainable Inequality Function.

For any measure of income inequality formulated in the preceding section, an *admissible inequality set*, $L(I)$, is the set of all states of income distribution yielding at most the measure of income inequality $I \in [0, +\infty)$, satisfying the following properties.

(P.1) $L(0) = \{ y \mid y = \lambda e, \lambda \geqq 0 \}$

(P.2) $0 \leqq I_1 \leqq I_2$ yield $L(I_1) \subset L(I_2)$

(P.3)   Consider $y \in L(I)$ such that $I \in [0, +\infty)$.

(i) For any bistochastic matrix P, $Py \in L(I)$.

(ii) For any bistochastic matrix P that is not a permutation matrix, there exists $I' \in [0, +I)$ such that $Py \in L(I')$.

(P.4) $\lambda y \in L(I)$ for any $\lambda > 0$, if $y \in L(I)$, $I \in [0, +\infty)$.

(P.4)'   For any $\lambda \in [1, +\infty)$, $I \in [0, +\infty)$,

$L(\lambda I) \subset (1/\lambda)L(I)$ and $\lambda L(I) \subset L(I/\lambda)$

(P.5) $L(I)$ is closed for any $I \in [0, +\infty)$.

(P.6) $\bigcap_{I \in (I_0, +\infty)} L(I) = L(I_0)$ for any $I_0 \in [0, +\infty)$.

---

6) $\psi[y]$ is called a strictly S-concave function on D if $-\psi[y]$ is strictly S-convex on D. It is readily seen that $\psi[y]$ is a strictly S-concave function if $\psi[y]$ is symmetric and strictly quasi-concave.

A function of y defined on an admissible set, $\phi[y]$, satisfying the requirement

$$\phi[y] = \text{Min} \ \{I \mid y \in L\,(I),\, I \in [0, +\infty)\}\,,\, y > 0, \tag{2.1}$$

is called an *attainable inequality function*.

An attainable inequality function possesses the following properties shown in Theorem 2.

(Theorem 2)   (i) if an admissible inequality set $L(I)$, $I \in [\,0, +\infty)$, satisfies (P.1), (P.2), (P.3),(P.4), (or (P.4)'), (P.5) and (P.6), then $\phi[y]$ is lower semi-continuous and homogeneous of degree zero (or negatively super-homogeneous) satisfying

   (a) $\phi[y]$ is strictly S-convex on $R_+^n - \{0\}$

   (b) $\phi[\mu e] = 0$, for any $\mu \in (0, +\infty)$.

(ii) $\phi[y]$ or its strictly increasing transformation $F(\phi[y]\,)$, being F mapping R_+ into R_+, is a measure of income inequality satisfying Postulates 1, 2 (or 2'), 3, 4 and 5, where it is assumed that $F(0) = 0$.

(Proof)   By (P.6) the function $\phi[y]$ is defined. (a) is direct from (P.3). (b) follows from (P.1), whereas the homogeneity of degree zero (or negative super-homogeneity) for $\phi[y]$ immediately results from (P.4) (or from (P.4)'). In order to show the lower semi-continuity of $\phi[y]$, it is necessary and sufficient to show that a set defined by

$$L_\phi[I] = \{y \mid \phi[y] \leqq I,\ y \geqq 0\},\ \ I \in R,$$

is closed for any I. By virtue of (P.5), it immediately follows that the set $L_\phi[I]$ defined above is closed. In the light of Theorem 1, it is not difficult to show that the statement (ii) of Theorem 2 is maintained.

   In the case of $n = 2$, a set of $L(I)$, $I \in [0, +\infty)$ which may be represented by a convex cone as Figure 1 exhibits. The boundary of each convex cone represents the state of income distribution that yields an equal level of the measure of income inequality. A ray from the origin defined by $y = \lambda e$ is called the equality line that expresses the state of equal distribution of incomes between the members of a society.

(Figure 1)   The Set of $L(I)$ and the Equality Line

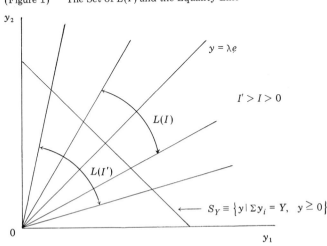

Suppose a function H is lower semi-continuous, strictly S-convex and homogeneous of degree -1 with respect to y mapping R_+^n into R_+^n and $H[\lambda e] = 0$, for any $\lambda \geq 0$. Let F stand for the transformation satisfying (ii) of Theorem 2. A function $L_F(I)$ defined in such a way that

$$L_F(I) = \{ y \mid F(H[y]) \leq I, y \in R_+^n \}, \quad I \in [0, +\infty), \tag{2.2}$$

also forms an admissible inequality set. Corresponding to $L_F(I)$, an attainable inequality function is formulated by

$$\psi[y] = \text{Min} \{ I \mid y \in L_F(I) \}, \qquad y \geq 0 \tag{2.3}$$

In view of (P.4)′, it is easy to see that

$$
\begin{aligned}
L_F(I) &= \{ y \mid F(H[y]) \leq I, y \in R_+^n \} \\
&= \{ y \mid H[y] \leq f(I) \} \\
&= (1/f(1))\{ y \mid H[y] \leq 1 \} \quad, \text{ where } f \text{ is the inverse of } F.
\end{aligned}
$$

Hence, we have

$$L_F(I) = (1/f(1))L_H(I), \text{ for } I > 0, \tag{2.4}$$

where

$$L_H(I) = \{ y \mid H[y] \leq 1 \}.$$

Thus, it is shown that

$$L_F(I) = g(I)L_F(1), \ g(I) = f(1)/f(I). \tag{2.5}$$

(2.4) states that a state of income distribution y which belongs to $L_F(I)$, $I \in [0, +\infty)$ is derived from the corresponding state of income distribution by the multiplication of a constant $g(I)$.

So far we have assumed that the size of the members in the society is fixed in n. It is conceivable to relax the assumption by establishing the Postulate 6 as below:

Postulate 6 For any state of income distribution $y = (y_i)$, $i = 1, 2, \ldots, n$, the level of the measure of income inequality is left unchanged, if the size of members that receive the amounts of income y_i $i = 1, \ldots n$, is changed proportionately. The postulate is termed the principle of proportionate addition to persons by Dalton.[7] The postulate is restated in the following manner. Let Z stand for a $n\lambda$ dimensional vector defined by

$$Z = (Z_{ir}), \text{ where } Z_{ir} = y_i, i = 1, 2, \ldots, n; r = 1, 2, \ldots, \lambda.$$

Measures of income inequality corresponding to y and Z are expressed by $I_n[y]$ and $I_{n\lambda}[Z]$ respectively. Postulate 6 states that

$$I_{n\lambda}[Z] = I_n[Z], \text{ for any } n, \ \lambda \in N \text{ such that } n > \bar{n} \in N. \tag{2.6}$$

3. Alternative Measures of Income Inequality and their Grouping.

Following measures of income inequality have been often and conveniently used in the literature for the measurement of income inequality. They are:[8]

---

7) H. Dalton (3), p. 357.
8) Further accounts of these measures of income inequality are given in A. Sen (6), ch. 2. For the convenience of reference, same notations as he uses are employed for the inequality measures.

(i) $E = [\,\text{Max}(y_i) - \text{Min}\,(y_i)\,]\,/\mu$ (3.1)

(ii) $M = \sum_i |\mu - y_i|\,/n\mu$ (3.2)

(iii) $V = \sum_i (\mu - y_i)^2 \,/n$ (3.3)

(iv) $C = (V)^{1/2}/\mu$ (3.4)

(v) $H = [\sum_i (\log \mu - \log y_i)^2 \,/n]^{1/2}$ (3.5)

(vi) $G = (1/2n^2\mu)\sum_i \sum_j |y_i - y_j|$ (3.6)

(vii) $T = \sum_i (y_i/Y) \log n(y_i/Y)$ (3.7)

E, M, V, C, H, G and T are respectively the range, the relative mean deviation, the variance, the coefficient of variation, the standard deviation of logarithms, Gini coefficient and Theil's entropy measure. It is interesting to see how the conventional measures of income inequality are associated with the postulates set forth in section 1. The association serves to grasp the hidden economic meaning for the distributional judgement that underlies in these statistical measures. Theorem 3 below indicates the association.

(Theorem 3)   (i) C, G and T satisfy the Postulates 1, 2, 3, 4, 5 and 6.

(ii) E and M satisfy the Postulates 1′, 2, 3, 4, 5 and 6.

(iii) H does not satisfy the Postulates 1 and 3, whereas V does not satisfy the Postulates 2 and 3. In place of the Postulates 2 and 3, the following properties are satisfied by V.

$$V[\lambda y] = \lambda^2 \,V[y]\,, \text{ for any } \lambda > 0;^{9)} \qquad (3.8)$$

$$V[y + te] = V[y]\,, \text{ for any } t \in R \text{ and } y + te \geqq 0. \qquad (3.9)$$

(Proof)   (i) It is easy to show that the conditions of (b) and (c) of Theorem 1 are fulfilled by C, G and T. Hence, it is sufficient to show that the condition (a) of Theorem 1 is maintained. Being $(y_i - \mu)^2$ strictly convex for a given μ

$$[\mu - (\theta y_i + (1 - \theta)y_i')]]^2 \leqq \theta(\mu - y_i)^2 + (1 - \theta)(\mu - y_i')^2$$

Hence, for any $\theta \in (0, 1)$ and $y \neq y'$

$$\Sigma\,[\mu - (\theta y_i + (1 - \theta)y_i')]^2 < \Sigma\theta(\mu - y_i)^2 + \Sigma(1 - \theta)(\mu - y_i')^2$$

and,

$$\Sigma\,[\mu - (\theta y_i + (1 - \theta)y_i')]^2 \,/n < \text{Max}\,[\Sigma(\mu - y_i)^2 \,/n, \,\Sigma(\mu - y_i')^2 \,/n]$$

Accordingly, for any $\theta \in (0, 1)$, $y \neq y'$

$$C[\theta y + (1 - \theta)y'] < \text{Max}\,(\,C[y],\,\,C[y']\,)$$

Thus, it is shown that $C[y]$ is strictly quasi-convex. Being $C[y]$ symmetric, it follows that $C[y]$ is strictly S-convex.

     Similarly,

$$T[y] = \Sigma\,(y_i/Y)[\log n + \log (y_i/Y)] = \log n + \Sigma\,(y_i/Y) \log (y_i/Y)$$

Denoting that

$$x_i = y_i/Y \text{ and } J[x] = \Sigma\,x_i \log x_i\,,$$

---

9) Apparently, $V[\lambda y] > V[y]$ if $\lambda > 1$ and $V[\lambda y] < V[y]$ if $\lambda < 1$.

it is ready to see that $J[x]$ is strictly convex with respect to x. Hence, $T[y]$ is also strictly convex for given Y. Being $T[y]$ symmetric, $T[y]$ is S-convex.

Some calculation directly leads $G(y^T(i, j)) < G(y)$ implying that $G(y)$ satisfies Postulate. 1. Hence, $G(y)$ is strictly S-convex and satisfies Postulate 4.

(ii) The decrease of E occurs only if the income is transferred between the members i and j that earn incomes Max y_i and/or Min y_j respectively. Otherwise, E remains unchanged in the process of income transfer. Hence, E satisfies Postulate 1'. By the similar reasoning, it easily turns out that M satisfies Postulate 1'. It is easy to show that E and M satisfy the remaining postulates.

(iii) It is not difficult to see that Postulates 4 and 6 are satisfied by V and $V[\mu e] = 0$. For a given μ, $(\mu - y_i)^2$ is strictly convex with respect to y_i. Hence, for any $\theta \in (0, 1)$, $y \neq y'$.

$$[\mu - (\theta y_i + (1 - \theta)y_i')]^2 < \theta \Sigma (\mu - y_i)^2 + (1 - \theta)\Sigma(\mu - y_i')^2$$

Accordingly, $V[y]$ is strictly convex on S_Y. Being $V[y]$ symmetric with respect to y, Postulate 1 is satisfied. By $V[\mu e] = 0$, Postulate 5 is also satisfied. It is ready to show that

$$V[\lambda y] = \lambda^2 V[y]$$

and

$$V[y + te] = V[y]$$

Being $H[y]$ not S-convex, it is easy to show that H satisfies the Postulates 2, 4, 5 and 6, but does not satisfy the Postulates 1 and 3.

In parallel reasoning with the corollaries to Theorem 1, an attainable inequality function, defined by (2.1) and possessing the properties indicated in Theorem 2, is generated by strictly increasing (or decreasing) transformation of $H[y]$ that is strictly S-convex (or S-concave), $F(H[y])$ such that

$$\phi(y) = F(H[y/\mu]) - F(H[e])$$
$$(\text{or } \phi(y) = F(H[e]) - F(H[y/\mu])).$$
(3.10)

Alternative measures of income inequality are derived from the specification of $H[y]$ such that (1) the distance function, (2) the type of Cobb-Douglas function, (3) the type of CES function, (4) the type of factor limitational Leontief function and (5) the type of the additive log-linear function. Theorem 4 states the derived measures of income inequality by such specification without giving the proof for the saving of space.

(Theorem 4) (i) Measures of income inequality $I_1[y]$, $I_2[y]$, $I_3[y]$ and $I_5[y]$ are derived from the specification of $H[y]$ that corresponds to (1) the distance function, (2) the Cobb-Douglas type function, (3) the CES type function and (5) the additive log-linear function applying the transformation of (3.10). They satisfy the Postulates 1, 2, 3, 4, 5 and 6.

(ii) The measure of income inequality $I_4[y]$ is derived from the specification of $H[y]$ by (4) the

Leontief type of factor liminational function. It satisfies the Postulates 1', 2, 3, 4, 5 and 6.

These measures of income inequality are expressed below:[10]

$$I_1[y] = (1/\mu)(\Sigma y_i^2)^{1/2} - n^{1/2} \tag{3.11}$$

$$I_2[y] = 1 - (1/\mu) \Pi y_i^{1/n} \tag{3.12}$$

$$I_3[y] = n^{1/\alpha} - (1/\mu)(\Sigma y_i^\alpha)^{1/\alpha}, \alpha \in (0, 1) \tag{3.13}$$

$$I_4[y] = 1 - (1/\mu) \mathrm{Min}(y_i) \tag{3.14}$$

$$I_5[y] = \Sigma(\log \mu - \log y_i)^{1/n} \tag{3.15}$$

The Daltonian principle of income transfer postulated in section 1 incorporates some relative evaluation of income transfer to different income classes. The point may be more explicitly spelled out by the following consideration. Suppose a couple of pairs of members of the society whose differences in income level are same between the pairs in such a way that for a couple of pairs (i, j) and (i', j').

$$y_i > y_j, \quad y_{i'} > y_{j'}, \quad y_{i'} > y_i \text{ and } y_i - y_j = y_{i'} - y_{j'} > 0 \tag{3.16}$$

Let us concider a couple of the states of income distribution, $y^T(i, j)$ and $y^T(i', j')$, resulting from the same amounts of income transfer for (i, j) and (i', j') that satisfies Postulate 1. It is said that a measure of income inequality is evaluated with greater weights to the members of lower incomes if the following condition (a) is always maintained.

$$\text{(a)} \qquad I[y] - I[y^T(i, j)] > I[y] - I[y^T(i', j')], \text{ for } y_{i'} > y_i \tag{3.17}$$

In parallel with the condition (a), it is said that a measure of income inequality is evaluated with greater weights to the members of upper incomes if the following condition (b) is always satisfied.

$$\text{(b)} \qquad I[y] - I[y^T(i, j)] < I[y] - I[y^T(i', j')], \text{ for } y_{i'} > y_i \tag{3.18}$$

It is also said that a measure of income inequality is evaluated with equal weights to the members of all incomes if the condition (c) is held.

$$\text{(c)} \qquad I[y] - I[y^T(i, j)] = I[y] - I[y^T(i', j')], \text{ for } y_{i'} > y_i \tag{3.19}$$

Suppose $I[y]$ is generated from a real valued function $G(y_i)$ applying a strictly increasing transformation F mapping R^+ into R^+ such that

$$I[y] = F(\sum_i G(y_i)) \text{ , for given } \mu \text{ .}$$

Then, it is noted that the conditions (a) and (b) are satisfied if a function $V(X)$ defined by

$$V(X) = G(X + t) - G(X), t > 0,$$

---

10) (3.11) is derived as a special case from a more generalized form,

$$I[y] = (1/\mu)(\Sigma y_i^\alpha)^{1/\alpha} - n^{1/\alpha}, \alpha > 1,$$

by putting $\alpha = 2$.

It is conceivable to use Max $|y_i|$ as a distance function R^n.

A function formulated by the distance function such that

$$I[y] = (1/\mu) \mathrm{Max} |y_i| - 1, y \in R_+^n - \{0\},$$

is also a measure of income inequality satisfying Postulates 1', 2, 3, 4, 5 and 6. It is readily seen that for this $I[y]$

$$E = I[y] + I_4[y]$$

is strictly concave (for (a)) or strictly convex (for (b)) and that the condition (c) is held if $V(X)$ is linear. The conditions (a), (b) and (c) cited above are associated with alternative measures of income inequality by Theorem 5 below.

(Theorem 5) (i) Measures of income inequality, T, I_2, I_3 and I_5 satisfy the condition (a).

(ii) Measures of income inequality, C and I_1, satisfy the condition (c).

(iii) A measure of income inequality G does not necessarily satisfy the conditions (a), (b) and (c).[11]

(iv) A measure of income inequality that is defined by

$$I[y] = (1/\mu)(\Sigma y_i{}^\alpha)^{1/\alpha} - n^{1/\alpha}$$

satisfies the condition (a) if $1 < \alpha < 2$, condition (b) if $\alpha > 2$ and condition (c) if $\alpha = 2$.

(Proof) (i) Nothing that

$$T[y] = -\log \mu + (1/Y) \Sigma y_i \log y_i$$

Or, by denoting

$$g(y_i) = y_i \log y_i{}'$$

$$T[y] = -\log \mu + (1/Y)\Sigma g(y_i)$$

Putting

$$V[y_i] = g[y_i + t] - g[y_i], \text{ for } t > 0,$$

it turns out that

$$V'[y_i] = \log (y_i + t) - \log y_i$$
$$V''[y_i] = (1/y_i + t) - (1/y_i), t > 0.$$

Hence, it follows that $V[y_i]$ is strictly concave for $t > 0$. $T[y]$ satisfies (a), because $T[y] + \log \mu$ satisfies (a) for given μ.

Noting that

$$I_s = \log \mu - (1/n) \Sigma \log y_i,$$

By putting

$$ng(y_i) = -\log y_i$$

and

$$V[y_i] = g(y_i + t) - g(y_i)$$

we have

$$nV''[y_i] = (1/[y_i + t]^2) - (1/y_i{}^2) < 0, \text{ for } t > 0.$$

Hence it follows that $V[y_i]$ is strictly concave. (a) immediately results from the strict concavity of $V[y_i]$. Recalling that

$$1 - I_2[y] = (1/\mu)\Pi y_i{}^{1/n},$$

we have

$$\log (1 - I_2[y]) = (1/n)\Sigma (\log y_i - \log \mu)$$
$$= -I_s[y]$$

Hence,

---

11) (ii) and (iii) of Theorem 5 have already been noted by A.B. Atkinson (1) and A. Sen (6) referring to the measures of C and G.

$$-I_5 [y^T(i, j)] > -I_5 [y^T(i', j')]$$

if $I_5 [y]$ satisfies (a). Accordingly, it turns out that

$$1 - I_2 [y^T (i, j)] > 1 - I_2 [y^T(i', j')]$$

The statement implies (a).

Noting that

$$I_3 = n^{1/\alpha} - (1/\mu)(\Sigma y_i{}^\alpha)^{1/\alpha}$$

we have

$$\mu^\alpha(n^{1/\alpha} - I_3 [y])^\alpha = \Sigma y_i{}^\alpha = \Sigma f(y_i)$$

where

$$f(y_i) = y_i{}^\alpha$$

By putting

$$g(y_i) = f(y_i + t) - f(y_i), \quad t > 0.$$

it is ready to see that

$$g'(y_i) = \alpha(y_i + t)^{\alpha - 1} - \alpha(y_i)^{\alpha - 1}$$
$$g''(y_i) = \alpha(\alpha - 1)[(y_i + t)^{\alpha - 2} - (y_i)^{\alpha - 2}] > 0$$

Hence, it follows that $g(y_i)$ is strictly convex. By the strict convexity of $g[y_i]$, we have

$$\mu^\alpha (n^{1/\alpha} - I_3 [y^T(i, j)])^\alpha > \mu^\alpha(n^{1/\alpha} - I_3 [y^T(i', j')])^\alpha$$

And

$$I_3 [y^T(i', j')] > I_3 [y^T(i, j)], \text{ for } y_{i'} > y_i$$

Accordingly, (a) immediately results.

(ii) Noting that

$$C = (1/\mu)[\Sigma(\mu - y_i)^2]^{1/2}$$

we have

$$\mu^2 C^2 = \Sigma(\mu - y_i)^2 = \Sigma f(y_i)$$

where

$$f(y_i) = (\mu - y_i)^2$$

By putting

$$g(y_i) = f(y_i + t) - f(y_i)$$
$$= (\mu - y_i - t)^2 - (\mu - y_i)^2$$
$$= -2t(\mu - y_i) + t^2$$

Hence, $g(y_i)$ is linear with respect to y_i. Then, it follows that

$$\mu^2 C^2 [y^T(i', j')] = \mu^2 C^2 [y^T(i, j)]$$

and

$$C[y^T(i', j')] = C[y^T(i, j)]$$

Similarly, noting that

$$I_1 = (1/\mu)(\Sigma y_i{}^2)^{1/2} - n^{1/2}$$

we have

$$\mu^2 (n^{1/2} + I_1)^2 = \Sigma\ y_i^2\ =\ \Sigma\ f(y_i)$$

where

$$f(y_i) = y_i^2$$

By putting

$$g(y_i) = f(y_i + t) - f(y_i)$$
$$= 2ty_i + t^2$$

It turns out that $g(y_i)$ is linear with respect to y_i. Hence, (c) immediately follows.

(iii) is direct from the consideration of $G[y^T(i, j)] - G[\dot{y}]$.

(iv) Noting that

$$I[y] = (1/\mu)(\Sigma y_i^\alpha)^{1/\alpha} - n^{1/\alpha}$$

we have

$$\mu^\alpha(1 + n^{1/\alpha})^\alpha = \Sigma\ y_i^\alpha = \Sigma\ f(y_i)$$

where

$$f(y_i) = y_i^\alpha$$

By putting

$$g(y_i) = f(y_i + t) - f(y_i) = (y_i + t)^\alpha - y_i^\alpha$$

It is seen that

$$g'(y_i) = \alpha(y_i + t)^{\alpha - 1} - \alpha y_i^{\alpha - 1}$$
$$g''(y_i) = \alpha(\alpha - 1)[(y_i + t)^{\alpha - 2} - y_i^{\alpha - 2}]$$

Hence, it follows that $g(y_i)$ is strictly convex if $\alpha > 2$. Then,

$$\mu^\alpha(I[y^T(i, j)] + n^{1/\alpha})^\alpha < \mu^\alpha(I[y^T(i, j)] + n^{1/\alpha})^\alpha$$

and

$$I[y^T(i', j')] < I[y^T(i, j)]$$

(b) Immediately follows. If $\alpha = 2$, then $g(y_i)$ is linear leading to (c).

$g(y_i)$ is strictly concave, if $1 < \alpha < 2$. Then, it turns out that

$$\mu^\alpha(n^{1/\alpha} + I[y^T(i', j')])^\alpha > \mu^\alpha(n^{1/\alpha} + I[y^T(i, j)])^\alpha$$

and

$$I[y^T(i', j')] > I[y^T(i, j)]$$

(a) immediately follows.

It is often the case that a state of income distribution is described as a vector of grouped data by income classes, whose measure of income inequality is known. It is interesting to see how the overall measure of income inequality is related to the corresponding measure of income inequality for grouped income classes. Theorem 6 discloses the relation by relaxing and extending the statement of Theorem 4. The proof of Theorem 6 is also omitted for the saving of space.

(Theorem 6) Suppose a state of income distribution is described by m grouped incomes such that

$$y = [y^S] \, ; S = 1, 2, \ldots, m,$$

$$y^S = (y_1^S, \ldots, y_{n_S}^s), \quad \sum_S n_S = n$$

denoting that y_i^S is the income of i-th individual who belongs to S-th income class and that y^S stands for a vector of incomes of members who belong to S-th income class. Letting

$$n_S \mu_S = \sum_i y_i^S = Y^S \text{ and } n\mu = \sum_i y_i = Y,$$

and $I[y]$ and $I_S[y^S]$ stand for an overall measure of income inequality and the corresponding measure of income inequality for S-th income class. Then, the following relations are established.[12]

$$I_1[y] = \left\{ \sum_S (\mu_S/\mu)^2 (I_S[y^S] + n_S^{1/2})^2 \right\}^{1/2} - n^{1/2} \tag{3.20}$$

$$I_2[y] = 1 - \prod_S (\mu_S/\mu)^{n_S/n} (1 - I_S[y^S])^{n_S/n} \tag{3.21}$$

$$I_3[y] = n^{1/\alpha} - \left\{ \sum_S (\mu_S/\mu)^\alpha (n_S^{1/\alpha} - I_S[y^S])^\alpha \right\}^{1/\alpha} \tag{3.22}$$

$$I_4[y] = 1 - \text{Min}\,[(\mu_S/\mu)(1 - I_S[y^S])] \tag{3.23}$$

$$I_5[y] = \log\mu - \sum_S (n_S/n)\,(\log \mu_S - I_S[y^S]) \tag{3.24}$$

$$T[y] = \sum_S (Y_S/Y)(T_S[y^S] + \log(\mu_S/\mu)) \tag{3.25}$$

12) If the measure of income inequality introduced in (iv) of Theorem 5 is adopted, then its decomposition into grouped measures of income inequality is implemented by the following formula:
$$I[y] = \left\{ \sum (\mu_s/\mu)^\alpha (I_s[y^s] + n_s^{1/\alpha})^\alpha \right\}^{1/\alpha} - n^{1/\alpha}$$

References

(1) Anthony B. Atkinson, "On the Measurement of Inequality", *Journal of Economic Theory*, 2, 1970, pp. 244-263.

(2) Claude Berge, *Topological Spaces*, Oliver and Boyd Ltd., London, 1963.

(3) Hugh Dalton, "The Measurement of the Inequality of Incomes", *Economic Journal*, 30, 1920, pp. 348-361.

(4) P. Dasgupta, A. Sen and D. Starrett, "Notes on the Measurement of Inequality", *Journal of Economic Theory*, 6, 1973, pp. 180-187.

(5) Michael Rothschild and Joseph E. Stiglitz, "Some Further Results on the Measurement of Inequality", *Journal of Economic Theory*, 6, 1973, pp. 188-204.

(6) Amartya Sen, *On Economic Inequality*, Clarendon Press, Oxford, 1973.

INVESTMENT ALLOCATION AND GROWTH IN A TWO-SECTOR ECONOMY

WITH NONSHIFTABLE CAPITAL[1]

Hajime Hori

I. Introduction

The well-known neoclassical two-sector model of economic growth first proposed by Uzawa [13, 14] is a simplified but elegant extension of disaggregate general equilibrium analysis in the sense that it describes the evolution of a disaggregate economy which is in equilibrium at each moment of time. As such, however, it has a rather serious drawback. It assumes that capital as well as labor can move instantaneously to bring about the uniformity of factor prices throughout the economy. But casual empiricism suggests that the uniformity of the rental rates on capital is achieved or approximated, if ever, not through the instantaneous movements of already installed capital equipment but through the allocation of newly produced investment goods; the distinction between the long run and the short run in the standard micro-economic theory may be regarded as a reflection of this observation. This means that the equalization of the rental rates on capital should not be regarded as a condition of each momentary equilibrium but as something that is attained or violated in the process of economic growth itself.

This problem was actually already posed and given some analysis by Inada [7], Kurz [8], and in a slightly different context, Shell and Stiglitz [12][2]. The purpose of the present paper is to further extend this line of analysis and systematically derive the implications of the nonshiftability of capital concerning the determination of momentary equilibria, the stability of a steady-state growth path, and the nature of possible oscillatory behaviors. Concerning the allocation of investment, I will basically follow Kurz, Stiglitz, and Shell and assume that all the savings of the economy will be invested in the sector enjoying the higher rental rate.

1)   This paper is based on a part of my Ph. D. thesis submitted to Brown University, U.S.A. I wish to thank Professors George H. Borts, James Hanson, Harl E. Ryder, Ryuzo Sato, and Jerome L. Stein (chairman of the thesis committee) of Brown University and Professor Kenichi Inada of Osaka University for their helpful comments and suggestions.
2)   The effects of the nonshiftabllity of capital on the dynamically optimum growth patterns are analyzed in [9] and [10].

Section II below presents the static structure of the model and analyzes the determination of each momentary equilibrium. Section III analyzes the problem of investment allocation. Section IV considers some geometric properties of the situations in which the rental rates of the two sectors are equal, and gives a comparison of the present model with the standard two-sector growth model in which capital is assumed to be shiftable. Section V considers the existence and stability of a steady-state growth path. Section VI analyzes the properties of possible oscillatory behaviors. The appendix analyzes the sensitivity of the growth paths to the investment allocation assumption adopted in this paper.

II.   *The model and momentary equilibria.*

This section presents the static structure of the model and discusses the determination of each momentary equilibrium. Some of the properties of the present model are common with the standard shiftable-capital model and are well known, and therefore will be simply presented without explanation.

The production functions are linearly homogeneous and continuously differentiable sufficiently many times. Let Y_i, K_i, and L_i denote the output, capital stock, and labor in the i-th sector, where $i = 1$ represents the investment-good producing sector and $i = 2$ represents the consumption-good producing sector. Define $y_i = Y_i/L_i$, $k_i = K_i/L_i$. Then the production relations in per capita form are given by $y_i = f_i(k_i)$, where $f_i(k_i)$ satisfies

$$f_i'(k_i) > 0, \quad f_i(k_i) - k_i f_i'(k_i) > 0, \quad f_i''(k_i) < 0, \quad \text{for} \quad k_i > 0,$$

(1)
$$\lim_{k_i \to 0} f_i(k_i) = 0, \qquad \lim_{k_i \to \infty} f_i(k_i) = \infty$$

$$\lim_{k_i \to 0} f_i'(k_i) = \infty, \qquad \lim_{k_i \to \infty} f_i'(k_i) = 0,$$

$$\lim_{k_i \to 0} (f_i(k_i) - k_i f_i'(k_i)) = 0, \qquad \lim_{k_i \to \infty} (f_i(k_i) - k_i f_i'(k_i)) = \infty,$$
$$i = 1, 2.$$

Although some of the conditions listed above are too strong for some purposes, we will stick to them throughout in order to minimize technicalities.

Total labor force of the economy denoted by L grows at an exogenously given rate n:

(2) $\dot{L} = nL.$

We also assume that total labor force is inelastically supplied, it is mobile between the sectors, and the labor market is perfectly competitive. Therefore the wage rates are equal to the marginal products of labor and are equal in the two sectors. Thus, if we let p denote the price of the investment good in terms of the consumption good, then

$$(3) \quad p = \frac{f_2 - k_2 f_2{}'}{f_1 - k_1 f_1{}'}$$

Our crucial assumption is that although the market for capital services within each sector is perfectly competitive, the capital installed in one sector cannot be shifted to the other sector. Let $x_i = K_i/L$, $\ell = L_i/L$. Then x_i, k_i, and ℓ are related by

$$(4) \quad k_1 = \frac{x_1}{\ell}, \qquad k_2 = \frac{x_2}{1-\ell}.$$

The rental rate on the capital employed in the i-th sector is given by the marginal product of capital in that sector.

Finally we assume that a constant proportion s_r of rental income and a constant proportion s_w of wage income are saved, where $0 \le s_r \le 1$, $0 \le s_w \le 1$, and that the commodity markets are perfectly competitive. The trivial case where $s_r = s_w = 0$ or $s_r = s_w = 1$ is excluded.

Let us turn to the determination of each momentary equilibrium. In the present context this reduces to finding an ℓ that brings equilibria in the investment-good market and the labor market simultaneously.

Let $H(x_1, x_2, \ell)$ denote the excess supply per capita of the investment good:

$$(5) \quad H(x_1, x_2, \ell) = \ell f_1 - s_r (f_1{}' x_1 + \frac{f_2{}'}{p} x_2) - s_w (f_1 - k_1 f_1{}'),$$

where k_i, f_i, $f_i{}'$, and p are functions of x_1, x_2, and ℓ through (3) and (4). If the equation

$$(6) \quad H(x_1, x_2, \ell) = 0$$

has a unique solution ℓ, $0 < \ell < 1$, for each given (x_1, x_2) such that $x_1 > 0$, $x_2 > 0$, then our economy has a unique momentary equilibrium at each moment of time.

First it is easy to see that, under assumption (1),

$$\lim_{\ell \to 0} H(x_1, x_2, \ell) = -\infty$$

and

$$\lim_{\ell \to 1} H(x_1, x_2, \ell) = (1 - s_w)(f_1(x_1) - x_1 f_1{}'(x_1)) + (1 - s_r) x_1 f_1{}'(x_1) > 0$$

if $x_1 > 0$, $x_2 > 0$. Thus equation (6) has at least one solution ℓ satisfying $0 < \ell < 1$. To see the uniqueness of such an ℓ, we differentiate $H(x_1, x_2, \ell)$ with respect to ℓ and evaluate this partial derivative at a point where (6) holds. Let H_ℓ denote the result. Then

(7) $H_\ell = f_1 - k_1 f_1' + (1 - s_r)k_1 f_1' \dfrac{1}{\sigma_1} + s_r(f_1 - k_1 f_1') \dfrac{k_2 f_2'}{f_2 - k_2 f_2'} \dfrac{1}{\sigma_2} > 0,$

where

(8) $\sigma_i = \dfrac{w_i}{k_i} \dfrac{1}{dw_i/dk_i} , \qquad i = 1, 2 ,$

and

(9) $w_i = \dfrac{f_i - k_i f_i'}{f_i'} , \qquad i = 1, 2 .$

Inequality (7) shows the uniqueness of an ℓ satisfying (6). Thus we have established that *in a two-sector model of economic growth with nonshiftable capital, each momentary equilibrium is determined unabiguously*[3]. In the following, the unique ℓ determined by (6) will be denoted by

(10) $\ell = \ell(x_1, x_2).$

k_1 and k_2 are also functions of x_1 and x_2 by (4) and (10):

(11)
$$k_1 = \frac{x_1}{\ell(x_1, x_2)}$$

$$k_2 = \frac{x_2}{1 - \ell(x_1, x_2)}$$

This unequivocal determination of each momentary equilibrium is one of the major differences between the present model and a standard shiftable-capital model because in a shiftable-capital model, momentary equilibria are not unique and the movements of the model are completely irregular unless an additional condition (the so-called causality condition) is satisfied. If the nonshiftability assumption can be regarded as more realistic than the shiftability assumption, then the above consideration shows that the movements of the actual economy are more regular and smooth than a shiftable-capital model suggests.

For later reference, the derivatives of the k_i's with respect to the x_i's are listed below:

(12)
$$\frac{\partial k_1}{\partial x_1} = \frac{1}{\ell H_\ell} \left[(1 - s_r)f_1 + s_r(f_1 - k_1 f_1') + s_r(f_1 - k_1 f_1') \frac{k_2 f_2'}{f_2 - k_2 f_2'} \frac{1}{\sigma_2} \right]$$

$$\frac{\partial k_1}{\partial x_2} = \frac{s_r k_1 (f_1 - k_1 f_1')f_2'}{\ell(f_2 - k_2 f_2')H_\ell} \left(\frac{1}{\sigma_2} - 1 \right)$$

$$\frac{\partial k_2}{\partial x_1} = \frac{(1 - s_r)k_2 f_1'}{(1 - \ell)H_\ell} \left(\frac{1}{\sigma_1} - 1 \right)$$

$$\frac{\partial k_2}{\partial x_2} = \frac{f_1 - k_1 f_1'}{(1 - \ell)H_\ell} \left[1 + s_r \frac{k_2 f_2'}{f_2 - k_2 f_2'} + (1 - s_r) \frac{k_1 f_1'}{f_1 - k_1 f_1'} \frac{1}{\sigma_1} \right]$$

---

3) Inada [7] derived this result for the case in which $s_w = 0$ and $s_r = 1$.

III.   *Investment allocation.*

Since the total investment of our economy at each moment of time is provided by the total output of the investment-good sector, we have

(13) $\dot{x}_1 + \dot{x}_2 = \ell f_1 - n(x_1 + x_2)$.

Our concern in this section is how this total investment is allocated between the two sectors.

As we noted Section I, we assume that if the rental rates are different between the two sectors, all the new investment goes to the sector with the higher rental rate. Define

(14) $E(x_1, x_2) = w_2 \left(\dfrac{x_2}{1 - \ell(x_1, x_2)} \right) - w_1 \left(\dfrac{x_1}{\ell(x_1, x_2)} \right)$,

where w_i is the wage-rental ratio in the i-th sector defined by (9). Since the wage rates are equal between the two sectors, we have

$$E \gtreqless 0 \qquad \text{if and only if} \qquad p f_1' \gtreqless f_2' \ .$$

Thus, all the investment will go to the investment-good sector if $E > 0$, and to the consumption-good sector if $E < 0$.

When all the investment goes to the investment-good sector, capital accumulation in each sector is governed by $\dot{x}_1 = \ell f_1 - nx_1$ and $\dot{x}_2 = -nx_2$. When all the investment goes to the consumption-good sector, it is governed by $\dot{x}_1 = -nx_1$ and $\dot{x}_2 = \ell f_1 - nx_2$. Let $x = (x_1, x_2)$ and define two vector-valued functions $g^+(x)$ and $g^-(x)$ by

$$g^+(x) = \begin{bmatrix} \ell f_1 - nx_1 \\ \\ -nx_2 \end{bmatrix}$$

(15)

$$g^-(x) = \begin{bmatrix} -nx_1 \\ \\ \ell f_1 - nx_2 \end{bmatrix}$$

Also define two sets of points S^+ and S^- by

(16)
$$S^+ = \left\{ x \geqq 0, \quad E(x) > 0 \right\}$$
$$S^- = \left\{ x \geqq 0, \quad E(x) < 0 \right\}$$

Then our assumption about investment allocation for the case where the rental rates are different can be represented by

$$(17)\ \dot{x} = \begin{cases} g^+(x) & \text{if } x \in S^+ \\ g^-(x) & \text{if } x \in S^- \end{cases}$$

Although formula (17) defines the investment allocation unambiguously when the rental rates are different between the two sectors, it does not determine the investment allocation when the economy is on the curve defined by $E(x) = 0$, which we shall call the *equi-rental curve*. The following consideration suggests how to treat this situation.

Suppose the investors allocate the investment at random when $pf_1' = f_2'$ because they are indifferent about which assets to hold as long as both assets yield the same reward. Further suppose that as a result of this random investment allocation the economy is driven off the equi-rental curve into S^+. As soon as the economy enters this region, formula (17) will start to work and the subsequent capital accumulation will proceed according to $\dot{x} = g^+(x)$. If the capital accumulation in this manner decreases the rental differential $pf_1' - f_2'$, then the economy will be pushed back to the equi-rental curve, but if this capital accumulation enlarges the rental differential $pf_1' - f_2'$, then the economy will further deviate from the curve. Similar consideration applies to the case where the economy happens to be driven off the equi-rental curve into S^-. Thus, after the economy reaches the equi-rental curve, we can expect it to move along the curve and preserve the equality of the rental rates if and only if the forces working on both sides of the curve are such as to push the economy back to the curve. In the following, a point on the equi-rental curve will be called a *normal point* if around this point the forces on both sides of the curve are such as to push the economy to the curve. A point on the curve will be called a *perverse point* if it is not a normal point.

In order to formalize the above idea, let $\dfrac{dE}{dx} = (E_1, E_2)$ be the gradient vector of $E(x)$ and consider

$$\frac{dE}{dx} \cdot g^+ = E_1(\ell f_1 - nx_1) + E_2(-nx_2),$$

$$\frac{dE}{dx} \cdot g^- = E_1(-nx_1) + E_2(\ell f_1 - nx_2).$$

Clearly, $\dfrac{dE}{dx} \cdot g^+$ and $\dfrac{dE}{dx} \cdot g^-$ express how $E(x)$ will change when x changes according to $\dot{x} = g^+(x)$ and $\dot{x} = g^-(x)$ respectively.

First suppose that at an x on the equi-rental curve,

$$\frac{dE}{dx} \cdot g^+(x) < 0 \qquad \text{and} \qquad \frac{dE}{dx} \cdot g^-(x) > 0.$$

Since these inequalities hold in a neighborhood of x by continuity, it follows that whether the economy is driven into S^+ or S^- by a random investment allocation on the equi-rental curve, it will be immediately pushed back to the curve by (17). Thus such an x is a normal point.

To find the differential equation governing the motion of the economy at a normal point, let the equation be denoted by

$$\dot{x} = g^0(x) \equiv \begin{bmatrix} g_1^0(x) \\ g_2^0(x) \end{bmatrix}.$$

$g^0(x)$ has to satisfy (13). It also has to keep the equality of the rental rates. Thus

$$g_1^0(x) + g_2^0(x) = \ell f_1 - n(x_1 + x_2),$$

$$\frac{dE}{dx} \cdot g^0(x) = E_1 g_1^0(x) + E_2 g_2^0(x) = 0.$$

These two equations yield

$$(18) \quad g^0(x) = \begin{bmatrix} \dfrac{E_2}{E_2 - E_1}(\ell f_1 - nx_1 - nx_2) \\ \dfrac{-E_1}{E_2 - E_1}(\ell f_1 - nx_1 - nx_2) \end{bmatrix}$$

It is easy to see that

$$(19) \quad \frac{dE}{dx} \cdot g^+(x) < 0 \quad \text{and} \quad \frac{dE}{dx} \cdot g^-(x) > 0 \quad \Rightarrow \quad E_2 - E_1 > 0.$$

Therefore equation (18) is well-defined.

Next suppose that at an x on the equi-rental curve,

$$\frac{dE}{dx} \cdot g^+(x) < 0 \quad \text{and} \quad \frac{dE}{dx} \cdot g^-(x) < 0 \ .$$

Again by continuity, these inequalities hold in a neighborhood of x. Thus, if the economy is driven into S^- by a random investment allocation, the economy will be caught in S^- and proceed to deviate from the curve, while if it is driven into S^+, equation (17) will push it back to the curve. Therefore x is a perverse point and the effective equation is given by $\dot{x} = g^-(x)$.

If

$$\frac{dE}{dx} \cdot g^+(x) > 0 \quad \text{and} \quad \frac{dE}{dx} \cdot g^-(x) > 0 \ ,$$

then a similar reasoning shows that $\dot{x} = g^+(x)$ is the effective equation.

Finally suppose that

$$\frac{dE}{dx} \cdot g^+(x) > 0 \quad \text{and} \quad \frac{dE}{dx} \cdot g^-(x) < 0 \ .$$

This case is the most troublesome for analysis because, into whichever of S^+ and S^- the economy is driven by a random investment allocation, that region will capture the economy. Hence the prediction of the future growth path of the economy is impossible until the economy actually enters one of the regions. Fortunately, however, since the economy will never come to such a point if it starts at any other point, the possibility of this situation will not cause a serious problem.

Summarizing the discussions, we obtain the following formula for investment allocation on the equi-rental curve:[4]

$$
(20) \quad \dot{x} = \begin{cases} g^0(x) & \text{if} \quad E(x) = 0, \quad \dfrac{dE}{dx} \cdot g^+(x) < 0, \quad \text{and} \quad \dfrac{dE}{dx} \cdot g^-(x) > 0, \\[2mm] g^+(x) & \text{if} \quad E(x) = 0, \quad \dfrac{dE}{dx} \cdot g^+(x) > 0, \quad \text{and} \quad \dfrac{dE}{dx} \cdot g^-(x) > 0, \\[2mm] g^-(x) & \text{if} \quad E(x) = 0, \quad \dfrac{dE}{dx} \cdot g^+(x) < 0, \quad \text{and} \quad \dfrac{dE}{dx} \cdot g^-(x) < 0, \\[2mm] \text{indeterminate} & \text{if} \quad E(x) = 0, \quad \dfrac{dE}{dx} \cdot g^+(x) > 0, \quad \text{and} \quad \dfrac{dE}{dx} \cdot g^-(x) < 0. \end{cases}
$$

Rigorously speaking, formula (20) is still incomplete because it does not specify what will happen if $\dfrac{dE}{dx} \cdot g^+(x) = 0$ or $\dfrac{dE}{dx} \cdot g^-(x) = 0$. In such cases, we have to examine the sings of $\dfrac{d}{dx}(\dfrac{dE}{dx} \cdot g^+(x)) \cdot g^+(x)$ and $\dfrac{d}{dx}(\dfrac{dE}{dx} \cdot g^-(x)) \cdot g^-(x)$. For example, it can be shown that if $E(x) = 0$, $\dfrac{dE}{dx} \cdot g^+(x) = 0$, $\dfrac{dE}{dx} \cdot g^-(x) > 0$, and $\dfrac{d}{dx}(\dfrac{dE}{dx} \cdot g^+(x)) \cdot g^+(x) > 0$, then $x = g^+(x)$ is effective; if $E(x) = 0$, $\dfrac{dE}{dx} \cdot g^+(x) < 0$, $\dfrac{dE}{dx} \cdot g^-(x) = 0$, and $\dfrac{d}{dx}(\dfrac{dE}{dx} \cdot g^-(x)) \cdot g^-(x) < 0$, then $\dot{x} = g^-(x)$ is effective, and so on.[5] For the moment, however, equations (17) and (20) will be sufficient to characterize the investment allocation of our economy.

It is of some interest to derive an economically meaningful sufficient condition for a point on the equi-rental curve to be normal, since around such a point the investment allocation specified in (20) will be such as to establish and preserve the equality of the rental rates and therefore the economy will behave as if capital were shiftable.

Let us confine our attention to the region R defined by

$$
(21) \quad R = \left\{ x \mid x > 0, \ \ell f_1 - n x_1 \geq 0, \ \ell f_1 - n x_2 \geq 0 \right\}.
$$

This is a region where the productivity in the investment-good producing sector is large enough to sustain or increase x_i if all the investment goes to the i-th sector. In region R, a point x is normal if $E_1(x) < 0$ and $E_2(x) > 0$. Written out more explicitly, a point is normal if

---

4) It should be noted that equation (20) has *not* been derived from equation (17) in a rigorous sense. It is known, however, that if we assume a positive time delay τ in the switching from one equation to the other in (17), namely if we assume that $\dot{x} = g^+$ starts working τ period after the economy crosses the equi-rental curve into S^+, and if we take the limit of a solution of this difference-differential equation as $\tau \to 0$, then this limit solution is a solution to equation (20). See [1].
5) For a fuller discussion of this subject, see [2].

$$w_2' \frac{\partial k_2}{\partial x_1} - w_1' \frac{\partial k_1}{\partial x_1} < 0, \quad \text{and}$$

(22)

$$w_2' \frac{\partial k_2}{\partial x_2} - w_1' \frac{\partial k_1}{\partial x_2} > 0,$$

where $w_i' = \dfrac{dw_i}{dk_i} > 0, \quad i - 1, 2$. Thus, using (12), we can conclude that *in region R, the economy will establish and preserve the equality of the rental rates around a point on the equi-rental curve if the elasticities of substitution in both sectors are greater than or equal to unity at this point.*

IV. *The equi-rental curve.*

Before proceeding to the analysis of a steady-state growth path, it is necessary to touch upon some properties of the equi-rental curve. On the equi-rental curve, the rental rates as well as the wage rates are equal between the two sectors and the commodity markets are cleared. Thus each point on the equi-rental curve corresponds to a momentary general equilibrium configuration in the corresponding shiftable-capital model (namely the shiftable-capital model which is identical to our nonshiftable-capital model except that capital is assumed to be shiftable). Therefore most of the properties of the equi-rental curve can be obtained by referring to the already known facts about the shiftable-capital model.[6]

It is well known that in a shiftable-capital model, (i) the capital-labor ratios k_1 and k_2 are uniquely determined for each positive wage-rental ratio w, (ii) $k_1(w)$ and $k_2(w)$ are increasing in w, and (iii) $\lim\limits_{w \to 0} k_1(w) = \lim\limits_{w \to 0} k_2(w) = 0, \lim\limits_{w \to \infty} k_1(w) = \lim\limits_{w \to \infty} k_2(w) = \infty$ under assumptions (1). Let

$$(23) \quad \psi(w) = \frac{k_1(w)k_2(w) + (s_w k_1(w) + (1-s_w)k_2(w))w}{(1-s_r)k_1(w) + s_r k_2(w) + w}$$

$\psi(w)$ gives the unique value of the overall capital-labor ratio k which is compatible with a momentary general equilibrium when the wage-rental ratio is w. It can be shown that

$$\lim_{w \to 0} \psi(w) = 0$$

(24)

$$\lim_{w \to \infty} \sup \psi(w) = \infty$$

under assumptions (1). It is clear from the meaning of $\psi(w)$ that the shiftable-capital model has a unique momentary equilibrium configuration for $k = \bar{k}$ if and only if the equation

$$(25) \quad \bar{k} = \psi(w)$$

is uniquely invertible[7].

---

6) For the properties of a shiftable-capital two-sector growth model, see [5] and [6].
7) For various sufficient conditions for the global invertibility of (25), see [5].

Let us turn to the equi-rental curve. The equi-rental curve has the following properties:

i)   it can be parametrized as a directed path

(26) $x = x(w) = (x_1(w), x_2(w))$

where

(27) $x_1(w) + x_2(w) = \psi(w)$;

ii)   it passes through the origin and has at least one intersection with the straight line $x_1 + x_2 = k$ for every positive k;

iii)   equation (25) is uniquely invertible for $k = \bar{k}$ if and only if the equi-rental curve has a unique intersection with $x_1 + x_2 = \bar{k}$;

iv)   if the corresponding shiftable-capital model has a unique momentary equilibrium for each $k > 0$, then the equi-rental curve has a unique intersection with the straight line $x_1 + x_2 = k$ for every positive k;

v)   if the equi-rental curve cuts $x_1 + x_2 = k$ from below as w increases, then $\psi'(w) \geq 0$ at the intersection, with the strict inequality holding unless the two curves are tangent. The converse also holds;

vi)   of the two regions divided by the equi-rental curve, the one on the left-hand side is S^+ and the one on the right-hand side is S^-. By the "left-hand side" ("right-hand side") we mean the left-hand side (right-hand side) as we face in the direction of the directed path $x = x(w)$.

Figure 1 illustrates these points. The arrow drawn along the equi-rental curve shows the direction of the directed path $x = x(w)$. The equi-rental curve has only one intersection with the straight line $x_1 + x_2 = k^1$ and hence equation (25) has a unique solution when $k = k^1$. But equation (25) has multiple solutions when $k = k^2$. Also, $\psi'(w) > 0$ at A, C, and D and $\psi'(w) < 0$ at B.

The rest of this section will be devoted to the proof of the assertions (i) to (vi).

To see (i), first note that equations (11) can be uniquely inverted for each positive (k_1, k_2) . In other words, for each positive (k_1, k_2), a pair (x_1, x_2) which establishes the equality of the wage rates and the investment-good-market equilibrium is unique. In fact, the market clearing condition (6) can be regarded as defining a relation among k_1, k_2, and ℓ:

$$\widetilde{H}(k_1, k_2, \ell) \equiv \ell f_1 - s_r(\ell k_1 f_1' + \frac{(1-\ell)k_2 f_2'}{p}) - s_w(f_1 - k_1 f_1') = 0,$$

where p is a function of k_1 and k_2 through (3). Thus

$$\ell = \mathcal{Y}(k_1, k_2) \equiv \frac{s_r \dfrac{k_2 f_2'}{p} + s_w(f_1 - k_1 f_1')}{f_1 - s_r k_1 f_1' + \dfrac{s_r k_2 f_2'}{p}}$$

where it is easy to see that $0 < \tilde{\ell}(k_1, k_2) < 1$ if $k_1 > 0$ and $k_2 > 0$.

Therefore

(28) $x_1 = \tilde{\ell}(k_1, k_2)k_1$, $x_2 = (1 - \tilde{\ell}(k_1, k_2))k_2$

provide the unique inverse of (11).

On the equi-rental curve, w uniquely determines k_1 and k_2 since it is so in the shiftable-capital model, and therefore w uniquely determines x_1 and x_2 through (28). On the other hand, since

$$w_1\left(\frac{x_1}{\ell(x)}\right) = w_2\left(\frac{x_2}{1-\ell(x)}\right)$$

on the equi-rental curve, each x on the equi-rental curve corresponds to a unique $w = w_1\left(\frac{x_1}{\ell(x)}\right) = w_2\left(\frac{x_2}{\ell(x)}\right)$. This proves the validity of the parametrization (26) of the equi-rental curve as a directed path. A mechanical calculation shows that (27) also holds.

(ii) follows from (24) and (27). (iii) and (v) follows from (27). (iv) follows from (iii).

Finaly, (vi) follows from

$$\liminf_{x_1 \to 0} E(x_1, x_2) > 0 \quad \text{for any} \quad x_2 > 0$$

and

$$\limsup_{x_2 \to 0} E(x_1, x_2) < 0 \quad \text{for any} \quad x_1 > 0,$$

which in turn follow from assumptions (1) and equation (6).

V. *The steady-state growth path and its stability.*

A steady-state growth path of our model is represented by an $x^* = (x^*_1, x^*_2)$ satisfying

(29)
$$\ell(x^*)f_1\left(\frac{x^*_1}{\ell(x^*)}\right) - n(x^*_1 + x^*_2) = 0$$

$$E(x^*) = 0$$

and

(30) x^* is a normal point.

Condition (30) is necessary for a steady state because otherwise $\dot{x} = g^+(x)$, $\dot{x} = g^-(x)$, or $\dot{x} = $ indeterminate, and therefore $x(t)$ will not stay at x^*. For convenience, we shall call a point x satisfying (29) *a quasi steady state.*

In Section III, we gave one sufficient condition for normality. But the normality condition for a quasi steady state takes a more revealing form. By (20) and (29), a quasi steady state x is normal if

$E_2 - E_1 > 0$.

But it can be shown that on the equi-rental curve,

$$(31)\ E_2 - E_1 = \frac{w^2 f_1 \{(1-s_r)k_1 + s_r k_2 + w\}^3}{k_1 k_2 \sigma_1 \sigma_2 H_\varrho (s_r k_2 + s_w w)\{(1-s_w)w + (1-s_r)k_1\}}\psi'(w(x)),$$

where $\psi'(w(x))$ is the derivative of $\psi(w)$ (defined by (23)) with respect to w evaluated at $w = w(x) = w_i(x)$, $i = 1, 2$. Thus *a quasi steady state is normal and therefore is a steady state if* $\psi'(w(x)) > 0$.

Now, the condition that $\psi'(w) > 0$ for all $w > 0$ is known as the causality condition that guarantees the existence of a unique momentary equilibrium in a shiftable-capital model for eash $k > 0$ (see (23) and (25)). Thus *the causality of a shiftable-capital model implies the normality of a quasi steady state of the corresponding nonshiftable-capital model.* This in turn implies, by the one-one correspondence between x and (k_1, k_2), that *if the causality condition is satisfied, then a steady state of a shiftable-capital model is also a steady state of the corresponding nonshiftable-capital model, and vice versa.* If the causality condition is violated, in particular if $\psi(w) = k^* \equiv x^*_1 + x^*_2$ is not invertible, then a shiftable-capital model is not well-defined around k^* but x^* may be a steady state for the corresponding nonshiftable-capital model, because normality is a local condition.

Figure 2 illustrates these points. By property (v) of the equi-rental curve, $\psi(w(x)) > 0$ if the equi-rental curve (as a directed path) cuts a negative $45°$ line from below at x. Thus in Figure 2, out of the three points satisfying (29), points A and C are normal while point B is not, and therefore A and C are the only steady states for the nonshiftable-capital model. If we let k_A and k_C denote the values of k at A and C, however, equation (25) cannot be inverted either for k_A or k_C, and thereforethe corresponding shiftable-capital model does not have a steady state.

To see the stability properties of a steady state, note that, at a normal point, a solution $x(t)$ behaves as if capital were shiftable, since the equality of the rental rates is preserved there. Therefore, *if the causality condition is satisfied, then a stable steady state of a shiftable-capital model is also a stable steady state of the corresponding nonshiftable-capital model, and vice versa.*[8]   But again, a nonshiftable-capital model may have a stable steady state even if the causality condition is not satisfied.

Since

$$\ell f_1 - n(x_1 + x_2) > 0 \quad \text{below the curve defined by } \ell f_1 - n(x_1 + x_2) = 0$$

and

---

[8]   For various sufficient conditions for the existence, uniqueness, and stability of a steady-state solution in a shiftable-capital model, see, e.g., [5] and [11].

$\ell f_1 - n(x_1 + x_2) < 0$ above the curve defined by $\ell f_1 - n(x_1 + x_2) = 0$,

we can see that a steady state x^* is stable if and only if the equi-rental curve cuts $\ell f_1 - n(x_1 + x_2) = 0$ from below at that point. Points A and C in Figure 2, which are not even steady states if capital is shiftable, are both stable steady states if capital is nonshitable.

VI. Cyclical solutions

In the preceding section, we saw that a nonshiftable-capital model might have a stable steady state even if equation (25) were not uniquely invertible. Another interesting possibility for the case where (25) is not uniquely invertible is a cyclical movement of the economy. Inada [6] conjectured that if equation (25) was not invertible, some additional regularizing assumptions would generate a cyclical solution. But the unreality of the shiftability assumption shows itself clearly in such cyclical solutions since they contain periodic sudden shifts of capital between the sectors (see [3]). As will be shown below, the friction in the economy introduced by the nonshiftability of capital provides a natural regularizing fremework for the analysis of cyclical solutions.

Assume that the equi-rental curve cuts $\ell f_1 - n(x_1 + x_2) = 0$ from below and that at this intersection,

$$\psi'(w) < 0.$$

In this case two types of cyclical solution around such a point are possible.

Both in Figures 3 and 4, all the points on the equi-rental curve between B and D are perverse points while all the other points on the curve are normal points. In particular,

$$\frac{dE}{dx} \cdot g^+(x) < 0 \quad \text{and} \quad \frac{dE}{dx} \cdot g^-(x) < 0 \text{ between } B \text{ and } M,$$

$$\frac{dE}{dx} \cdot g^+(x) > 0 \quad \text{and} \quad \frac{dE}{dx} \cdot g^-(x) > 0 \text{ between } N \text{ and } D,$$

and

$$\frac{dE}{dx} \cdot g^+(x) > 0 \text{ and } \frac{dE}{dx} \cdot g^-(x) < 0 \text{ between } M \text{ and } N.$$

Furthermore,

$$\frac{dE}{dx} \cdot g^+(x) = 0, \quad \frac{dE}{dx} \cdot g^-(x) < 0, \quad \text{and}$$

$$\frac{d}{dx}(\frac{dE}{dx} \cdot g^+(x)) \cdot g^+(x) < 0 \quad \text{at } B,$$

and

$$\frac{dE}{dx} \cdot g^+(x) > 0 , \quad \frac{dE}{dx} \cdot g^-(x) = 0 , \quad \text{and}$$

$$\frac{d}{dx}(\frac{dE}{dx} \cdot g^-(x)) \cdot g^-(x) > 0 \quad \text{at } D .$$

(See the remarks following equation (20)).

In Figure 3, a solution leaving the equi-rental curve at B (or D) returns to it at a normal point C (or F). In this case, the trajectory $BCDFB$ describes a complete cycle, which is characterized by an alteration of a higher rental for the consumption-good sector (BC), uniform rental rates (CD), a higher rental rate for the investment-good sector (DF), and uniform rental rates (FB). As can be seen by following the movement of a solution starting at I, for example, a solution starting off the cycle reaches it in finite time.

In Figure 4, a solution leaving the equi-rental curve at B (or D) returns to it at a perverse point C (or F). In this case, a solution which leaves the equi-rental curve at B, for example, follows the trajectory $BCG...$ with an ever shrinking width of oscillation. Using an argument similar to the Poincaré-Bendixon limit cycle theorem,[9] it can be shown that there exists a limit cycle, such as $PRQSP$ in Figure 4, to which a solution starting off the cycle approaches asymptotically. This limit cycle is characterized by an alteration of a higher rental rate for the consumption-good sector (PRQ) and a higher rental rate for the investment-good sector (QSP).

Appendix

In the text, we analyzed the growth of a two-sector economy with non-shiftable capital assuming that the investment allocation was governed by (20).

The extreme sensitivity of the investors to the rental rate differential, implicity assumed in (20), may seem unrealistic. An alternative formulation that is more realistic in this respect will be

$$(A\text{-}1) \quad \dot{x} = h(x) \equiv \begin{bmatrix} h_1(x) \\ h_2(x) \end{bmatrix} \equiv \begin{bmatrix} \alpha(x)\ell f_1(x) - n x_1 \\ (1-\alpha(x))\ell f_1(x) - n x_2 \end{bmatrix} ,$$

where $\alpha(x)$ is a continuously differentiable function such that $0 \le \alpha(x) \le 1$.[10]

In the following, we will present, without proofs,[11] two theorems which compare the short-run and long-run behavious of the solutions of (20) and (A-1).

I] It is well known that, roughly speaking, solutions of two differential equations which are lipschitzian

---

9) For the Poincaré-Bendixon limit cycle theorem, see, e.g., [4].
10) In [7], Inada used this type of investment function, together with an additional assumption (A-7) on $\alpha(x)$ stated below.
11) The proofs are available from the author upon request.

and close to each other are also close to each other. Although differential equation (20) has a discontinuous right-hand side, a similar conclusion holds for (20) and (A-1). But to state formally and prove this assertion, we have to define the distance between the two functions $g(\cdot)$ and $h(\cdot)$.

Let Ω be a compact set in R^2_+ with nonempty interior and let

$$\bar{\delta} = \max\left\{ |E(x)| \ \bigg| \ x \in \Omega \right\}.$$

$\bar{\delta}$ is positive since Ω^0 (interior of Ω) $\neq \phi$ implies the existence of an $x \in \Omega$ such that $E(x) \neq 0$. For each $\delta > 0$, define

$$\rho(\delta) = \max\left\{ |g(x) - h(x)| \ \bigg| \ x \in \Omega, \ |E(x)| \geq \min(\delta, \bar{\delta}) \right\},$$

where $|g(x) - h(x)|$ is the Euclidean norm of the two-dimensional vector $g(x) - h(x)$. $\rho(\delta)$ is well difined since $g(x)$ is continuous as long as $E(x) \neq 0$. Cleary $\rho(\delta)$ is decreasing in δ. Now we define the distance between $g(\cdot)$ and $h(\cdot)$ in Ω by

(A-2) $\quad \|g(\cdot) - h(\cdot)\| = \sup\left\{ \delta \mid \rho(\delta) \geq \delta, \ 0 < \delta \leq \bar{\delta} \right\}.$

Some remarks may be in order. If $\rho(\bar{\delta}) \leq \bar{\delta}$, then by the monotonicity of $\rho(\delta)$, there is a unique δ, $0 < \delta \leq \bar{\delta}$, such that $\delta = \rho(\delta)$, and $\|g(\cdot) - h(\cdot)\|$ is given by this δ . If $\rho(\bar{\delta}) > \bar{\delta}$, then $\|g(\cdot) - h(\cdot)\| = \bar{\delta}$. The magnitude $\|g(\cdot) - h(\cdot)\|$ measures the closeness between $g(\cdot)$ and $h(\cdot)$ in the sense that if $\|g(\cdot) - h(\cdot)\|$ is small, then, except for a *small* neighborhood of the equi-rental curve, the difference between $g(x)$ and $h(x)$ is *small*.

Now we can state and prove a theorem which shows that if $g(\cdot)$ and $h(\cdot)$ are close to each other, then the solution of $\dot{x} = g(x)$ and $\dot{x} = h(x)$ are also close to each other *in the short-run*.

Theorem 1: Let $x(t)$ and $\xi(t)$ be the solutions of (20) and (A-1) with $x(0) = \xi(0) = x^0$. Let Ω be a compact set in R^2_+ such that

$$\left| \frac{dg^+(x)}{dx} \right| < \infty \ \text{ and } \ \left| \frac{dg^-(x)}{dx} \right| < \infty \quad \text{ for all } \ x \in \Omega,$$

$$\left\{ x(t) \mid 0 \leq t \leq T \right\} \subset \Omega^0.$$

If $x(t)$ and T satisfy

   (i) $E(x(t)) \neq 0$, $0 \leq t \leq T$,   or

   (ii) $E(x^0) = 0$, $(\dfrac{dE}{dx} \cdot g^+(x^0))(\dfrac{dE}{dx} \cdot g^-(x^0)) > 0$, *and*

        $E(x(t)) \neq 0, \ 0 < t \leq T$,   or

   (iii) $E(x(t)) = 0$, $\dfrac{dE}{dx} \cdot g^+(x(t)) < 0$, *and* $\dfrac{dE}{dx} \cdot g^-(x(t)) > 0$, $0 \leq t \leq T,$

then, for every $\epsilon > 0$, there exists a $\delta > 0$ such that

$$\|g(\cdot) - h(\cdot)\| \leqq \delta$$

implies

$$|x(t) - \xi(t)| \leqq \epsilon, \quad 0 \leqq t \leqq T.$$

II]   In the text, we have shown that a quasi steady state x^* of (20) defined by (29) is a stable steady state if,

(A-3) $\dfrac{dE}{dx} \cdot g^+(x^*) < 0$ and $\dfrac{dE}{dx} \cdot g^-(x^*) > 0,$

and if, along the equi-rental curve,

(A-4) $-\dfrac{d}{dw}(\ell f_1(x(w^*)) - n(x_1(w^*) + x_2(x^*))) < 0$

where w^* is the wage-rental ratio at x^*.   (A-3) ensures that x^* is a normal point, while (A-4) ensures that the equi-rental curve cuts the curve $\dot{k} = 0$ from below.

In order to make the stability properties of (20) and (A-1) comparable, let us make an additional assumption concerning $\alpha(x)$:

(A-5) $\dfrac{\alpha(x)}{1 - \alpha(x)} \gtreqqless \dfrac{x_1}{x_2}$ as $E(x) \gtreqqless 0.$

Clearly this is equivalent to

$$\dfrac{\dot{x}_1}{x_1} \gtreqqless \dfrac{\dot{x}_2}{x_2} \quad \text{as} \quad E(x) \gtreqqless 0 .$$

Under this additional assumption, the steady states of (A-1) coincide with those of (20) and are therefore given by (29). Furthermore, the following theorem obtains:

Theorem 2:   *Suppose the system of differential equations (A-1) satisfies (A-5). Then a steady state x^* of (A-1) is stable if (A-3), (A-4), and*

(A-6) $\dfrac{d}{dx_1}\left(\dfrac{\alpha}{1-\alpha} - \dfrac{x_1}{x_2}\right)\Big|_{x_1 + x_2 = \text{const.}} < 0$ at x^*

are satisfied.

Remark: As was shown in the text (see (19)), the normality condition (A-3) implies that

$$\dfrac{d}{dx_1} E(x)\Big|_{x_1 + x_2 = \text{const.}} = E_1 - E_2 < 0.$$

Hence, under assumption (A-3), (A-5) implies that

$$\frac{d}{dx_1}\left(\frac{\alpha}{1-\alpha} - \frac{x_1}{x_2}\right)\bigg|_{x_1 + x_2 = \text{const.}} \leqq 0.$$

Therefore assumption (A-6) slightly strengthens assumption (A-5).

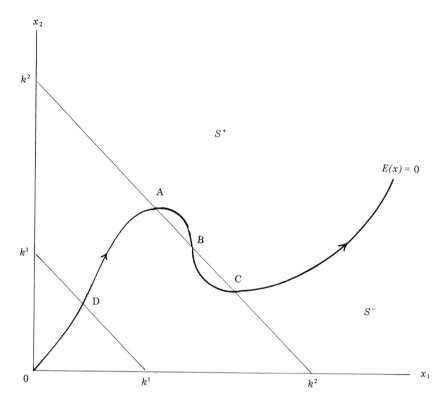

Figure 1

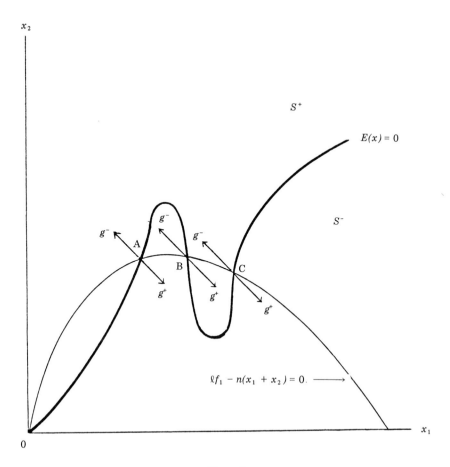

Figure 2

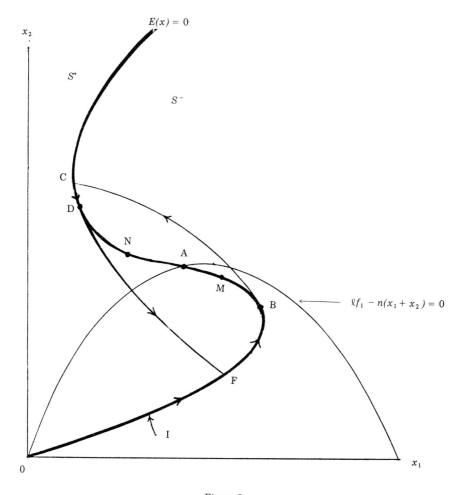

Figure 3

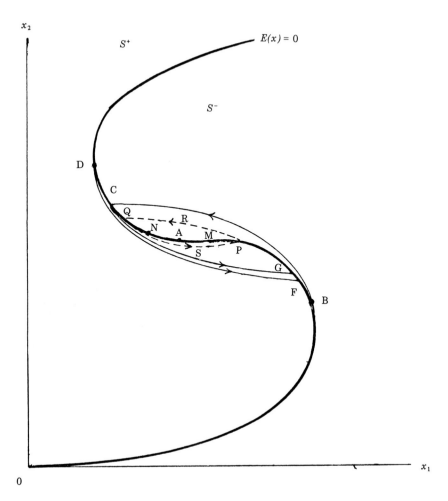

Figure 4

Bibliography

[1]   André, J. and P. Seibert, "Über stückweise lineare Differentialgleichungen, die bei Regelungs-problemen auftreten I, " *Archiv der Mathematik*, vol.VIII(1956).

[2]   André, J. and P. Seibert, "The Local Theory of Piecewise Continuous Differential Equations, " *Contributions to the Theory of Nonlinear Oscillations*, vol.V, edited by L. Cesari, J. Lasalle, and S. Lefschetz, 1960.

[3]   Burmeister, E. and A.R. Dobell, *Mathematical Theories of Economic Growth*, London, 1970.

[4]   Coddington, E.A., and N. Levinson, *Theory of Ordinary Differential Equations*, New York, 1955.

[5]   Drandakis, E.M., "Factor Substitution in a Two-Sector Growth Model," *Review of Economic Studies*, XXX (1963).

[6]   Inada, K., "On a Two-Sector Model of Economic Growth: Comments and a Generalization," *Review of Economic Studies*, XXX (1963).

[7]   Inada, K., "Investment in Fixed Capital and the Stability of Growth Equilibrium," *Review of Economic Studies*, XXXIII (1966).

[8]   Kurz, M., "A Two-Sector Extension of Swan's Model of Economic Growth: The Case of No Technical Change, "*International Economic Review*, IV (1963).

[9]   Kurz, M., "Optimal Patterns of Capital Accumulation under the Minimum Time Objective," *Econometrica*, XXXIII (1965).

[10]   Ryder, H.E., Jr., "Optimal Accumulation in a Two-Sector Neoclassical Economy with Non-Shiftable Capital," *Journal of Political Economy*, LXXVII (1969).

[11]   Sato, R., "Stability Conditions in Two-Sector Models of Economic Growth," *Journal of Economic Theory*, I (1969).

[12]   Shell, K. and J.E. Stiglitz, "The Allocation of Investment in a Dynamic Economy," *Quarterly Journal of Economics*, LXXXI (1967).

[13]   Uzawa, H., "On a Two-Sector Model of Economic Growth," *Review of Economic Studies*, XXIX (1961).

[14]   Uzawa, H., "On a Two-Sector Model of Economic Growth: II," *Review of Economic Studies*, XXX (1963).

FACTOR SPECIFICITY AND THE RYBCZINSKI THEOREM

by Koji Okuguchi

1. Introduction

It has recently been recognized that capital is specific in the short run in the sense that once installed, it can not temporarily be shifted from one industry to another. In a two factor, two goods, small open economy characterized by specificity of capital, the short run and long run behaviors of factor prices induced by an exogenous change in the product price in general differ. W. Mayer (1974), M. Mussa (1974) and K. Okuguchi (1975) have been concerned with implications of factor specificity in the short run for the comparative static, long run Stolper-Samuelson theorem for a two industry model. R. Jones (1975) has analyzed the same problem for a more general model with n industries.

The specificity of factor(s) has the same effects on factor prices as factor market imperfections as has been shown by H. Herberg and M. Kemp (1972) for a two factor, two goods, neoclassical model of economic growth.

The implications of the short run specificity of capital for the Rybczinski theorem which concerns only with the long run equilibrium have been analyzed by Mayer (1974). He decomposes the total effects of a once for all change in total labor on factor prices and industry outputs into two components, that is, the immediate short run effects involving no change in inter-industrial re-allocation of capital and the effects associated with the long run inter-industrial re-allocation of specific capital.

In this paper we shall also be concerned with analyzing effects, under factor specificity, of an exogenous change in total labor on factor prices and industry outputs for a two factor, two goods, small open economy where not only capital but also labor may be completely or partially specific in the short run. Mayer's analysis is restricted to the case where only capital is completely specific. Section 2 is devoted to explicit derivations of expressions for changes in factor prices and industry outputs caused by a change in the amount of labor available. In Section 3 we shall analyze time-absorbing processes of inter-industrial re-allocations of factors. It will be shown that the long run equilibrium for which the Rybczinski theorem is relevant is globally stable provided only that capital intensities in two industries differ.

2. The Short Run Changes in Factor Prices and Industry Outputs.

Let us introduce the following notation. Subscripts and superscripts i's run from 1 to 2.

X_i : output of the i-th industry

L : total labor

L_i : labor employed in the i-th industry

K : total capital

K_i : capital allocated to the i-th industry

$k \equiv K/L$, aggregate capital intensity

$k_i \equiv K_i/L_i$, capital intensity in the i-th industry

$\eta_i \equiv K_i/K$, proportion of capital in the i-th industry

$1_i \equiv L_i/L$, proportion of labor in the i-th industry

p : price of the second goods in terms of the first goods

w_i : wage rate in the i-th industry in terms of the first goods

r_i : rental of capital in the i-th industry in terms of the first goods

σ_i : elasticity of factor substitution in the i-th industry

θ^i_L : share of labor in the unit price of the i-th goods

θ^i_K : share of capital in the unit price of the i-th goods

"*" over a variable: relative rate of change of the variable, e.g. $X^*_i = dX_i/X_i$, $p^* = dp/p$

The production function for the i-th industry is

(1) $X_i = F^i.(L_i , K_i), \quad i = 1, 2$,

where F^i is assumed to be linear homogeneous and twice differentiable. As both capital and labor are assumed to be under full employment,

(2) $L_1 + L_2 = L,$

(3) $K_1 + K_2 = K.$

Though inter-industrial factor price differentials do not exist in the long run equilibrium where inter-industrial re-allocation of factors induced by an exogenous change in factor endowment ceases, they may exist in the short run due to factor specificity. Assuming incomplete specialization we have,

(4) $w_1 = F^1_1 (L_1 , K_1),$

(5) $w_2 = pF^2_1 (L_2 , K_2),$

(6) $r_1 = F^1_2 (L_1 , K_1),$

(7) $\quad r_2 = pF_2^2 (L_2, K_2)$,

where F_j^i denotes partial derivative of F^i with respect to the j-th argument. We define partial derivative of F_j^i with respect to the 1-th argument by F_{jl}^i. To see the short run effects of a change in total labor on changes in factor prices under factor specificity, differentiate (4-7) totally and rearrange in view of

$$p^* = 0, \quad dK_2 = -dK_1, \quad L_2^* = (L^* - L_1^* l_1)/l_2$$

to get,

(4') $\quad w_1^* = (K_1^* - L_1^*)\theta_K^1 /\sigma_1$,

(5') $\quad w_2^* = (K_2^* - L_2^*)\theta_K^2 /\sigma_2$

$$= ((L_1^* l_1 - L^*)/l_2 - K_1^* \eta_1 /\eta_2)\theta_K^2 /\sigma_2 ,$$

(6') $\quad r_1^* = (L_1^* - K_1^*) \theta_L^1 /\sigma_1$,

(7') $\quad r_2^* = ((L^* - L_1^* l_1)/l_2 + K_1^* \eta_1 /\eta_2) \theta_L^2 /\sigma_2$.

We have to consider five cases depending on which factor is specific and whether specificity is partial or complete.

Case 1: Suppose that only capital is completely specific in the short run. Since $K_1^* = K_2^* = 0$, we have by letting $w_1^* = w_2^*$,

(8) $\quad L_1^* = \sigma_1 \theta_K^2 L^*/(\sigma_1 l_1 \theta_K^2 + \sigma_2 l_2 \theta_K^1)$,

(9) $\quad L_2^* = \sigma_2 \theta_K^1 L^*/(\sigma_1 l_1 \theta_K^2 + \sigma_2 l_2 \theta_K^1)$.

Hence labors in both industries increase and the uniform wage rate decreases. The degree of decline in the wage rate depends, among other things, on elasticities of factor substitution in two industries as the following expression reveals.

(10) $\quad w^* = -\theta_K^1 \theta_K^2 L^*/(\sigma_1 l_1 \theta_K^2 + \sigma_2 l_2 \theta_K^1)$,

where $w^* \equiv w_1^* = w_2^*$. From this we see that *ceteris paribus*, the larger σ_1 and/or σ_2, the smaller the rate of decrease in the wage rate. This point can be made more clear by use of a diagram. See Fig. 1 below.

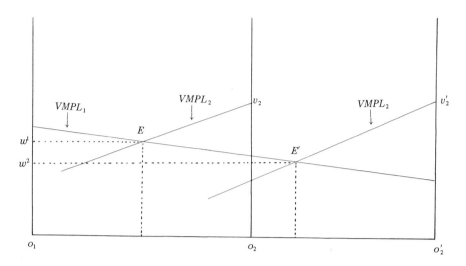

Figue. 1   Increase of labor under complete specificity of capital.

Let the distance between o_1 and o_2 equal the initial total amount of labor and that between o_1 and o_2' denote total labor after increase. Given K_1, K_2 and L, value of marginal product of labor in the first industry is depicted as a downward sloping curve $VMPL_1$ and that in the second industry also by a downward sloping curve $VMPL_2$ emanating from v_2. The long run equilibrium is attained at E where the uniform wage rate equals ow_1. If labor increases without accompanying inter-industrial re-allocation of capital, the new short run equilibrium is attained at E', the intersection of the old $VMPL_1$ curve and $VMPL_2$ curve emanating from v_2'. Note $o_2 v_2 = o_2' v_2'$. The new short run wage rate equals ow^2 which is less than ow^1. The difference between ow^1 and ow^2 depends on values of elasticities of factor substitution in two industries. The larger (smaller) σ_i, the flatter (steeper) $VMPL_i$ curve[1].

Outputs in two industries both increase in the short run with increase in total labor since $K_1^* = K_2^* = 0$, $L_1^* > 0$ and $L_2^* > 0$.

Case 2:   We next consider a case where only capital is partially specific in the sense that partial inter-industrial re-allocation of capital occurs in the short run. Since inter-industrial shiftability of

1)   Note $F_{11}^1 = -K_1/L_1 \cdot F_{12}^1 = -\theta_K^1 w_1/\sigma_1 L_1$
$F_{11}^2 = -\theta_K^2 \omega/\sigma_2 L_2$, $\omega \equiv w_2/p$.

labor entails no inter-industrial wage differential, we have from $w_1^* = w_2^* \equiv w^*$,

(11) $K_1^* = \eta_2 ((\sigma_1 l_1 \theta_K^2 + \sigma_2 l_2 \theta_K^1)L_1^* - \sigma_1 \theta_K^2 L^*)/l_2(\sigma_1 \eta_1 \theta_K^2 + \sigma_2 \eta_2 \theta_K^1)$,

(12) $w^* = (K_1^* - L_1^*)\theta_K^1 /\sigma_1$

$$= ((l_1 \eta_2 - l_2 \eta_1)\sigma_1 \theta_K^2 L_1^* - \sigma_1 \eta_2 \theta_K^2 L^*)\theta_K^1 /\sigma_1 l_2(\sigma_1 \eta_1 \theta_K^2 + \sigma_2 \eta_2 \theta_K^1).$$

If $k_2 > k_1$, $l_1 \eta_2 - l_2 \eta_1 > 0$. Thus w^* might take a positive value provided L_1^* is positive and sufficiently large. This point can be illustrated in Fig. 2. In Fig. 2, $w^* = 0$ at E; $w^* > 0$ in the north-eastern direction of E and along the line corresponding to (11); $w^* < 0$ in the south-western direction of E and along the same line. Fig. 3 depicts the situation where $k_1 > k_2$.

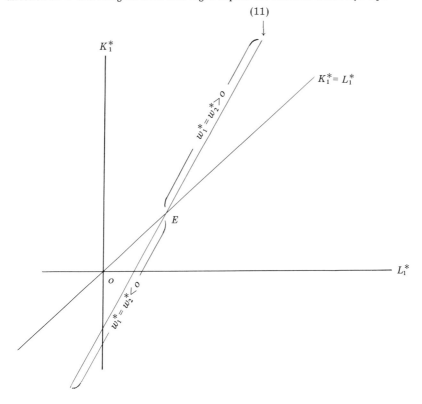

Fig. 2 $k_2 > k_1$ and only capital partially specific.

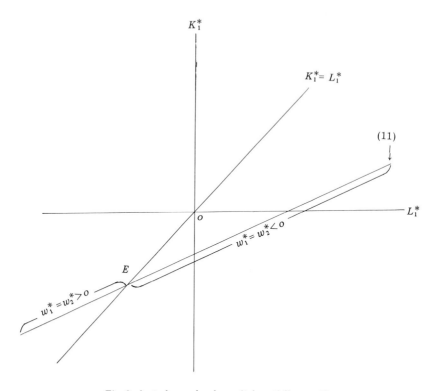

Fig. 3 $k_1 > k_2$ and only capital partially specific.

Cases 3 and 4:   In contrast with Cases 1 and 2, in these cases only labor is completely and partially specific, respectively. Similar arguments as for Cases 1 and 2 will reveal the impacts of a change in L on factor prices.

Case 5:   This is the general case where both labor and capital are assumed to be partially specific in the short run[2]. In this case w_1^* (and r_1^*) and w_2^* (and r_2^*) in general differ in the short run. The directions of changes in factor prices can be ascertained based on (4′) and (5′) as in Fig. 4 and 5.

---

2)   Mayer (1974), Mussa (1974) and Jones (1975) have assumed that only capital is completely specific. Herberg and Kemp (1972) have assumed that both capital and labor markets are imperfect. Okuguchi (1975) have analyzed the general situation where both factors may be completely or partially specific.

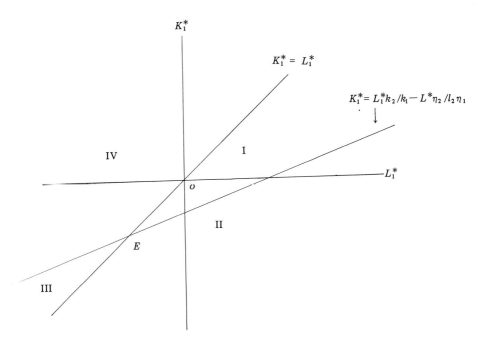

Fig. 4 $k_2 > k_1$ and both factors partially specific.

Legend:

In Region I, $w_1^* \geq 0,\quad w_2^* \geq 0$

In Region II, $w_1^* \leq 0,\quad w_2^* \geq 0$

In Region III, $w_1^* \leq 0,\quad w_2^* \leq 0$

In Region IV, $w_1^* \geq 0,\quad w_2^* \leq 0$

Equality holds only on boundaries.

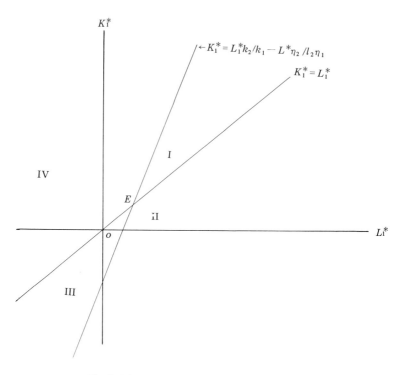

Fig. 5 $k_1 > k_2$ and both factors partially specific.

Legend:

In Region I, $\quad w^* \leq 0, \quad w_2^* \leq 0$

In Region II, $\quad w_1^* \leq 0, \quad w_2^* \geq 0$

In Region III, $\quad w_1^* \geq 0, \quad w_2^* \geq 0$

In Region IV, $\quad w_1^* \geq 0, \quad w_2^* \leq 0$

Equality holds only on boundaries.

The difference between relative rate of change in the wage rate in the first industry and that in the second industry is given by

(13) $w_1^* - w_2^* = K_1^*(\sigma_1\eta_1\theta_K^2 + \sigma_2\eta_2\theta_K^1)/\sigma_1\sigma_2\eta_2$

$$-L_1^*(\sigma_1 l_1\theta_K^2 + \sigma_2 l_2\theta_K^1)/\sigma_1\sigma_2 l_2 + L^*\theta_K^2/\sigma_2 l_2 .$$

Since $L^* > 0$, the difference becomes positive provided

$$dK_1/dL_1 \geq (\sigma_1 l_1\theta_K^2 + \sigma_2 l_2\theta_K^1)/(\sigma_1\eta_1\theta_K^2 + \sigma_2\eta_2\theta_K^1) \cdot k_1 k_2/k .$$

In order to see changes in outputs in two industries, we differentiate (1) totally to derive,

(14) $X_1^* = \theta_L^1 L_1^* + \theta_K^1 K_1^*$,

(15) $X_2^* = -(L_1^*\theta_L^2 l_1/l_2 + K_1^*\theta_K^2\eta_1/\eta_2) + L^*\theta_L^2/l_2$.

Hence

$$X_1^* \gtreqless 0 \quad \text{according as} \quad K_1^* \gtreqless -L_1^*\theta_L^1/\theta_K^1 ,$$

$$X_2^* \gtreqless 0 \quad \text{according as} \quad K_1^* \lesseqgtr L^*\theta_L^2\eta_2/\theta_K^2\eta_1 l_2 - L_1^*\theta_L^2 l_1\eta_2/\theta_K^2 l_2\eta_1 .$$

Taking into account

$$\theta_L^1/\theta_K^1 = \theta_L^2 l_1\eta_2/\theta_K^2 l_2\eta_1 ,$$

we get Fig. 6.

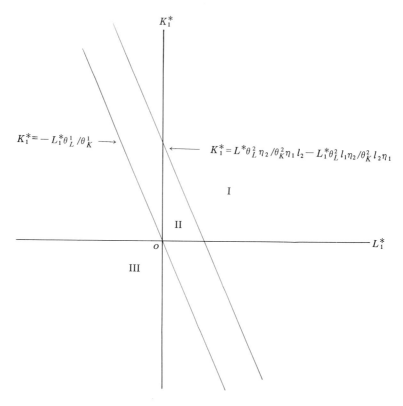

Fig. 6   Changes in industrial outputs.

Legend:

In Region I, $X_1^* \geq 0,\quad X_2^* \leq 0$

In Region II, $X_1^* \geq 0,\quad X_2^* \geq 0$

In Region III, $X_1^* \leq 0,\quad X_2^* \geq 0$

Equality holds holds only on boundaries.

We are now in a position to compare our results with those associated with the Rybczinski theorem which is of a comparative static nature and holds only in the long run equilibrium. As is well known, in the case of Rybczinski, factor prices do not undergo change with a change in factor endowment provided the product price remains constant. In our cases where capital and/or labor are (or is) completely or partially specific in the short run, factor prices may change and the directions of the changes are not determinate *a priori.* According to the Rybczinski theorem, changes of outputs are given by the following expressions[3].

$$L/X_1 \cdot (\partial X_1 /\partial L)^{LR} = k_2 /l_1 (k_2 - k_1) \gtrless 0 \text{ according as } k_1 \lessgtr k_2,$$

$$L/X_2 \cdot (\partial X_2 /\partial L)^{LR} = -k_1 /l_2 (k_2 - k_1) \lessgtr 0 \text{ according as } k_1 \lessgtr k_2,$$

where "*LR*" over a rate of change refers to the long run rate of change. As we have seen above, nothing definite can be said about the directions of changes in outputs when factor specificity is explicitly taken into account.

3. Global Stability of the Long Run Equilibrium.

In this section we shall prove that the long run equilibrium associated with the Rybczinski theorem is globally stable provided $k_1 \neq k_2$ always. Since both factors are assumed to be partially or completely specific, inter-industrial factor price differentials may arise if total labor changes once for all. The inter-industrial factor price differentials in turn cause sluggish re-allocations of factors between two industries as described by

(16) $dL_1 /dt = H_1 (w_1 - w_2), \text{ sgn}H_1 = \text{sgn}(w_1 - w_2), H_1 (0) = 0, H_1' > 0,$

(17) $dK_1 /dt = H_2 (r_1 - r_2), \text{ sgn}H_2 = \text{sgn}(r_1 - r_2), H_2 (0) = 0, H_2' > 0.$

Taking into account (2-7) we can show:

(18) $\partial H_1 /\partial L_1 = H_1' (F_{11}^1 + pF_{11}^2),$

(19) $\partial H_1 /\partial K_1 = H_1' (F_{12}^1 + pF_{12}^1),$

(20) $\partial H_2 /\partial L_1 = H_2' (F_{21}^1 + pF_{21}^2),$

(21) $\partial H_2 /\partial K_1 = H_2' (F_{22}^1 + pF_{22}^2).$

Hence

(22) $\partial H_1 /\partial L_1 + \partial H_2 /\partial K_1 < 0,$

---

3)   See Kemp (1969).

$$(23) \quad \begin{vmatrix} \partial H_1 / \partial L_1 & \partial H_1 / \partial K_1 \\ \\ \partial H_2 / \partial L_1 & \partial H_2 / \partial K_1 \end{vmatrix} = H_1' \, H_2' \, p F_{22}^1 \, F_{11}^2 \, (1 - k_1 / k_2)^2$$

$$> 0 \quad \text{if} \quad k_1 \neq k_2 \, ,$$

$$(24) \quad \partial H_1 / \partial L_1 \cdot \partial H_2 / \partial K_2 \neq 0.$$

Applying the Olech theorem[4] the global stability of the long run equilibrium follows provided $k_1 \neq k_2$ always. The global stability is established without any stringent assumption on relative capital intensities between two industries or that on elasticities of factor substitution provided $k_1 \neq k_2$, which is in a sharp contrast with the global stability of the long run growth equilibrium for a two factor, two goods, neoclassical model of economic growth[5].

---

4)   See Olech (1963).

5)   See R. Sato (1969) for the comprehensive stability conditions for the long run growth equilibrium for a two factor, two goods, neoclassical model of economic growth.

References

Herberg, H. and M.C. Kemp, "Growth and Factor Market Imperfections", *Zeitschrift für Gesamtestaatswissenschaft*, 128(1972), 590-604.

Kemp, M.C., *The Pure Theory of International Trade and Investment*, Prentice-Hall Inc., N.J. 1969.

Jones, R., "Income Distribution and Effective Protection in a Multicommodity Trade Model", *Journal of Economic Theory*, 11(1975), 1-15.

Mayer, W., "Short-Run and Long-Run Equilibrium for a Small Open Economy", *Journal of Political Economy*, 82(1974), 955-967.

Mussa, M., "Tariffs and Distribution of Income: The Importance of Factor Specificity, Substitutability, and Intensity in the Short and Long Run", *Journal of Political Economy*, 82(1974), 1191-1203.

Okuguchi, K., "Product Price Change and Inter-sectoral Re-allocation of Specific Factors", *Economic Record*,   September, 1976.

Olech, C., "On the Global Stability of an Autonomous System on the Plane", *Contributions to Differential Equations*, 1(1963), 389-400.

Sato, R., "Stability Conditions in Two-Sector Models of Economic Growth", *Journal of Economic Theory*, 1(1969), 107-117.

Devaluation and Financial Controls

in the Multi-Commodity World*

Akira Takayama

I.   *Introduction*

There are three purposes in writing this paper. The first is to examine the "dual" relations between devaluation and an autonomous change in the home or the foreign money supply. In this sense it extends the analysis of Kemp [12]. We shall obtain the generalization of some of his results in a much simpler way. The second purpose of this paper is to examine the uniqueness and stability of the steady state under the specie flow mechanism. We shall conclude that the steady state is stable if the devaluation condition is satisfied, which is more or less contradictory to a recent result by Chacholiades ([6], p. 473), but rather recovers the old result by Lerner to which Chacholiades objected. The analysis here thus completely parallels that of Anderson and Takayama [3]. Thirdly, we investigate the effects of devaluation and financial controls on the steady state values of the money and real prices, the nominal and real cash balances of each country and the level of the welfare of each country. This paper thus extends Anderson and Takayama [3] to a many commodity world, where A-T assumes only that there are two traded commodities and non no-traded goods.

In the main, our basic model is an extension of the one developed and utilized by Hahn [9], Kemp [10], [11], [12], Sieper [19], Negishi [15], Takayama [20], Amano [1] [2], and Dorbush [7], [8], for example. We shall make use of the separability assumption in the utility function, whose consequences are successfully exploited by Morishima [14], Pearce [16], Sieper [19], Negishi ([15], Chap. 17), and in some recent works by Samuelson [17], Amano [1] and Dornbusch [7], etc. Note, however, that the major results of this paper (theorems 1-4) also hold without separability. Samuelson [17] considers a multicommodity world.

2.   *Model*

We consider a trading world of two countries (home and foreign). There are n commodities which are traded internationally, and there are m non-traded goods in the home country, while there are m_f non-traded goods in the foreign country. The two countries' currencies are assumed to be the

---

* This paper was first presented in my lecture at Purdue in September 1975. As can be seen easily, it is a natural extension of Anderson and Takayama [3], at least in some part.

only marketable assets. Let C_i, X_i and p_i be the consumption, output and money price of the i-th commodity in the home country, where $i = 1, 2, \ldots, n + m$. Letting H be home real hoarding (the excess demand for the home currency), in terms of commodity 1, we can write the budget condition of the home country as

$$(1) \quad \sum_{i=1}^{n+m} \bar{p}_i C_i + H = \sum_{i=1}^{n+m} \bar{p}_i X_i$$

where $\bar{p}_i \equiv p_i/p_1$, the relative price (or the "real" price) of the i-th commodity in terms of commodity 1, $i = 1, 2, \ldots, n, n + 1, \ldots, n + m$, with $\bar{p}_1 \equiv 1$.

Assuming the separability of the utility function between the real commodities and money, we can write the demand functions of the i-th commodity and the hoarding function as

$$(2) \quad C_i = C_i(\bar{p}, \bar{q}, Z), \ i = 1,2, \ldots, n + m, \ H = H(\bar{p}, \bar{q}, M/p_1)$$

where $\bar{p} \equiv (\bar{p}_2, \ldots, \bar{p}_n), \bar{q} \equiv (\bar{p}_{n+1}, \ldots, \bar{p}_{n+m})$, and Z is defined by

$$(3) \quad Z \equiv \sum_{i=1}^{n+m} \bar{p}_i X_i - H$$

so that the budget condition (1) can be rewritten as

$$(4) \quad \sum_{i=1}^{n+m} \bar{p}_i C_i = Z$$

I.e., Z signifies total real expenditures in the home country.

Assuming the full employment of all resources, we may write the output of each commodity as

$$(5) \quad X_i = X_i(\bar{p}, \bar{q}), \ i = 1, 2, \ldots, n + m$$

where we assume the usual strictly concave production transformation surface; and the tangency condition of production may be written as

$$(6) \quad \sum_{i=1}^{n+m} \bar{p}_i \, dX_i = 0$$

Using (3) and (5), we define the expenditure function Z by

$$(7) \quad Z(\bar{p}, \bar{q}, H) \equiv \sum_{i=1}^{n+m} \bar{p}_i X_i(\bar{p}, \bar{q}) - H$$

Letting E_i be the excess demand for the i-th commodity $(E_i \equiv C_i - X_i)$, we have

$$(8) \quad E_i = E_i(\bar{p}, \bar{q}, H), \quad i = 1, 2, \ldots, n + m$$

where $E_i(\bar{p}, \bar{q}, H) \equiv C_i[\bar{p}, \bar{q}, Z(\bar{p}, \bar{q}, H)] - X_i(\bar{p}, \bar{q})$. In terms of the E_i's, the home budget condition (1) can be rewritten as

(1') $\displaystyle\sum_{i=1}^{n+m} \bar{p}_i E_i + H = 0$

We denote the foreign variables by adding the subscript f.   Thus the foreign budget condition can be written as

(9) $\displaystyle\sum_{i=1}^{n+m_f} \bar{p}_{if} E_{if} + H_f = 0$

Assuming away tariffs, transport costs and other impediments to trade, the free trade arbitrage condition can be written as

(10) $p_i = ep_{if}$, $i = 1, 2, \ldots, n$

where e denotes the exchange rate (the price of the foreign currency in terms of the home currency). (10) clearly implies

(11) $\bar{p}_i = \bar{p}_{if}$, $i = 2, \ldots, n$

Hence (1') and (9) are combined to yield

(12) $\displaystyle\sum_{i=1}^{n} \bar{p}_i(E_i + E_{if}) + \sum_{i=n+1}^{n+m} \bar{p}_i E_i + \sum_{i=n+1}^{n+m_f} \bar{p}_{if} E_{if} + H + H_f = 0$

which may be called *Walras' law* of the present system.

We are now ready to write the equilibrium conditions of the present model

(13) $E_i + E_{if} = 0$, $i = 1, 2, \ldots, n$

(14) $E_i = 0$, $i = n + 1, \ldots, n + m$

(15) $E_{if} = 0$, $i = n + 1, \ldots, n + m_f$

(16) $H = 0$

(17) $H_f = 0$

where one of the equations in $(13) - (17)$ is superfluous due to Walras' law. Under the flexible exchange rate system, these equations determine the equilibrium values of p_i , $i = 1, 2, \ldots, n+m$, p_{if}, $i = n+1, \ldots, n+m_f$, and e.   Under the fixed exchange rate system, (16) and (17) do not necessarily hold, and these monetary disequilibria create a balance of payments disequilibrium.

Assume that commodity i is a home exportable for $i = 1, 2, \ldots n_1$, and it is a home importatable for $i = n_1 + 1, \ldots, n$, in equilibrium. Then we may define the real balance of payments of the home country in terms of commodity 1 by

$$(18) \quad \bar{B} \equiv \sum_{i=1}^{n_1} \bar{p}_i E_{if} - \sum_{i=n_1+1}^{n} \bar{p}_i E_i$$

where the home balance of payments in terms of the home currency is simply $B \equiv p_1 \bar{B}$.   Assume that the market for non-traded goods for each country is held in equilibrium, and rewrite the budget conditions of the two countries as

$$(19) \quad \sum_{i=1}^{n} \bar{p}_i E_i + H = 0, \quad \sum_{i=1}^{n} \bar{p}_i E_{if} + H_f = 0$$

Given (14) and (15), we may rewrite (13) in the following equivalent way

$$(20) \quad H = \bar{B}, \quad H_f = -\bar{B}$$

and

$$(21) \quad E_i + E_{if} = 0, \quad i = 2, \ldots, n_1 \; ; n_1 + 2, \ldots, n$$

I.e., the equilibrium conditions of the first exportable commodity of each country (i.e., $i = 1$ and $n_1 + 1$) are replaced by (20).

3.   Devaluation and Financial Controls

We confine ourselves to the fixed exchange rate system, and write out the equilibrium conditions as

$$(22) \quad H(\bar{p}, \bar{q}, M/P_1) = \bar{B}$$

$$(23) \quad H_f(\bar{p}, \bar{q}_f, eM_f/p_1) = -\bar{B}$$

$$(24) \quad E_i(\bar{p}, \bar{q}, \bar{B}) + E_{if}(\bar{p}, \bar{q}_f, -\bar{B}) = 0, \quad i = 2; \ldots, n_1 \; n_1 + 2, \ldots, n$$

$$(25) \quad E_i(\bar{p}, \bar{q}, \bar{B}) = 0, \quad i = n + 1, \ldots, m$$

$$(26) \quad E_{if}(\bar{p}, \bar{q}_f, -\bar{B}) = 0, \quad i = n + 1, \ldots, m_f$$

$$(27) \quad \bar{B} = \sum_{i=1}^{n_1} \bar{p}_i E_{if}(\bar{p}, \bar{q}_f, -\bar{B}) - \sum_{i=n_1+1}^{n} \bar{p}_i E_i(\bar{p}, \bar{q}, \bar{B})$$

These $(n + m + m_f + 1)$ equations determine the equilibrium values of $(n + m + m_f + 1)$ variables, $\bar{p}_2, \ldots, \bar{p}_n, \bar{p}_{n+1}, \ldots \bar{p}_m, \bar{p}_{n+1,f}, \ldots, \bar{p}_{m_f,f}, p_1$, and $\bar{B}$, for given values of e, M, and M_f. The money prices are then determined.[1])   The balance of payment of the home country in terms of the home currency

---

1)   The home money prices p_i are determined from $\bar{p}_i$ and p_1 by using $\bar{p}_i \equiv p_i/p_1$. The foreign money prices p_{if} are then determined by (10).

may simply be computed by $B \equiv p_1 \bar{B}$. Since the parameters of this short-run equilibrium are e, M, and M_f , we may write these equilibrium values as[2]

(28) $\bar{B} = \bar{B}(e, M, M_f), \ \ B = B(e, M, M_f)$

(29) $\bar{p}_i = \bar{p}_i \ (e, M, M_f), \ \ p_i = p_i(e, M, M_f), \ \ \ i = 1, 2, \ldots, n, n + 1, \ldots, n + m$

(30) $\bar{p}_{if} = \bar{p}_{if} \ (e, M, M_f), \ p_{if} = p_{if} \ (e, M, M_f), \ i = 1, 2, \ldots, n, n + 1, \ldots, n + m_f$

The effect of devaluation on the balance of payments can be determined by computing $\partial \bar{B}/\partial e$. Recent articles such as Amano [1] and Dornbusch [7], for example, are concerned with computing $\partial \bar{B}/\partial e$ or $\partial B/\partial e$ (assuming $B = 0$ initially), where they assume $n = 2$ and $m = m_f = 0$; i.e., there are only two traded commodities and that there are no non-tradables in each country. The computation of $\partial \bar{B}/\partial e$ is not the purpose of this paper, and is left to the interested reader.

Instead, we shall investigate the dual relations between devaluation and the monetary controls, which was perceived by Komiya[3], and later fully clarified by Kemp [11], who assumes that there are two traded goods and one non-traded good for each country. In particular we prove the following theorem.

Theorem 1: In the above system of the fixed exchange rate system, (22) — (27), we have the following "dual relations", which, hold whether or not $B = 0$ initially.[4]

(31) $e\partial \bar{B}/\partial e = M_f \partial \bar{B}/\partial M_f, \ e\partial \bar{p}_i/\partial e = M_f \partial \bar{p}_i/\partial M_f, \ i = 2, \ldots, n + m$

(32) $e\partial B/\partial e = M_f \partial B/\partial M_f, \ \ e\partial p_i/\partial e = M_f \partial p_i/\partial M_f, \ i = 1, 2, \ldots, n + m$

(33) $e\partial \bar{B}/\partial e = - M\partial \bar{B}/\partial M, \ \ e\partial \bar{p}_i = - M\partial \bar{p}_i/\partial M, \ i = 2, \ldots, n + m$

(34) $\partial \log p_i/\partial \log e + \partial \log p_i/\partial \log M = 1, \ \ i = 1, 2, \ldots, n + m$

(35-a) $\partial \log p_i/\partial \log e + \partial \log B/\partial \log M = 1$, if $B \neq 0$ initially

(35-b) $e\partial B/\partial e + M\partial B/\partial M = B$

Proof: Observe that e and M_f always appear in the same place, i.e., in (23), as (eM_f/p_1)

---

2) We assume the existence of such single-valued functional relationships. With differentiability, comparative statics analysis is then concerned with computing such partial derivatives as $\partial \bar{B}/\partial e$, $\partial p_i/\partial e$, etc.

3) See footnote 19 of Komiya [13]. A slip in this footnote was pointed out by Shizuki [18]. Komiya corrected this slip in footnote 18 in the Japanese version of the paper (1975).

4) As should be clear from the proof, the conclusion here does not particularly depend on the separability assumption on the utility function. To see this, simply rewrite the excess demand functions as $E_i(\bar{p}, \bar{q}, M/p_1)$ for the home country and $E_{if}(\bar{p}, \bar{q}_f, eM_f/p_1)$ for the foreign country. We can then utilize the same argument as used in the present proof. Kemp [13] did not impose the separability assumption.

in the above system, from which (31) and (32) immediately follows.[5] Next, rewrite M/p_1 in (22) as $M/(ep_{1f})$, and then observe that this is the only place in the above system in which e and M appear, from which (33) follows immediately.[6]   To show (34), observe $(1/e)\partial p_{if}/\partial(1/e) = M\partial p_{if}/\partial M$, $i = 1, 2, \ldots, n, \ n + 1, \ldots, n + m_f$, from the second relation of (32) by switching the home country with the foreign country. Then using $\ p_{if} = p_i/e, \ \ i = 1, 2, \ldots, \ n$, we obtain (34) for $\ i = 1, 2, \ldots, n$. Also, using the second relation of (33) for $\ i = n + 1, \ldots, n + m$, we have $\partial \log p_i/\partial \log e + \partial \log p_i/\partial \log M = \partial \log p_1/\partial \log e + \partial \log p_1/\partial \log M, i = n + 1, \ldots, n + m$.   Since (34) holds for $i = 1$, this proves that (34) holds $i = n + 1, \ldots, n + m$. (35) follows from the first relation of (33), together with (34) for $i = 1$. The latter is required only to show (35-a). (Q.E.D.)

Equations (31) and (32) say that the devaluation of the home currency has a similar effect to that of an autonomous increase of the foreign currency, while (33) says that devaluation and tight money policy have similar effects on the real variables such as $\bar{B}$ and the $\bar{p}_i$'s. (34) and (35) reveal the dual relation between devaluation and tight money policy with respect to their effect on nominal variables, i.e., the money prices and the nominal balance of payments.

Kemp ([12], his theorem 2) obtained similar relations as (31) — (33) for $n = 2$ and $m = m_f = 1$, by differentiating the entire system, and actually computing the partial derivatives such as $\partial\bar{B}/\partial e$, $\partial\bar{B}/\partial M_f$, etc., where be assumed that $B = 0$ initially. Not only is our theorem more general than his, but also our proof is much simpler.

4. *Specie Flow Mechanism and Steady States*

If for example, the home country has a balance of payments surplus ($B > 0$) for the current period, the stock of the home currency increases by that amount at the beginning of the next period, while the stock of the foreign currency decreases, provided that the two currencies are completely convertible with a fixed exchange rate and that no autonomous monetary policies are taken by either of the two countries. With different amounts of the money stocks, the equilibrium values of the endogenous variables including B are different, and there is, of course, no guarantee that B is zero, which then changes the amount of the money stock in each country at the beginning of the third period. This process, which exists whether monies are fiat or gold, will continue until B becomes zero. This process may be termed as the "specie flow mechanism" in analogy to a similar process under the classical gold standard system. The question is whether this process leads to the steady state in which $B = 0$.

In examining this question, we first consider the basic dynamic equation of the specie flow

---

5)   For example, write $\bar{B}(e, M, M_f) = \beta(M, eM_f)$ and observe that $(1/M_f) (\partial\bar{B}/\partial e) = \partial\beta/\partial(eM_f) = (1/e) (\partial\bar{B}/\partial M_f)$, which proves $e\partial\bar{B}/\partial e = M_f\partial\bar{B}/\partial M_f$.

6)   In this case, p_1 is dropped from the list of the endogenous variables in the above system, and it is replaced by p_{1f} .

mechanism, which may be specified by

(36) $\dot{M} = B(e, M, M_f)$

where the dot signifies the derivative with respect to time. We assume that the exchange rate is fixed and that there are no autonomous changes in the money supplies during the process, so that we have

(37) $M + eM_f = \text{constant} \ (\equiv G)$

Substituting (37) into (36), we obtain

(38) $\dot{M} = \varphi(M) \ (\equiv B[e, M, (G - M)/e])$

where e and G are fixed. Observe that

(39) $e\partial B/\partial e = -M\partial B/\partial M = M_f \partial B/\partial M_f$, for $B = 0$ initially

from (32) and (35-6). Using this, we can compute

(40) $\dfrac{d\varphi}{dM} = -\dfrac{G}{MM_f} \dfrac{\partial B}{\partial e}$

where $d\varphi/dM$ and $\partial B/\partial e$ are both evaluated at $B = 0$, i.e., at $\dot{M} = 0$. Hence we can at once obtain

(41) $\dfrac{d\varphi}{dM}\Big|_{\dot{M}=0} < 0$ if and only if $\dfrac{\partial B}{\partial e}\Big|_{B=0} > 0$

and conclude:

Theorem 2:   The steady state value of M under the specie flow mechanism is unique and globally stable, if the devaluation of the home currency, beginning with the payment equilibrium, improves the balance of payments, i.e., if $\partial B/\partial e$ evaluated at $B = 0$ is always positive.[7]

Given the uniqueness and stability of the steady state, we now investigate the effect of devaluation and monetary controls on the steady state values of various variables, which we denote by adding an asterisk such as M^*, p_i^*, M_f^*, p_{if}^*, etc.

First note that the steady state can be defined by the following set of equations.[8]

---

7)   Assuming away the knife-edge case of $d\varphi(M^*)/dM=0$, the "devaluation condtion"($\partial B/\partial e > 0$ with $B=0$ initially) is necessary as well as sufficient for stability. Needless to say, $\partial B/\partial e$ *evaluated at* $B = 0$ *may not always be positive*. This is the case of multiple steady states, and the devaluation condition then provides the condition for *local* (instead of global) stability. As mentioned earlier, Amano [1] and Dornbusch [7] obtained the explicit expression for the devaluation contion for $n = 2$ and $m = m_f = 0$. Under the gross substitutability assumption, it can be shown that the devaluation condition is always satisfied.

8)   Suppose that there are only two traded commodities and no non-traded commodities, so that $\bar{p} \equiv p_2/p_1$, and $\bar{p}_i \equiv 0$, $i = 3, \ldots, n$, $\bar{q} \equiv 0$ and $\bar{q}_f \equiv 0$. Thus (27') reduces to $0=E_f(p^*,0,0) - p^*E_2(p^*,0,0)$. This means that the equilibrium "terms of trade" p^* are determined by the balance of payments equilibrium condition alone, regardless of the initial quantity of money supplies. I.e., the usual textbook exposition of the determination

(22') $\quad H(\bar{p}^*, \bar{q}^*, M^*/p_1^*) = 0$

(23') $\quad H_f(\bar{p}^*, \bar{q}_f^*, eM_f^*/p_1^*) = 0$

(24') $\quad E_i(\bar{p}^*, \bar{q}^*, 0) + E_{if}(\bar{p}^*, \bar{q}_f^*, 0) = 0, \quad i = 2, \ldots, n_1, \quad n_1 + 2, \ldots, n$

(25') $\quad E_i(\bar{p}^*, \bar{q}^*, 0) = 0, \quad i = n + 1, \ldots, m$

(26') $\quad E_{if}(\bar{p}^*, \bar{q}_f^*, 0) = 0, \quad i = n + 1, \ldots, m_f$

(27') $\quad 0 = \sum_{i=1}^{n_1} \bar{p}_i^* E_{if}(\bar{p}^*, \bar{q}_f^*, 0) - \sum_{i=n_1+1}^{n} \bar{p}_i^* E_i(\bar{p}^*, \bar{q}^*, 0)$

where $\bar{p}^* = (\bar{p}_2^*, \ldots, \bar{p}_n^*)$, $\bar{q}^* = (\bar{p}_{n+1}^*, \ldots, \bar{p}_{n+m}^*)$, $\bar{q}_f^* = (\bar{p}_{n+1,f}^*, \bar{p}_{n+m_f}^*, f)$ and $\bar{p}_i^* = \bar{p}_i^*/p_1^*$, $\bar{p}_{if}^* = p_{if}^*/p_{1f}^*$.

The steady state values of the various variables should, in general, depend on the initial values of the exchange rate e and the initial supply of each county's currency, M and M_f. Hence, in general, we have

(42) $\quad p_i^* = p_i^*(e, M, M_f), \quad \bar{p}_i^* = \bar{p}_i(e, M, M_f),$

$\quad M^* = M^*(e, M, M_f), \quad M_f^* = M_f^*(e, M, M_f),$

$\quad \bar{M}^* = \bar{M}^*(e, M, M_f), \quad \bar{M}_f^* = \bar{M}_f^*(e, M, M_f), \quad \text{etc.}$

where $\bar{M}^* \equiv M^*/p_1^*$ and $\bar{M}_f^* \equiv M_f^*/p_{1f}^*$ ($= eM_f^*/p_1^*$). However, as is clear from (22') $-$ (27'). the steady state values of the *real* variables $\bar{p}^*, \bar{q}^*, \bar{q}_f^*, \bar{M}^*$ and $\bar{M}_f^*$ are obtained from (22')$-$(29') alone, and thus independent of the initial values of $e, M,$ and M_f. In other words,

(43-a) $\partial \bar{p}_i^*/\partial e = 0, i = 1, \ldots, n + m; \quad \partial \bar{p}_{if}^*/\partial e = 0, \ i = 1, \ldots, n + m_f$

(43-b) $\partial \bar{M}^*/\partial e = \partial \bar{M}_f^*/\partial e = 0$

(44-a) $\partial \bar{p}_i^*/\partial M = \partial \bar{p}_i^*/\partial M_f = 0, \quad i = 1, \ldots, n + m;$

$\quad \partial \bar{p}_{if}^*/\partial M = \partial \bar{p}_{if}^*/\partial M_f = 0, \ i = 1, \ldots, n + m_f$

(44-b) $\partial \bar{M}^*/\partial M = \partial \bar{M}^*/\partial M_f = 0; \quad \partial \bar{M}_f^*/\partial M = \partial \bar{M}_f^*/\partial M_f = 0$

---

of p^* in terms of the Mill-Marshall offer curves is valid in the steady state. It should be clear that the same conclusion also holds under the flexible exchange rate system in which $\bar{B} = H = H_f = 0$. These conclusions are, as is well-known, the remarkable consequence of the separability assumption on the utility function.

(44-a) and (44-b) constitute the neoclassical doctrine of the *neutrality of money*.

Once the steady state values of the real variables are determined from $(22')-(27')$, the steady state values of the *nominal* variables are determined as follows. First observe from the definition of G in (37)

(45) $\bar{M}* + \bar{M}_f^* = G/p_1^*$

which determines p_1^* for a given value of G. The values of p_i^*, p_{if}^*, M^*, and M_f^* are then determined by $p_i^* = \bar{p}_i^* p_1^*$, $p_{if}^* = \bar{p}_{if}^* \, p_1^*/e$, $M^* = \bar{M}^* p_1^*$ and $M_f^* = \bar{M}_f^* p_{1f}^*$.

Since $\bar{M}^*$ and $\bar{M}_f^*$ are independent of e, M and M_f, we also have

(46) $d(p_1^*/G) = 0$ for all values of e, M, and M_f

although each value of p_1^* and G clearly depends on e, M and M_f. Next utilizing (43) and (44) together with (46), we at once obtain

(47-a) $\partial(p_i^*/G)/\partial e = 0$, $i = 1, \ldots, n + m$; $\partial(ep_{if}^*/G)/\partial e = 0$, $i = 1, \ldots, n + m_f$

(47-b) $\partial(M^*/G)/\partial e = \partial(eM_f^*/G)/\partial e = 0$

(48-a) $\partial(p_i^*/G)/\partial M = \partial(p_i^*/G)/\partial M_f = 0$, $i = 1, \ldots, n + m$;

$\partial(p_{if}^*/G)/\partial M = \partial(p_{if}^*/G)/\partial M_f = 0$, $i = 1, \ldots, n + m_f$

(48-b) $\partial(M^*/G)/\partial M = \partial(M^*/G)/\partial M_f = 0$; $\partial(M_f^*/G)/\partial M = \partial(M_f^*/G)/\partial M_f = 0$

Recalling $M + eM_f \equiv G$, we obtain the following relations for the effects of devaluation and financial controls on the steady state values of nominal variables.

(49-a) $\dfrac{1}{p_i^*}\dfrac{\partial p_i^*}{\partial e} = \dfrac{1}{M^*}\dfrac{\partial M^*}{\partial e} = \dfrac{M_f}{G} > 0$, $i = 1, 2, \ldots, \quad n + m$

(49-b) $\dfrac{1}{p_{if}^*}\dfrac{\partial p_{if}^*}{\partial e} = \dfrac{1}{M_f^*}\dfrac{\partial M_f^*}{\partial e} = -\dfrac{M}{eG} < 0$, $i = 1, 2, \ldots, \quad n + m_f$

(50-a) $\dfrac{1}{p_i^*}\dfrac{\partial p_i^*}{\partial M} = \dfrac{1}{M^*}\dfrac{\partial M^*}{\partial M} = \dfrac{1}{G} > 0$, $\quad \dfrac{1}{p_i^*}\dfrac{\partial p_i^*}{\partial M_f} = \dfrac{1}{M_f^*}\dfrac{\partial M_f^*}{\partial M_f} = \dfrac{e}{G} > 0$, $i = 1, 2, \ldots, n + m$

(50-b) $\dfrac{1}{p_{if}^*}\dfrac{\partial p_{if}^*}{\partial M} = \dfrac{1}{M_f^*}\dfrac{\partial M_f^*}{\partial M} = \dfrac{1}{G} > 0$, $\dfrac{1}{p_{if}^*}\dfrac{\partial p_{if}^*}{\partial M_f} = \dfrac{1}{M_f^*}\dfrac{\partial M_f^*}{\partial M_f} = \dfrac{e}{G} > 0$, $i = 1, 2, \ldots, \quad n + m$

We may summarize $(43) - (44)$ and $(49) - (50)$ as follows.

Theorem 3:

(i)   The steady state values of all the real prices ($\bar{p}_i^*$ and $\bar{p}_{if}^*$) and the real cash balances ($\bar{M}^*$ and $\bar{M}_f^*$) are not affected by devaluation, nor by an autonomous change in either of the two currencies.

(ii) The devaluation of the home currency increases (resp,. decreases) the steady state values of all the home (resp. foreign) money prices and of the nominal supply of the home (resp. foreign) currency.

(iii) An autonomous increase in the money supply of either of the two currencies increases the steady state values of all the (home and foreign) money prices, and of the nominal supply of each currency.

Finally, let us determine the steady state effect of devaluation and financial controls on welfare. For this purpose, we use the aggregate utility function of the home country defined by[9]

$$(51) \quad u = u(C_1, \ldots, C_{n+m}, L/P)$$

where L denotes the demand for nominal cash balances, and P denotes the general price index of the home country defined by

$$(52) \quad P \equiv \sum_{i=1}^{n+m} \theta_i p_i$$

and $\theta_i \equiv \bar{p}_i C_i / Z$, $i = 1, 2, \ldots, n + m$ (with $\bar{p}_1 \equiv 1$). Next, recalling (2) and (3) noting $H = 0$ in the steady state, we have

$$(53) \quad C_i^* = C_i [\bar{p}^*, \bar{q}^*, Y(\bar{p}^*, \bar{q}^*)]$$

where $Y(p^*, q^*) \equiv \sum_{i=1}^{n+m} \bar{p}_i^* X_i (\bar{p}^*, \bar{q}^*)$, the real output in terms of commodity 1. Since $Z = Y(p^*, q^*)$ in the steady state in which $H = 0$, and since C_i^*, $i = 1, 2, \ldots, n + m$ are constant in the steady state, we can at once conclude that θ_i, $i = 1, 2, \ldots, n + m$, are also constant in the steady state.[10] Also, from the constancy of the C_i^*'s, it is apparent that whether or not the steady state value of u changes or not depends on L/P. But by recalling $L = M$ in the steady state in which $H = 0$, we obtain

$$(54) \quad L/P \equiv \bar{M}/(\sum_{i=1}^{n+m} \theta_i \bar{p}_i)$$

where $\bar{M} \equiv M/p_1$. Since the steady state values of the $\bar{p}_i$' s, $\bar{M}$ and θ_i's are all constant, L/P is also constant. Thus we obtain.[11]

---

9) The separability assumption on the utility function, which is crucial to the discussion of this paper, is not needed here. Needless to say, the author fully realizes the sins committed in representing the level of commodity welfare by an aggregate utility function. Given this limitation, the discussion here simply follows the pattern of the exercise in the usual optimal tariff argument.

10) Therfore, our analysis here will be unaltered if we replace the general price index defined in (52) by $p = p(p_1, \ldots, p_{n+m})$ where the function P is homogeneous of degree one in $p_1, p_2, \ldots, p_{n+m}$.

11) The argument obtaining this theorem is conveyed to me by Richard K. Anderson. It is then used in Anderson and Takayama [3].

Theorem 4:   A change in the exchange rate or an autonomous change in the supply of either of the two currencies does not alter the steady state values of the home welfare.

In a similar fashion, we can also conclude that the steady state values of the foreign welfare are unaffected by devaluation and financial controls. However, if the utility function (51) is replaced by[12]

(55) $u = u(C_1, \ldots, C_{n+m}, L)$

we can conclude that the devaluation of the home currency and/or an autonomous increase in the money supply of either of the two currencies increases the steady state value of the home welfare. To show this, again recall $L^* = M^*$, and theorem 3. Since the devaluation of the home currency decreases the steady state value of the nominal supply of the foreign currency (by Theorem 3-ii), we can readily conclude, using a similar argument as above, that the devaluation of the home currency decreases the steady state value of foreign welfare. Similarly, an autonomous increase in the nominal money supply of either of the two currencies increases the steady state value of the nominal supply of the foreign currency (by Theorem 3), and thus increases the steady state value of foreign welfare.

------

[12]   Such a utility function is used by Arrow-Hahn ([41], eg. p. 339) and Negishi [15], for example. One justification is simply to assume that the public expects the future prices are identical to the present ones (static foresight), in which case the level of P stays constant (see Negishi [15], 255-256, for example, for this justification).

References:

1. Amano, A., "Stability Conditions in the Real and Monetary Models of International Trade," *International Economics and Development, Essays in Honor of Raul Prebisch*, ed. by L.E. DiMarco, New York: Academic Press, 1972, 47-59.

2. Amano, A., "Non-Traded Goods and the Effects of Devaluation," *Economic Studies Quarterly*, XXIII, August 1972, 1-9.

3. Anderson, R.K. and Takayama, A., "Devaluation, Specie Flow Mechanism, and the Steady State," presented at the Zushi Conference of the Tokyo Economic Research Center, March 1975 (forthcoming in *Review of Economic Studies*, XLIV, June 1977).

4. Arrow, K.J. and Hahn, F.H., *General Competitive Analysis*, San Francisco, Holden-Day 1971.

5. Berglas, E. and Razin, A., "A Note on the 'Balance of Payments and the Terms of Trade in Relation to Financial Controls'," *Review of Economic Studies*, XXXIX, October 1972, 511-513.

6. Chacholiades, M., "The Classical Theory of International Adjustment: A Restatement," *Econometrica*, 40, May 1972, 463-486.

7. Dornbusch, R., "Currency Depreciation, Hoarding, and Relative Prices," *Journal of Political Economy*, July/August 1973, 81, 893-915.

8. Dornbusch, R., "Devaluation Money, and Nontraded Goods," *American Economic Review*, December 1973, LXIII, 871-880.

9. Hahn, F., "The Balance of Payments in a Monetary Economy," *Review of Economic Studies*, February 1959, XXVI, 110-125.

10. Kemp, M.C., "The Rate of Exchange, the Terms of Trade and the Balance of Payments in Fully Employed Economies," *International Economic Review*, 3, September 1962, 314-327.

11. Kemp, M.C., *The Pure Theory of International Trade and Investment*, Englewood Cliffs, Prentice-Hall, 1969, Chapter 14.

12. Kemp, M.C., "The Balance of Payments and the Terms of Trade in Relation to Financial Controls," *Review of Economic Studies*, XXXVII, January 1970, 25-31.

13. Komiya, R., "Monetary Assumptions, Currency Depreciation and the Balance of Trade," *Economic Studies Quarterly*, XVII, December 1966, 9-22: Reproduced with revisions in his *Studies in International Economics* (in Japanese), Tokyo, Iwanami-Shoten, 1975, Chapter 1.

14. Morishima, M., "Consumer Behavior and Liquidity Preference," *Econometrica*, 20, April 1952, pp. 223-246.

15. Negishi, T., *General Equilibrium Theory and International Trade*, Amsterdam: North Holland Publishing, 1972, Chapters 15-17.

16. Pearce, I.F., *A Contribution to Demand Analysis*, Oxford, Clarendon Press, 1964.

17. Samuelson, P.A., "An Exact Hume-Ricardo-Marshall Model of International Trade," *Journal of International Economics*. 1. February 1971, pp. 1-18.

18. Shizuki, T., "On the 'Equivalence' of Currency Depreciation and Monetary Policy," *Economic Studies Quarterly*, XX, December 1969.

19. Sieper, E., "Economic Policy and the Balance of Trade," presented at the Christchurch Meeting of the Australian and New Zealand Associations for the Advancement of Science, January 1968.

20 Takayama, A., "The Role of Money in the Neoclassical System of International Trade," in his *International Trade, an Approach to the Theory*, New York: Holt, Rinehart and Winston, 1972, 251-278.

AN ECONOMIC DEVELOPMENT MODEL

BY

THE THEORY OF CONCENTRATED ACCUMULATION

Takayoshi Umeshita

I Introduction

Many kinds of development theory have been developed from the view-point of space. But they are all classified into either a balanced development theory or an unbalanced one.[1]

When we consider a nation which consists of spaces, it will conflict with a real economy that one space always develops more rapidly and the other more slowly, or each space always tends to develop with the same rate. It will be a general spatial development pattern that a space develops more rapidly in one phase and more slowly in the other.

The aim of this paper is to develop a new spatial development model in which a balanced development model and an unbalanced development one will be united, making a concentrated accumulation theory by T. Fujii [4, 5] more theoretical and operational.

II   An Economic Development Model by the Theory of Concentrated Accumulation

The model developed in this paper is a closed model consisting of two spaces. The basic equations of this model consist of two functions, i.e., *CA* production function and capital movement function. Capital will be chiefly analysed here by putting a severe assumption of labor.

1.   *CA* Production Function

In developing a dynamic spatial development model, it is decisively important how to build endogenously and flexibly the economy and diseconomy of concentrated accumulation into space production function which will be expressed in the production function with increasing and diminishing returns to scale.

A homothetic production function tied with R. Frisch's point of view, "regular ultra-passum law" [3], is developed here, because of returns to scale being managed as a variable.

---

1) Borts and Stein [1] stands for a representative balanced development theory, and contrarily Hirschman [6], Myrdal [8], Perróux [10], C. Clark [2] and A. Peaker [9] do an unbalanced development theory.

In the sense that this production function endogeneously builds in the economy and diseconomy of concentrated accumulation and that it has the potential power to provoke the mechanism of concentrated accumulation, this production function is named the *CA* production function [11].

For simplification, production factors are only capital and labor and the ratio of capital to labor is assumed to be fixed.

Now, the *CA* production function of each space is represented as the following.

$$Y_i = A \cdot \exp(-\frac{\eta}{K_i}), \qquad A, \eta = \text{Const.} > 0, \qquad i = \text{I, II} \tag{II-1}$$

where Y_i and K_i represent the income and the capital of space i respectively, and subscript i represents space I and II.[2]

This *CA* production function has the following characteristics.

(i) $\quad \dfrac{dY}{dK} \cdot \dfrac{K}{Y}\Big|_{d\log K = d\log L} = \dfrac{\eta}{K}$ $\hspace{4cm}$ (II-2)

(ii) $\quad \dfrac{d^2Y}{dK^2} = \dfrac{\eta Y}{K}(\eta - 2K)$ $\hspace{4cm}$ (II-3)

or

(ii′) $\quad \dfrac{d^2Y}{dK^2} \lesseqgtr 0 \quad \text{as} \quad K \lesseqgtr \dfrac{\eta}{2}$ $\hspace{3cm}$ (II-4)

(iii) $\begin{cases} \displaystyle\lim_{K \to 0} A \cdot \exp(-\dfrac{\eta}{K}) = 0 & \text{(II-5)} \\[4mm] \displaystyle\lim_{K \to \infty} A \cdot \exp(-\dfrac{\eta}{K}) = A & \text{(II-6)} \end{cases}$

From the above consideration, returns to scale of *CA* production function is variable; increasing returns to scale where $K < \eta$, constant returns to scale where $K = \eta$ and diminishing returns to scale where $K > \eta$, and marginal productivity of capital is highest where $K = \eta/2$. *CA* production function is depicted as Fig. 1.

---

2) Capital is assumed to be a limiting factor in our model.

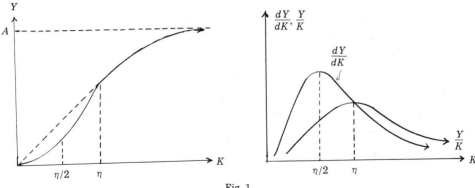

Fig. 1

2. Capital Movement Function between Spaces

The most basic concentrated accumulation mechanism is that of capital. Therefore, to develop operationally a concentrated accumulation mechanism, the analysis of capital movement between spaces is indispensable [12].

Capital movement between spaces will be specified by two factors; the difference of profit rate between spaces and the spatial stickiness of capital.

The difference of profit rate between spaces is prescribed in this model by the difference of marginal productivity of capital.[3]

The spatial stickiness of capital is the inclination of capital to remain in the proper space despite the profit rate of the other space being higher than that of the proper space. It will be caused by the shortage of information and risk coming from economic distance as a general term and more by managial strategy of enterprises etc.

As a result, the difference of profit rate between spaces has a positive effect and the spatial stickiness of capital has a negative effect for capital movement. And under the condition that spatial stickiness of capital is constant, if the difference of profit rate between spaces gets larger, capital mobility will generally rise at a higher rate.

The sources of mobil capital can be roughly classified into two categories; the monetary

---

3) Profit rate is not always equal to marginal productivity of capital. It is said, however, that profit rate is an increasing function of marginal productivity of capital because wage rate is implicitly assumed to be constant by the above notes (2).

capital from gross saving and the existing capital stock. But it does not happen so often in the usual economic society that all monetary capital from gross saving move out, or further, that existing capital stock moves, no matter how high capital mobility may be. It is considered at most that a part of monetary capital from depreciation will move out and the capital stock level of that space will consequently decrease. Therefore, just the mobility of monetary capital will be analysed here and the differences of stickiness among the monetary capital from gross saving will be neglected because of their smallness.

Now, if the depreciation rate of capital is μ and the propensity to saving s is constant and the same in the two spaces, the gross saving of each space S_i is represented as the following.

$$S_i = sY_i + K_i \qquad i = \text{I, II} \tag{II-7}$$

Next, if the ratio of moving monetary capital to total mobile monetary capital is defined as a mobility response coefficient of monetary capital ϵ, it is represented as the following, it being specified by the profit rate difference and the spatial stickiness of capital.

$$_i\epsilon_j = \frac{_iS_j}{S_i} = f_i(_j\gamma_i, \lambda_i)$$

$$_j\gamma_i = \gamma_j - \gamma_i \qquad i, j = \text{I, II} \quad i \neq j \tag{II-8}$$

where γ_i and λ_i each represents profit rate and stickiness of capital of space i, and $_iS_j$ represents monetary capital moving from space i into space j.

If λ_i is constant, $_i\epsilon_j$ will rise at a higher rate, as $_j\gamma_i$ does. But, in the following for simplification, spatial stickiness of monetary capital is assumed to be constant over time and the same in the two spaces. And function f_i is also assumed to be a linear function of $_j\gamma_i$.

Now, on the assumption of $\lambda_I = \lambda_{II} = \text{const.}$, the largest profit rate difference $\hat{\gamma}$ is determined from $_i\epsilon_j = 1$. Therefore, the monetary capital movement function of each space in the case that profit rate difference is smaller than $\hat{\gamma}$ is represented as the following.

$$_IS_{II} = -\alpha \cdot _I\gamma_{II} \cdot S_I \tag{II-9}$$

$$_{II}S_I = \alpha \cdot _I\gamma_{II} \cdot S_{II} \qquad \alpha = \text{Const.} > 0 \tag{II-10}$$

where it goes without saying that α depends on λ and $\hat{\gamma} = 1/\alpha$.

From the above analysis, the concentrated accumulation function of capital of each space in the case of $|_I\gamma_{II}| < \hat{\gamma}$ is represented as the following.

$$\dot{K}_I = S_I - \mu K_I - \delta \cdot _IS_{II} + \Delta \cdot _{II}S_I \tag{II-11}$$

$$\dot{K}_{II} = S_{II} - \mu K_{II} + \delta \cdot {}_{I}S_{II} - \Delta \cdot {}_{II}S_{I} \tag{II-12}$$

where $dK_i/dt = \dot{K}_i$,

$${}_{I}\gamma_{II} > 0 \rightarrow \delta = 0, \ \Delta = 1, \ {}_{I}\gamma_{II} = 0 \rightarrow \delta = \Delta = 0, \ {}_{I}\gamma_{II} < 0 \rightarrow \delta = 1, \ \Delta = 0$$

III Model Development under the Case of $|{}_{I}\gamma_{II}| < \hat{\gamma}$

Uniting CA production function and capital movement function between spaces, a spatial dynamic model under the case of $|{}_{I}\gamma_{II}| < \hat{\gamma}$ will be developed here.

Substituting (II-1) into (II-7) and further them into (II-9) and (II-10), we get

$${}_{I}S_{II} = -\alpha \cdot {}_{I}\gamma_{II} \{ sA\exp(-\eta/K_I) + \mu K_I \} \tag{III-1}$$

$${}_{II}S_{I} = \alpha \cdot {}_{I}\gamma_{II} \{ sA\exp(-\mu/K_{II}) + \mu K_{II} \} \tag{III-2}$$

Now, assuming that the profit rate is represented by marginal productivity of capital, the difference of profit rate between spaces will become from (II-2),

$${}_{I}\gamma_{II} = \gamma_I - \gamma_{II} = \eta A \left\{ \frac{\exp(-\eta/K_I)}{K_I^2} - \frac{\exp(-\eta/K_{II})}{K_{II}^2} \right\} \tag{III-3}$$

So, putting this into (III-1) and (III-2) and further them into (II-11) and (II-12), the concentrated accumulation function of capital of each space under the case of $|{}_{I}\gamma_{II}| < \hat{\gamma}$ will become (III-4) and (III-5).

$$\dot{K}_I = sA\exp\left(-\frac{\eta}{K_I}\right) + \alpha\eta A \left\{ \frac{\exp(-\eta/K_I)}{K_I^2} - \frac{\exp(-\eta/K_{II})}{K_{II}^2} \right\}$$
$$\cdot \left[sA \left\{ \delta \cdot \exp\left(-\frac{\eta}{K_I}\right) + \Delta \cdot \exp\left(-\frac{\eta}{K_{II}}\right) \right\} + \mu(\delta \cdot K_I + \Delta \cdot K_{II}) \right] \tag{III-4}$$

$$\dot{K}_{II} = sA\exp\left(-\frac{\eta}{K_{II}}\right) - \alpha\eta A \left\{ \frac{\exp(-\eta/K_I)}{K_I^2} - \frac{\exp(-\eta/K_{II})}{K_{II}^2} \right\}$$
$$\cdot \left[sA \left\{ \delta \cdot \exp\left(-\frac{\eta}{K_I}\right) + \Delta \cdot \exp\left(-\frac{\eta}{K_{II}}\right) \right\} + \mu(\delta \cdot K_I + \Delta \cdot K_{II}) \right] \tag{III-5}$$

In the following, they are analysed by cases first and put together later.

Case I $\quad {}_{I}\gamma_{II} = 0$

From (III-3)= 0,

$$K_I^2 \, e^{\frac{\eta}{K_I}} = K_{II}^2 \, e^{\frac{\eta}{K_{II}}} \tag{III-6}$$

First, as a trivial solution,

$$K_I = K_{II} \tag{III-7}$$

Secondly, as Fig. 1 explains, besides (III-7), $_I\gamma_{II}=0$ occurs only in $\{\,K_I\ |K_I<\eta/2\,,\,K_{II}\,|\,K_{II}>\eta/2\,\}$ and $\{\,K_I\ |\ K_I>\eta/2,\,K_{II}\ |\,K_{II}<\eta/2\,\}$.

Concerning the nature of the curve $_I\gamma_{II}=0$ in these domains, the next three points can be pointed out.

i) K_{II} (or K_I) is a monotonous decreasing function of $K_I(K_{II})$.

ii)   This curve is symmetric with a line of $K_I=K_{II}$ on the $(K_I,\,K_{II})$ plane.

iii)   It approaches asymptotically each K_I and K_{II} axis.

As to point i), differentiating (III-6) and arranging it,

$$\frac{dK_{II}}{dK_I}=\frac{e^{\eta/K_I}\;(2K_I-\eta)}{e^{\eta/K_{II}}\;(2K_{II}-\eta)}\ <0$$

The reason why it is negative is the following: when the denominator is negative, the numerator is positive and vice versa.

Point ii) will be self-evident if K_I is replaced with K_{II} in Fig. 1.

Point iii) comes from the fact that dY/dK approaches the K axis asymptotically with the increase of K, as Fig. 1 shows.

From the above deduction, the curve of $_I\gamma_{II}=0$ is drawn as Fig. 2.

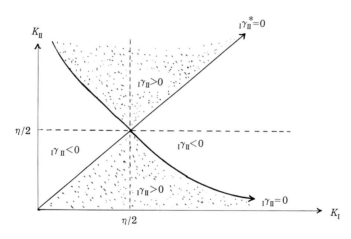

Fig. 2

Case 2 $_I\gamma_{II}>0$

First, the domains of $_I\gamma_{II}>0$ and $_I\gamma_{II}<0$ will be depicted as Fig. 2.

Next, putting $\delta=0$ and $\Delta=1$ in the case of $_I\gamma_{II}>0$ into (III-4) and (III-5), the concentrated accumulation function of capital of each space is each as follows,

$$\dot{K}_{\mathrm{I}} = \frac{Ae^{-\eta/K_{\mathrm{I}}}}{K_{\mathrm{I}}^2}\left\{ sK_{\mathrm{I}}^2 + s\alpha\eta Ae^{-\eta/K_{\mathrm{II}}} + \alpha\eta\mu K_{\mathrm{II}}\right\}$$

$$+ \frac{\alpha\eta Ae^{-\eta/K_{\mathrm{II}}}}{K_{\mathrm{II}}^2}\left\{ sAe^{-\eta/K_{\mathrm{II}}} + \mu K_{\mathrm{II}}\right\} \tag{III-8}$$

$$\dot{K}_{\mathrm{II}} = \frac{Ae^{-\eta/K_{\mathrm{II}}}}{K_{\mathrm{II}}^2}\left\{ sK_{\mathrm{II}} + s\alpha Ae^{-\eta/K_{\mathrm{II}}} + \alpha\eta\mu K_{\mathrm{II}}\right\}$$

$$- \frac{\alpha\eta Ae^{-\eta/K_{\mathrm{I}}}}{K_{\mathrm{I}}^2}\left\{ sAe^{-\eta/K_{\mathrm{II}}} + \mu K_{\mathrm{II}}\right\} \tag{III-9}$$

As (III-8) explains, $\dot{K}_{\mathrm{I}}$ is always positive in the domain of $_{\mathrm{I}}\gamma_{\mathrm{II}} > 0$. The question is $\dot{K}_{\mathrm{II}}$. To examine the nature of $\dot{K}_{\mathrm{II}}$, suppose $\dot{K}_{\mathrm{II}} = 0$. Then, (III-9) may be rewritten as (III-10).

$$K_{\mathrm{I}}^2 e^{\eta/K_{\mathrm{I}}} = \alpha\eta K_{\mathrm{II}}^2 e^{\eta/K_{\mathrm{II}}}\left\{ \frac{\mu K_{\mathrm{II}} e^{\eta/K_{\mathrm{II}}} + sA}{sK_{\mathrm{II}}^2 e^{\eta/K_{\mathrm{II}}} + \alpha\eta\mu K_{\mathrm{II}} e^{\eta/K_{\mathrm{II}}} + s\alpha\eta A}\right\} \tag{III-10}$$

By the total differential of (III-10),

$$(2K_{\mathrm{I}} - \eta)e^{\eta/K_{\mathrm{I}}} \cdot dK_{\mathrm{I}} = \frac{\alpha\eta e^{\eta/K_{\mathrm{II}}} \cdot dK_{\mathrm{II}}}{B^2}\left\{ C \cdot (2K_{\mathrm{II}} - \eta) \cdot (s\alpha\eta A + \alpha\eta\mu K_{\mathrm{II}} e^{\eta/K_{\mathrm{II}}})\right.$$

$$+ (K_{\mathrm{II}} - \eta)\, s\mu K_{\mathrm{II}}^3\, e^{2\eta/K_{\mathrm{II}}}\bigg\} \tag{III-11}$$

where $\quad B = sK_{\mathrm{II}}^2 e^{\eta/K_{\mathrm{II}}} + \alpha\eta\mu K_{\mathrm{II}} e^{\eta/K_{\mathrm{II}}} + s\alpha\eta A, \quad C = \mu K_{\mathrm{II}} e^{\eta/K_{\mathrm{II}}} + sA$

From the left side of this equation, the curve of the left side of (III-10) will be graphed as Fig. 3, where it takes the minimum value $\eta^2 e^2/4$ at $K_{\mathrm{I}} = \eta/2$.

And, the right side of (III-11) makes it clear that the curve of the right side of (III-10) decreases till $K_{\mathrm{II}} \leq \eta/2$ and increases at least from $K_{\mathrm{II}} \geq \eta$.

To analyse this more fully, suppose that the right side of (III-10) is J and that the value of J when $K_{\mathrm{II}} = \eta/2$ and $K_{\mathrm{II}} = \eta$ is $J_{\eta/2}$ and J_η respectively. Then, they will become

$$J_{\eta/2} = \frac{\eta^2 e^2}{4}\left\{ \frac{4s\alpha\eta A + 2\alpha\mu\eta^2 e^2}{4s\alpha\eta A + 2\alpha\mu\eta^2 e^2 + s\eta^2 e^2}\right\} < \frac{\eta^2 e^2}{4} \tag{III-12}$$

$$J_\eta = \frac{\eta^2 e^2}{4}\frac{4}{e}\left\{ \frac{s\alpha\eta A + \alpha\mu\eta^2 e^2}{s\alpha\eta A + \alpha\mu\eta^2 e^2 + s\eta^2 e^2}\right\} \tag{III-13}$$

But, not knowing precisely the J curve in $\eta/2 < K_{\mathrm{II}} < \eta$, the most probable case is shown by the dotted line. And K_{II}^{**} is not accurately decided except that it locates in $\eta/2 < K_{\mathrm{II}} < \eta$ (this is explained later), either.

Now, it is clear from Fig. 3 and Fig. 4 that the curve of $\dot{K}_{\mathrm{II}} = 0$ is when K_{I} (or K_{II}) approaches zero or infinity, K_{II} (or K_{I}) also zero or infinity, respectively.

Next, by arranging (III-11),

$$\frac{dK_{\mathrm{II}}}{dK_{\mathrm{I}}} = \frac{(2K_{\mathrm{I}}-\eta)e^{\eta/K_{\mathrm{I}}}}{\alpha\eta e^{\eta/K_{\mathrm{II}}} \cdot V/B^2} \tag{III-14}$$

where V is $\{\ \ \}$ of (III-11).

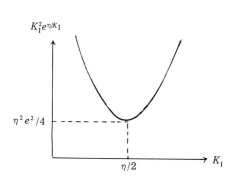

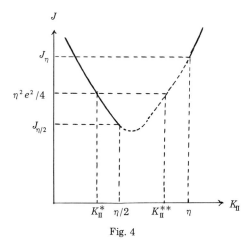

Fig. 3   Fig. 4

From (III-14), the following can be said about the curve of $\dot{K}_{\mathrm{II}}=0$.

(a) $K_{\mathrm{I}}<\dfrac{\eta}{2}$, $K_{\mathrm{II}}<\dfrac{\eta}{2}$ $\rightarrow \dfrac{dK_{\mathrm{II}}}{dK_{\mathrm{I}}}>0$ (d) $K_{\mathrm{I}}>\dfrac{\eta}{2}$, $K_{\mathrm{II}}\geqq\eta$ $\rightarrow \dfrac{dK_{\mathrm{II}}}{dK_{\mathrm{I}}}>0$

(b) $K_{\mathrm{I}}>\dfrac{\eta}{2}$, $K_{\mathrm{II}}<\dfrac{\eta}{2}$ $\rightarrow \dfrac{dK_{\mathrm{II}}}{dK_{\mathrm{I}}}<0$ (e) $K_{\mathrm{I}}=\dfrac{\eta}{2}$ $\rightarrow \dfrac{dK_{\mathrm{II}}}{dK_{\mathrm{I}}}=0$

(c) $K_{\mathrm{I}}<\dfrac{\eta}{2}$, $K_{\mathrm{II}}\geqq\eta$ $\rightarrow \dfrac{dK_{\mathrm{II}}}{dK_{\mathrm{I}}}>0$

From the above stated, the curve of $\dot{K}_{\mathrm{II}}=0$ is depicted as the following.

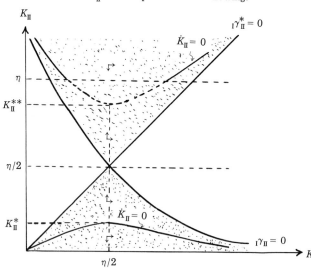

Fig. 5

As the curve of $\dot{K}_{II} = 0$ in $\eta/2 < K_{II} < \eta$ is not so clear, the most probable case is showed by the dotted line. And it is clear from (d) and (e) that K_{II}^{**} is in $\eta/2 < K_{II} < \eta$.

Under $_I\gamma_{II} > 0$, as $\dot{K}_I$ is always positive, the direction of the arrow in the phase diagram is as Fig. 5.

Case 3 $_I\gamma_{II} < 0$

Just as the domain of $_I\gamma_{II} < 0$ is symmetrical with that of $_I\gamma_{II} > 0$ about a $45°$ line, so the phase diagram of this case is symmetrical with that of $_I\gamma_{II} > 0$ about a $45°$ line.

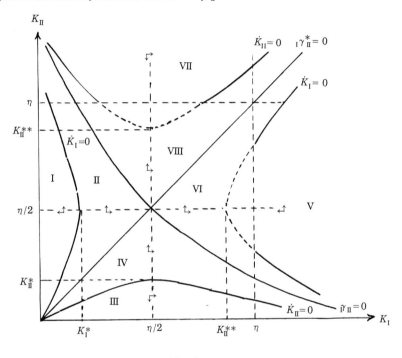

Fig. 6

To combine the above three cases, the phase diagram in the case of $|_I\gamma_{II}| < \hat{\gamma}$ is figured as Fig. 6.

If each domain surrounded by vertical and horizontal axes, $\dot{K}_I = 0$ and $\dot{K}_{II} = 0$ curves, and $_I\gamma_{II} = 0$ and $_I\gamma_{II}^* = 0$ $(=45°$ line) curves is divided from domain I to VIII, showed in Fig. 6, the following can be said about the relation between K_I and K_{II} in each domain.

Domain I

The capital stock of space I keeps decreasing, absorbed by space II and that of space II keeps increasing. Therefore, the economy in this domain traces a very drastic unbalanced development course.

Domain II

i) Though both capital stock of space I and that of space II increase, the economy in this domain traces an unbalanced development course in the meaning that the capital stock of space II increases relatively more than that of space I.

ii) Though i) holds good all over the domain II, it becomes gradually drastic, as to the degree of unbalanced development, a maximum, and gradually gentle as K_{II} gets near $\eta/2$, at $\eta/2$, and after that.

iii) The curve which shows the relation between K_I and K_{II} surely strikes against the curve ${}_I\gamma_{II} = 0$.

Domain III

As to K_I and K_{II}, just the contrary to the case of domain I holds good.

Domain IV

As to K_I and K_{II}, just the contrary to i) and ii) of domain II holds good. About iii) the same holds good.

Domain V

i) In the form that the capital stock I keeps decreasing and that of space II increasing, the economy traces an unbalanced development course.

ii) The degree of unbalanced development behaves in a fashion similar to that described in ii) of domain II.

iii) The curve which shows the relation between K_I and K_{II} surely strikes against the curve $\dot{K}_I = 0$.

Domain VI

i) Behavior is similar to that described in i) and ii) of domain II.

ii) In the place surrounded by the curve ${}_I\gamma_{II} = 0$, the straight line $K_I = K_I^{**}$ and the curve of $\dot{K}_I = 0$, the curve strikes against the curve of $\dot{K}_I = 0$.

iii) The curve asymptotically approaches the straight line of ${}_I\gamma_{II}^* = 0$.

Domain VII

As to K_I and K_{II}, just the contrary to domain V holds good.

Domain VIII

As to K_I and K_{II}, just the contrary to i)-iii) of domain VI holds good. And about iv) the same holds good.

Besides these, the following can be said as a whole.

(1) As the profit rate between spaces becomes equal on $_I\gamma_{II}=0$, the economy shows a balanced development. In other words, when the curve which shows the relation between K_I and K_{II} crosses the curve $_I\gamma_{II} = 0$, it runs parallel to the curve $_I\gamma_{II}^* = 0$.

(2) On the curve $\dot{K}_I=0$, because the concentrated accumulation rate of capital of space I is zero, when the curve which shows the relation between K_I and K_{II} crosses the curve $\dot{K}_I = 0$, it runs parallel to the vertical axis.

(3) On the curve $\dot{K}_{II} = 0$, because the concentrated accumulation rate of space II is zero this time, when the curve which shows the relation between K_I and K_{II} crosses the curve $\dot{K}_{II}=0$, it runs parallel to the horizontal axis.

From the above, if the curve which shows the relation between K_I and K_{II} is figured in Fig. 6, it will be figured as Fig. 7.

As this figure also explains, the general conclusion gotten from the analysis of economic development model by the concentrated accumulation theory may be represented as the following:

(1) When the early capital stock level between space I and space II is equal, the economy traces a balanced development course.

(2) When the early capital stock level of space I and that of space II exist in domain I and domain II, the economy keeps tracing a very drastic unbalanced development course such that the capital stock level of either of the two spaces comes to zero.

(3) When the early capital stock level of space I and that of space II exists in the part excluding domain I and domain II, we can generally say as the following. At first, in a form favorable to one space the degree of unbalanced development increases. It attains maximum at a certain stage and after that it gradually becomes gentle. Passing a certain breaking point, this time in a form conversely profitable to the other space, the degree of unbalanced development increases. It attains maximum at a certain stage and after that it gradually becomes gentle. Through the

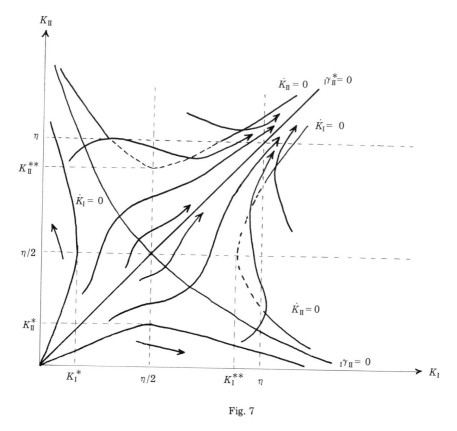

Fig. 7

cycle of such unbalanced development, the economy is finally moving in the direction of balanced development.

Thus, as stated in the beginning, our development model unites a balanced development model and an unbalanced development model.

References

[1] Borts,,G.H. and Stein, J.L., *Economic growth in a Free Market*, 1964.

[2] Clark, C., "Industrial location and economic potential", *Lloyds Bank Review*.

[3] Frisch, R., *Theory of Production*, 1965.

[4] Fujii, T., "The Concentrated Accumulation of Population and Capital and Economic Growth", *Keizai Kenkyu* (in Japanese), 1966.

[5] _____ , "Metropolis Formation in the Age of Industrialization", *Problems of Modern Metropolises* (in Japanese), 1965.

[6] Hirschman, A.O., *The Strategy of Economic Development*, 1958.

[7] Meyer, A., "An Aggregate Homothetic Production Function", *Southern Economic Journal*, 1970.

[8] Myrdal, G., *Economic Theory and Under-Developed Regions*, 1957.

[9] Peaker, A., "Regional Growth and Economic Potential — A Dynamic Analysis", *Regional Studies*, 1971.

[10] Perróux, S., "Economic Space: Theory and Applications", *Q.J.E.*, vol. 64.

[11] Umeshita, T., "On Spatial Production Function — Towards a New Economic Development Theory —", *Keizai Kagaku* (in Japanese), 1972.

[12] _____ , "On Capital Movement Function — In the Case of Two Spaces —", *Keizai Kagaku* (in Japanese), 1972.

SPATIAL EQUILIBRIUM:

A NEW APPROACH TO URBAN DENSITY

by Martin J. Beckmann

1. The Equilibrium Model Described.

Spatial equilibrium may be discussed in various contexts and from many different points of view. In contemporary research the most interesting application of the spatial equilibrium concept appears to be to problems of urban structure and design. How do we explain the observed patterns of density distributions of economic activities in cities? An understanding of these problems must precede any attempts at control through economic policies.

Most urban land is used for residential purposes, i.e., housing. The central problem of urban economics is, therefore, an explanation of the equilibrium patterns of residential land uses. [References 1-4.]

The standard analysis of residential density is modelled on the typical United States city. It assumes a single central business district in which all jobs and all shopping facilities are concentrated. This is an oversimplification which can sometimes be remedied. But it proves a blind alley when one attempts to understand the structure of older cities in other parts of the world.

In [5] I have proposed a model in which by contrast economic activity is decentralized. The aggregate density of economic activities is assumed to be proportional to the distribution of population. Concerning the locational preferences of population we make the following simple but not implausible assumptions.

(1) A larger amount of housing is preferred to a smaller one.

(2) A smaller density of housing in the area of one's residence is preferred to a higher density. This is assumed to be true even when the amount of housing occupied by the household itself is the same.

(3) Other things equal households prefer greater proximity to other households and economic activities to lesser proximity, i.e., to a larger average distance from other households.

(4) The amount of interaction with other households is not predetermined but is the result of a utility maximization.

In order to obtain an operational model it is necessary to specify the utility function having the above four properties. Our specification will be along the lines of recent approaches to the study of spatial interaction [6]. Namely utility is assumed to be an additive function consisting of a utility of housing, of urban density, of interaction, and of general consumption. Furthermore,

(5)   The utility function for interaction is the entropy function; the utility of general consumption is linear.

For a representative household we then have the following utility maximization problem.

$$(1) \quad \max_{h, \, x_i} \quad y - ph - k\sum_i r_i x_i + \phi(h) + \psi(m) + \sum_i a_i x_i - \sum_i x_i \log x_i$$

where

y	income
h	housing
k	unit transportation (that is, interaction) cost
p	housing rent
$\phi(h)$	the utility of housing expressed in money terms
$\psi(m)$	the utility of housing density m in the neighborhood also expressed in money terms
a_i	the attraction of destination i
x_i	the number of trips to destination i per period.

Here, the first three terms represent the utility of general consumption, and the last two terms are the utility of interaction with (trips to) other households.

Although housing and density appear as two separate variables in the utility function and hence in housing demand, it turns out that in equilibrium they are linked. This is due to the fact that the market price of housing p governs both the supply of housing s per unit of land area and the demand h for housing per household.

Assuming a Cobb-Douglas production function for the production of housing (from land and and capital, say) the quantity of housing supplied per unit of land area turns out to be a power function of the housing price

$$(2) \quad s = s_0 p^\gamma \qquad \text{(say)}$$

Consider now the demand for housing. Maximizing with respect to h in (1)

$$(3) \quad \phi'(h) = p.$$

Equations (2) and (3) may be used to express p and h in terms of the housing density m. Observe first that

$$h = (\phi')^{-1}(p)$$

and that, by definition of density

(4) $\quad m = \dfrac{s}{h} = \dfrac{\text{housing/area}}{\text{housing/housholds}} = \dfrac{\text{housholds}}{\text{area}}$

Now

$$m = \frac{s_0 \, p^\gamma}{(\phi')^{-1}(p)} = m(p).$$

Inverting we have

(5) $\quad p = p(m).$

All terms in the utility function (1) involving housing h and density m may now be combined

$$-ph + \phi(h) + \psi(m) = -p\,(\phi')^{-1}(p) + \phi(\,(\phi')^{-1}(p)\,) + \psi(m(p)\,)$$

or upon substituting (5)

(6) $\hspace{3cm} = g\,(m), \text{ say.}$

Thus housing demand and density are linked and the utility function turns out to depend on density m only. The utility function becomes

(7) $\quad u = y + g(m) - k\sum_i r_i x_i + \sum_i a_i x_i - \sum_i x_i \, \log x_i.$

Maximizing (7) with respect to the number of trips x_i

$$a_i - kr_i - \log x_i - 1 = 0$$

(8) $\quad x_i = e^{a_i - 1 - kr_i}$.

Substituting in the utility function we obtain as the indirect utility function in terms of the density m, of income y, and distances r_i

$$v = y + g(m) + \sum_i e^{a_i - 1 - kr_i}\ .$$

Assume now that every household is potentially an equally attractive object of interaction so that $a_i = \text{constant} = 1$ (say). In a one-dimensional continuum, where destinations, i.e., housholds are distributed with a density m, the indirect utility function for a household located at point r is then

(9) $\quad v = y + g(m) + \int e^{-k\,|x - r|} m(x)\ dx.$

Assume that the city is of this one-dimensional (long narrow) shape and that it extends between points $-R$ and R. The utility of a household located at r is given by (9). In equilibrium households must be equally satisfied in all locations. Upon standardizing the distance units so that $k = 1$ the condition of spatial equilibrium becomes

(10) $\quad g(m) + \int_{-R}^{R} e^{-|x-r|} m(x)\, dx = u_o$

where u_o is a constant. This constant depends on the total number of households to be housed and on the space $2R$ available. In the next section we study the equation of equilibrium (10).

2. The Equation of Equilibrium Discussed

In this section we study general properties of solutions to (1.10) which can be derived without specifying the functional form of $g(m)$. We merely assume that $g(m)$ is decreasing. We show first:

Lemma 1

There always exists a symmetric solution of (1.10)

(1) $\quad m(x) = m(-x)$.

Proof:

Writing (1.10) for $r = r_o$ and

$$r = -r_o$$

$$g(m(r_o)) + \int_{-R}^{R} e^{-|x-r_o|} m(x)\, dx = u_o$$

$$g(m(-r_o)) + \int_{-R}^{R} e^{-|x+r_o|} m(x)\, dx = u_o$$

and substituting

$$|x + r_o| = |-x-r_o| \quad \text{and (1)}$$

in the second equation we obtain the first equation, proving the assertion.

Since $g(m)$ is decreasing, its inverse exists and we can define the following iteration

(2) $\quad m_{n+1}(r) = g^{-1}\{u_o - \int_{-R}^{R} e^{-|x-r|} m_n(x)\, dx\}$.

We now restrict the function g further so that the mapping (2) is a contraction. Then a fixed point exists and the iteration (2) converges to a fixed point of the contraction. The iteration preserves some fundamental properties of the solution.

Lemma 2: Let m_n be symmetric

$$m_n(x) = m_n(-x).$$

Then the iterated function $m_{n+1}(x)$ is also symmetric, and so is the limit function

(3) $\quad m(x) = \lim_{n \to \infty} m_n(x)$.

Proof:

$$m_{n+1}(-r) = g^{-1}\left\{ u_o - \int_{-R}^{R} e^{-|x+r|} m_n(x)dx \right\}$$

$$= g^{-1}\left\{ u_o - \int_{-R}^{R} e^{-|-x-r|} m_n(-x)\, dx \right\}$$

since m_n is symmetric. Changing notation

$$= g^{-1}\left\{ u_o - \int_{-R}^{R} e^{-|t-r|} m(t)dt \right\}$$

$$= m_{n+1}(r).$$

Since $m_o = 0$ may be chosen symmetric, it follows by induction that $m_n(r)$ is symmetric for all n.

Therefore,

$$m(r) = \lim_{n \to \infty} m_n(r) \quad \lim_{n \to \infty} m_n(-r)$$

$$= m(-r).$$

This completes the proof.

Lemma 3:   Among the symmetric solutions there exists one such that density $m(r)$ decreases with distance from the center $m'(r) < 0$ for $r > 0$.

Proof: Let $m_o = 0$ and assume that $m_n(r)$ is decreasing

$$m_n'(r) < 0 \quad \text{for} \quad r > 0.$$

Consider

$$m_{n+1}'(r) = -(g^{-1})'\left(u_o - \int_{-R}^{R} e^{-|x-r|} m_n(x)\, dx\right) \cdot \frac{d}{dr} \int_{-R}^{R} e^{-|x-r|} m_n(x)dx.$$

Sincs g' is negative

$$\text{sign } m_{n+1}' = \text{sign } \frac{d}{dr} \int_{-R}^{R} e^{-|x-r|} m_n(x)dx.$$

Now

$$I = \int_{-R}^{R} e^{-|x-r|} m(x)\, dx = \int_{0}^{R} e^{-r-x} m_n(x)\, dx$$

$$+ \int_{0}^{R} e^{-r+x} m_n(x)\, dx + \int_{r}^{R} e^{+r-x} m_n(x)\, dx$$

where the first integral on the right-hand side expresses the symmetry assumption $m_n(x) = m_n(-x)$

$$= e^{-r}\int_{0}^{R} e^{-x} m(x)dx + \int_{0}^{r} e^{-x} m(r-x)\, dx + \int_{0}^{R-r} e^{-x} m(r+x)\, dx.$$

Taking the derivative

(4) $\dfrac{dI}{dr} = -e^{-r}\int_0^R e^{-x} m(x)\, dx + \int_0^r e^{-x} m'\,(r-x)dx$

$\qquad + \int_0^{R-r} e^{-x} m'\,(r+x)\, dx + e^{-r}m(0)$

$\qquad - e^{-R+r}\, m(R).$

For the first integral integration by parts yields

$\qquad + e^{-r}[e^{-x}m(x)]_0^R - \int_0^R e^{-r-x} m'\,(x)\, dx$

$\qquad = e^{-r-R}\, m(R) - e^{-r}m(0) - \int_0^R e^{-r-x}m'\,(x)\, dx.$

Substituting in (4)

$\qquad \dfrac{dI}{dr} = m_n\,(R)\cdot e^{-R}\cdot[e^{-r} - e^r]$

$\qquad\qquad + \int_0^r e^{-x}\, m_n'\,(x)\, dx\cdot[1 - e^{-r}]$

$\qquad\qquad + \int_r^R e^{-x}\, m_n'\,(x)\, dx\,[e^r - e^{-r}]$

$\qquad\qquad < 0,$

by the induction hypothesis $m_n'\,(r) < 0.$

It follows that $m_{n+1}'\,(r) < 0$ and by induction that the limit function $m(x)$ is decreasing.

3. Solution of the Linear Case.

In this section we treat the case of a linear $g(m)$

(1) $g(m) = \alpha - \beta m.$

Upon substitution, the equation of equilibrium may be rewritten

(2) $m(r) = \dfrac{\alpha - u_0}{\beta} + \dfrac{1}{\beta}\int_{-R}^R e^{-|x-r|}\, m(x)\, dx.$

Lemma 4

The sequence

$\qquad m_{n+1}\,(r) = \dfrac{a}{\beta} + \dfrac{1}{\beta}\int_{-R}^R e^{-|x-r|}\, m_n\,(x)dx.$

$\qquad\qquad = \dfrac{a}{\beta} + P(m_n), \qquad\qquad$ say, converges when

$$\frac{1}{\beta} \int_{-R}^{R} e^{-|x-r|} dx < 1 \qquad\qquad \text{all } r,$$

i.e., when

(3) $\quad \beta > 2 (1 - e^{-R})$.

Proof:

$$|m_{n+1} - m_n| = |Pm_n - Pm_{n-1}|$$

$$\leqq |P| |m_n - m_{n-1}|.$$

From this

$$|m_{n+1} - m_n| \leqq \lambda |m_n - m_{n-1}|$$

where $|\ \ |$ denote the sup norm. Condition (3) implies $\lambda < 1$. Repeated application yields

$$|m_{n+1} - m_n| \leqq \lambda^n |m_1 - m_0| = \lambda^n \cdot |m_1|$$

and

$$|m_{n+k} - m_n| \quad \leqq |m_{n+k} - m_{n+k-1}| + \dots |m_{n+1} - m_n|$$

$$\leqq |m_1| \lambda^n \cdot (1 + \lambda + \lambda^2 + \dots \lambda^{n-k-1})$$

$$= |m_1| \lambda^n \frac{1-\lambda^{n-k}}{1-\lambda}$$

$$\leqq \frac{|m_1|}{1-\lambda} \lambda^n$$

and this may be made arbitrarily small by choosing n sufficiently large.

Lemma 5: The solution of the equilibrium equation (2) is unique provided condition (3) holds.

Proof: Let m^1, m^2 be two solutions. (3) implies that they are bounded. Therefore,

$\quad \cdot m^1 - m^2 = \mu \qquad\qquad$ is bounded. Now

$\quad \mu = P\mu = P^n \mu$

and so

$\quad |\mu| \leqq |P^n \mu| \leqq \lambda^n |\mu|$

and $\quad |\mu| \leqq \lim_{n \to \infty} \lambda^n \cdot |\mu| = 0$

since $|\mu|$ is bounded.

The equation (2) may now be transformed into a differential equation as follows. Rewrite (2)

$$m(r) = \frac{\alpha - u_\rho}{\beta} + \frac{1}{\beta} \int_{-R}^{r} e^{x-r} m(x) dx + \frac{1}{\beta} \int_{r}^{R} e^{r-x} m(x) dx.$$

Differentiating

$$m'(r) = -\frac{1}{\beta} \int_{-R}^{r} e^{x-r} m(x) dx + \frac{1}{\beta} \int_{r}^{R} e^{r-x} m(x) dx.$$

Differentiating again

$$m''(r) = \frac{1}{\beta} \int_{-R}^{r} e^{x-r} m(x) dx + \frac{1}{\beta} \int_{r}^{R} e^{r-x} m(x) dx \qquad \text{or}$$

(4) $m''(r) = m(r) - \frac{\alpha - u_\rho}{\beta}$

The general solution of the differential equation (4) is

(5) $m(r) = \dfrac{a}{\beta-2} + Ae^{wr} + Be^{-wr}.$

Symmetry requires

(6) $A = B.$

Upon substituting

$$m(r) = \frac{a}{\beta-2} + A(e^{wr} + e^{-wr})$$

in (2) one obtains by a straightforward but tedious calculation

(7) $A = -\dfrac{a}{\beta-2} \cdot \dfrac{1}{\dfrac{e^{-wr}}{1+w} + \dfrac{e^{wr}}{1-w}}$

Thus, except for a linear transform, the solution is a hyperbolic cosine function. It is concave. Its coefficients depend on R, the size of the region, and on the utility level attainable, that is, the total number of households to be housed.

4. Generalization and Conclusion.

The uniqueness proof for the linear case may be extended in straightforward fashion when the following Lipschitz condition applies to the inverse function g^{-1}.

Lemma 6:   Let

(1) $|g^{-1}(m_1) - g^{-1}(m_2)| < K |m_1 - m_2|$

and let

(2) $\quad K \cdot \int_{-R}^{R} e^{-|x-r|} dx \leqq K \; 2|1 - e^{-R}| < 1.$

Then the solution of (1.10) is unique. The proof is an immediate adaptation of the uniqueness proof in the linear case.

It follows that for general decreasing functions $g(m)$ satisfylng the Lipschitz condition (1) the equilibrium density is symmetric and decreases with absolute distance from the center.

An interesting question is this: What happens when the Lipschitz condition is not satisfied, i.e., when utility is not sufficiently sensitive to density. In that case there need not exist, and when the sensitivity is too small, there does not exist a spatial equilibrium of the type examined here. This means that the advantages and disadvantages of distance from other households, i.e., the factor of accessibility cannot be balanced through the housing market to bring about an equilibrium. Presumably in the face of market failure some other rationing mechanism becomes necessary. This observation throws some new light on the persistence of rent control and administered housing allocation in some economies. However, the situation of insensitivity is unlikely to occur when housing is in drastically short supply. For then, on the contrary, households are eager to sacrifice accessibility for an ampler provision of housing space.

Can the analysis be extended to a two-dimensional city? In principle, this is straightforward, but in doing so, one must make certain prior specifications with regard to the transportation system. In the case of a square grid, for instance, we have immediately

(3) $\quad u_o = g(m(r_1, r_2)) + \int_R \int e^{-|x_1 - r_1| - |x_2 - r_2|} m(x_1, x_2) dx_1 dx_2$

where the integral is to be extended over the city's region R. Unfortunately, the equation does not factor into two equations except in the singular case where $g = u_o - \beta m$ so that the constant term vanishes.

Except in this case of "pre-established harmony" the solution of the integral equation raises some difficult problems, even in the case of a region of regular (square or circular) shape.

The case of a concentric and radial road system generates a density function which depends only on distance from the center so that the integral equation becomes once more one in terms of a function of a single variable $m = m(r)$. However, the second-order differential equation is difficult. For linear functions $g(m)$ it is a linear differential equation with coefficients composed of exponential and power functions. This equation is currently under investigation.

References

[1] Beckmann, Martin, "On the Distribution of Urban Rent and Residential Density", *Journal of Economic Theory*, 1 (1969), 60-67.

[2] Casetti, Emilio, " Equilibrium Land Values and Population Densities in an Urban Setting", *Economic Geography*, Vol. 47, No. 1, January, 1971.

[3] Mills, Edwin S., "An Aggregative Model of Resource Location in a Metropolitan Area", *American Economic Review*, May, 1967.

[4] Muth, Richard F., *Cities and Housing*, University of Chicago Press, Chicago, Illinois, 1969.

[5] Beckmann, Martin, "Spatial Equilibrium in the Dispersed City", in *Mathematical Land Use Theory* (George J. Papageorgiou, editor), Lexington Books, Lexington, Massachusetts, 1976, 117-125.

[6] Wilson, A.G., "Developments of Some Elementary Residential Location Models", *Journal of Regional Science*, 9 (1969), 377-385.

On Changes of Urban Space Structure

Kenji Kojima

I. Introduction

The purpose of this paper is to consider the changes of land use in an urban space where management-service activity and physical-production activity each have specialized sites, and are surrounded with residental districts.

Urban economic activities can be divided into the functions of management, production and consumption,[1] and each of them might correspond to a business district, a factory district and a residental district in an urban space.

Management activities supply production activities with necessary information for them. Workers are employed in management or production activities and commute from a residental district, which is a place to consume goods in, to their offices. Goods produced by production activities are demanded by consumers.

The necessity of access between management and production activities can be diminished by the development of means of communication and traffic. The problem of the transportation of goods from producers to consumers can be diminished by the development of a means of transportation, too. But the problem of commuting between the residental districts and the business, or factory districts, which is restricted by twice a day commuting, can not be so diminished as in the above two cases. Management and production activities are concentrated in space because of the agglomeration effect of the same kind of activity respectively.[2] As a result, it seems to bring about the inevitable occurence of an urban space which has centers of management and production activities surrounded with residental districts. In actual urban space, especially in Japan, we can find many urban areas where a management town and manufacturing town adjoin.

Such an urban land use pattern alters on account of economic growth and changes of demand and supply in various markets, while it keeps its spatial relationship relatively.

In this paper, supposing that such an urban land use pattern has already been shaped, changes of urban land use will be discussed by means of a price-theoretical approach.

---

1) Fujii [1], Kojima [2].
2) Fujii [1]. The consumption function has its agglomeration effect, too. But we suppose here that it is not so strong as those of the management and production functions.

Needless to say, it does not mean to deny the dynamic approach containing agglomeration effects.

II. Model

The above-mentioned subject will be analysed, based on Muth's urban land use theory [3, 4]. This paper adopts the following assumptions about an urban space.

(Assumption-I)

Imagine a one-dimensional space which straight extends in the lengthwide direction with a constant width. The operational meaning of this assumption is that the difference in distance which indicates the difference of commuting cost here is considered in the lengthwide direction but neglected in the breadthwide direction.[3] Distance (t) is measured from origin (0).

(Fig. 1)

$$0 \qquad\qquad \hat{t}_1$$

(Assumption-II)

1. The management-service industry (the first industry) is located at the point 0, and the pysical-production industry (the second industry) at the point $\hat{t}_1$.

2. The 1st industry has a Cobb-Douglas production function with constant returns to scale; that is:

$$O_1 = B_1 K_1{}^\gamma L_1^\delta , \qquad\qquad \gamma + \delta = 1 \qquad\qquad (1)$$

where O_1 = the output of industry 1

$\qquad\qquad K_1$ = the input of capital in the production of industry 1

$\qquad\qquad L_1$ = the input of labour in the production of industry 1.

3. Similarly the production function for the 2nd industry is written as follows:

$$O_2 = B_2 K_2{}^\epsilon L_2^\zeta, \qquad\qquad \epsilon + \zeta = 1 \qquad\qquad (2)$$

where O_2 = the output of industry 2

$\qquad\qquad K_2$ = the input of capital in the production of industry 2

$\qquad\qquad L_2$ = the input of labour in the production of industry 2.

---

3) Solow and Vickrey [6].

4. The management-service input produced in this area in the supply of good 2, O_{12}, is in proportion to the product of the industry 2, O_2:

$$O_{12} = gO_2 \ . \tag{3}$$

5. When the price of good 1 is denoted by P_1, the amount after subtracting a unit management-service cost from the price of good 2 by P_2, and a unit cost of management services produced in other areas by θ, then the price of good 2 is $P_2 + gP_1 + \theta$ from (3).

(Assumption-III)

1. The firms in the housing-service industry have identical, Cobb-Douglas functions with constant returns to scale,[4] that is:

$$q = B_3 K_3^{\alpha} R_3^{\beta} \ , \qquad\qquad \alpha + \beta = 1 \tag{4}$$

where q = the output of a firm in the housing-service industry

K_3 = the input of capital in the production of a firm in the housing-service industry

R_3 = the input of land in the production of a firm in the housing-service industry.

2. A household unit supplies a labour unit. When $\bar{q}$ denotes the amount of housing-service consumption of a household unit, and is constant, then the amounts of housing-service demand of all households employed in industries 1 and 2 are $\bar{q}L_1$ and $\bar{q}L_2$ respectively.

3. It is conceivable that the demand price for housing-service for households employed in industry 1, P_{31}, is different from the one for households employed in industry 2, P_{32}, on account of the difference of commuting cost. And the former declines with the distance from the point O and the latter from the point $\hat{t}_1$. We shall assume that they are given by the following exponential functions of distance:

$$P_{31} = p_{10} e^{-\lambda |t|} \tag{5}$$

$$P_{32} = p_{20} e^{-\lambda |t - \hat{t}_1|} \tag{6}$$

(Assumption-IV)

Entry and exit on all industries is free for the firms. And therefore the profits are equal

---

4) Though the optimum output of the firm is indeterminate from (4) under the condition of perfect competition, we shall assume that it has very small weight in the industry on accout of the scale restriction, for example, entrepreneurship and so on.

to zero for industry equilibrium.

(Assumption-V)

There are perfect mobilities of capital and labour. The expenditure of every household has a trade-off relationship between the housing-service expenditure and the commuting cost. That is, the amounts of the housing-service expenditure plus the commuting cost of a household employed in industry 1 and 2 in any location are equal to $p_{10}\bar{q}$ and $p_{20}\bar{q}$ respectively.[5] Under the assumption of perfect mobility of labour, it is conceivable that the amount subtracting these costs from the wage in every household is equal. That is; $w = w_1 - p_{10}\bar{q} = w_2 - p_{20}\bar{q}$.

Therefore: $w_1 = w + p_{10}\bar{q}$, (7)

$$w_2 = w + p_{20}\bar{q},$$ (8)

where w_1 = the wage rate in industry 1

w_2 = the wage rate in industry 2.

w and the capital rental price, ρ, are given.

Bid Rent Function

In the housing-service firm we will have the following necessary conditions for firm equilibrium under industry equiliblium:

$$K_3{}^* = P_{3i}{}^* + \alpha{}^* + q{}^* - \rho{}^*,$$ (9)

$$R_3{}^* = P_{3i}^* + \beta{}^* + q{}^* - r_i^*,$$ (10)

$$(i = 1, 2)$$

where X^* is written for the natural logarithm of X and r_i is land rent.

From (4), $q^* = B_3^* + \alpha K_3^* + \beta R_3^*$. (11)

From (9) (10) (11),

$$r_i^* = \frac{1}{\beta}B_3^* + \frac{\alpha}{\beta}\alpha^* + \beta^* - \frac{\alpha}{\beta}\rho^* + \frac{1}{\beta}P_{3i}^* .$$ (12)

This is called a bid rent function.

Substituting (5) into (12),

---

5) $p_{10}\bar{q}$ is the amount of the housing-service expenditure of a household employed in industry 1 at the point 0, and $p_{20}\bar{q}$ is the one of a household employed in industry 2 at the point $\hat{r}_1$. In these two cases, we assume that the commuting cost is equal to zero.

$$r_1^*(t) = M + \frac{1}{\beta}p_{10}^* - \frac{\lambda}{\beta}|t|, \tag{13}$$

where $\qquad M = \frac{1}{\beta}B_3^* + \frac{\alpha}{\beta}\alpha^* + \beta^* - \frac{\alpha}{\beta}\rho^*.$

Or, $\qquad r_{1_I}^*(t) = M + \frac{1}{\beta}p_{10}^* + \frac{\lambda}{\beta}t, \qquad (t < 0) \tag{14}$

$$r_{1_{II}}^*(t) = M + \frac{1}{\beta}p_{10}^* - \frac{\lambda}{\beta}t. \qquad (t \geq 0) \tag{15}$$

Rewriting $M + \frac{1}{\beta}p_{10}^*$ as follows;

$$r_{10}^* = t_{1_I}^*(0) = r_{1_{II}}^*(0) = M + \frac{1}{\beta}p_{10}^*. \tag{16}$$

Similarly substituting (6) into (12),

$$r_2^*(t) = M + \frac{1}{\beta}p_{20}^* - \frac{\lambda}{\beta}|t - \hat{t}_1|. \tag{17}$$

Or, $\qquad r_{2_{III}}^*(t) = M + \frac{1}{\beta}p_{20}^* + \frac{\lambda}{\beta}(t - \hat{t}_1), \qquad (t < \hat{t}_1) \tag{18}$

$$r_{2_{IV}}^*(t) = M + \frac{1}{\beta}p_{20}^* - \frac{\lambda}{\beta}(t - \hat{t}_1). \qquad (t \geq \hat{t}_1) \tag{19}$$

$$r_{20}^* = r_{2_{III}}^*(\hat{t}_1) = r_{2_{IV}}^*(\hat{t}_1) = M + \frac{1}{\beta}p_{20}^*. \tag{20}$$

Boundaries

The point O and the residental district where the workers in industry 1 live is called the 1st region, and the point $\hat{t}_1$ and the residental district where the workers in industry 2 live is called the 2nd region. We shall assume that there is constant land rent value for other purposes, $\hat{r}_0$,[6] independent of distance.

The boundary on the first region side of this urban area which is composed of the 1st region and the 2nd region, $\hat{t}_{01}$,[7] will be calculated, assuming that r_{1_I} in (14) is equal to $\hat{r}_0$:

$$\hat{r}_0 = r_{10} e^{\frac{\lambda}{\beta}\hat{t}_{01}}, \tag{21}$$

$$\hat{t}_{01} = \frac{\beta}{\lambda}(\hat{r}_0^* - r_{10}^*). \tag{22}$$

The boundary between region 1 and region 2, $\hat{t}_{12}$, will be calculated, assuming that $r_{1_{II}}$ in (15) is equal to $r_{2_{III}}$ in (18)[8]:

---

6) Imagine the agricultural land rent for example. See Sakashita [5] for the operational meanings of $\hat{r}_0$.
7) $\hat{t}_{01} < 0.$
8) We assume that regions 1 and 2 adjoin. Therefore, $r_{1_{II}}(\hat{t}_{12}) = r_{2_{III}}(\hat{t}_{12}) > \hat{r}_0.$

$$r_{10}\, e^{-\frac{\lambda}{\beta}\hat{t}_{12}} = r_{20}\, e^{\frac{\lambda}{\beta}(\hat{t}_{12}-\hat{t}_1)}, \tag{23}$$

$$\hat{t}_{12} = \frac{\beta}{2\lambda}(r_{10}^* - r_{20}^*) + \frac{\hat{t}_1}{2}. \tag{24}$$

The boundary on the region 2 side of this area, $\hat{t}_{02}$, will be calculated, assuming that $r_{2\,\text{IV}}$ in (19) is equal to $\hat{r}_0$:

$$\hat{r}_0 = r_{20}\, e^{\frac{\lambda}{\beta}(\hat{t}_1 - \hat{t}_{02})}, \tag{25}$$

$$\hat{t}_{02} = \frac{\beta}{\lambda}(r_{20}^* - \hat{r}_0^*) + \hat{t}_1. \tag{26}$$

Hereupon all boundaries are calculated. The relation mentioned above will be illustrated with Fig. 2. Region 1 is divided into I and II. Region 2 is divided into III and IV.

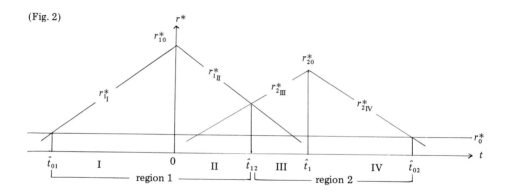

(Fig. 2)

Housing-Service Market Equilibrium

The housing-service product per unit of land at point t is; in region 1,

$$\left(\frac{q}{R}\right)_{\text{I}} = N_{10}\, e^{\frac{\alpha\lambda}{\beta}t}, \qquad (t < 0) \tag{27}$$

$$\left(\frac{q}{R}\right)_{\text{II}} = N_{10}\, e^{-\frac{\alpha\lambda}{\beta}t}, \qquad (t \geqq 0) \tag{28}$$

where $\qquad N_{10} = B_3^{\frac{1}{\beta}}\, \alpha^{\frac{\alpha}{\beta}}\, \rho^{-\frac{\alpha}{\beta}}\, p_{10}^{\frac{\alpha}{\beta}}, \tag{29}$

in region 2,

$$\left(\frac{q}{R}\right)_{\mathrm{III}} = N_{20} e^{\frac{\alpha\lambda}{\beta}(t-\hat{t}_1)}, \qquad\qquad (t < \hat{t}_1) \qquad\qquad (30)$$

$$\left(\frac{q}{R}\right)_{\mathrm{IV}} = N_{20} e^{\frac{\alpha\lambda}{\beta}(\hat{t}_1 - t)}, \qquad\qquad (t \geq \hat{t}_1) \qquad\qquad (31)$$

where $\qquad N_{20} = B_3^{\frac{1}{\beta}} \alpha^{\frac{\alpha}{\beta}} \rho^{-\frac{\alpha}{\beta}} p_{20}^{\frac{\alpha}{\beta}}.$ $\qquad\qquad\qquad\qquad$ (32)

Now there is the relationship, $\dfrac{dR}{dt} = a$, between distance and land for the space expressed in Assumption I, where a is constant and smaller than the width of this space.

The increment to housing-service output per unit increase in distance is written as follows:

$$\left(\frac{q}{R}\right)_{\mathrm{I}} \frac{dR}{dt} = aN_{10} e^{\frac{\alpha\lambda}{\beta} t}, \qquad\qquad (t < 0) \qquad\qquad (33)$$

$$\left(\frac{q}{R}\right)_{\mathrm{II}} \frac{dR}{dt} = aN_{10} e^{-\frac{\alpha\lambda}{\beta} t}, \qquad\qquad (t \geq 0) \qquad\qquad (34)$$

$$\left(\frac{q}{R}\right)_{\mathrm{III}} \frac{dR}{dt} = aN_{20} e^{\frac{\alpha\lambda}{\beta}(t-\hat{t}_1)}, \qquad\qquad (t < \hat{t}_1) \qquad\qquad (35)$$

$$\left(\frac{q}{R}\right)_{\mathrm{IV}} \frac{dR}{dt} = aN_{20} e^{\frac{\alpha\lambda}{\beta}(\hat{t}_1 - t)}. \qquad\qquad (t \geq \hat{t}_1) \qquad\qquad (36)$$

As a result, the amount of housing-service supply in region 1, Q_1, is;

$$Q_1 = \int_{\hat{t}_{01}}^{0}\left(\frac{q}{R}\right)_{\mathrm{I}}\frac{dR}{dt}dt + \int_{0}^{\hat{t}_{12}}\left(\frac{q}{R}\right)_{\mathrm{II}}\frac{dR}{dt}dt$$

$$= \frac{\beta aN_{10}}{\alpha\lambda}(2 - e^{\frac{\alpha\lambda}{\beta}\hat{t}_{01}} - e^{-\frac{\alpha\lambda}{\beta}\hat{t}_{12}}). \qquad\qquad (37)$$

And the amount of housing-service supply in region 2, Q_2, is;

$$Q_2 = \int_{\hat{t}_{12}}^{\hat{t}_1}\left(\frac{q}{R}\right)_{\mathrm{III}}\frac{dR}{dt}dt + \int_{\hat{t}_1}^{\hat{t}_{02}}\left(\frac{q}{R}\right)_{\mathrm{IV}}\frac{dR}{dt}dt$$

$$= \frac{\beta aN_{20}}{\alpha\lambda}(2 - e^{\frac{\alpha\lambda}{\beta}(\hat{t}_1 - \hat{t}_{02})} - e^{\frac{\alpha\lambda}{\beta}(\hat{t}_{12} - \hat{t}_1)}). \qquad\qquad (38)$$

Considering Assumption III-2, the conditions of housing-service market equilibrium in two regions are;

$$\bar{q}L_1 = Q_1, \qquad\qquad\qquad\qquad (39)$$

$$\bar{q}L_2 = Q_2. \qquad\qquad\qquad\qquad (40)$$

Market Equilibria for Goods 1 and 2

In industries 1 and 2, the following conditions for industry equilibrium will be obtained: In industry 1,

$$K_1 = \frac{\gamma P_1 O_1}{\rho}, \tag{41}$$

$$L_1 = \frac{\delta P_1 O_1}{w_1}. \tag{42}$$

Substituting (41) (42) into (1),

$$P_1 = B_1^{-1} \gamma^{-\gamma} \delta^{-\delta} \rho^{\gamma} w_1^{\delta}. \tag{43}$$

In industry 2,

$$K_2 = \frac{\epsilon P_2 O_2}{\rho}, \tag{44}$$

$$L_2 = \frac{\zeta P_2 O_2}{w_2} \tag{45}$$

Substituting (44) (45) into (2),

$$P_2 = B_2^{-1} \epsilon^{-\epsilon} \zeta^{-\zeta} \rho^{\epsilon} w_2. \tag{46}$$

Concerning demand for goods 1 and 2, we shall assume the following.

(Assumption-VI)

The demand for management-service in this area is the sum of the demand of industry 2 expressed in (3) and that of activities in other areas. When the latter demand is denoted by D_1, the demand for good 1 is written as follows;

$$O_1^D = D_1 + g O_2. \tag{47}$$

(Assumption-VII)

The demand for good 2 produced in this area is denoted by O_2^D. The price of good 2 is $P_2 + g P_1 + \theta$ from Assumption II-5. We shall assume that the price elasticity of the demand for good 2, η, is constant and the demand function is;

$$O_2^D = D_2 (P_2 + g P_1 + \theta)^{-\eta}. \tag{48}$$

The conditions of market equilibria for goods 1 and 2 are;

$$O_1 = O_1^D, \tag{49}$$

$$O_2 = O_2^D. \tag{50}$$

There are 23 equations; (7), (8), (16), (20), (22), (24), (26), (29), (32), (37), (38), (39),

(40), (41), (42), (43), (44), (45), (46), (47), (48), (49), (50), and 23 endogenous variables; $p_{10}, p_{20}, w_1, w_2, r_{10}, r_{20}, \hat{t}_{01}, \hat{t}_{12}, \hat{t}_{02}, N_{10}, N_{20}, Q_1, Q_2, O_1, O_2, K_1, K_2, L_1, L_2, P_1, P_2, O_1^D,$ O_2^D. It follows that the model is completed.

III.   Comparative Statics Analysis

In this section, we shall analyse the effects on boundaries ($\hat{t}_{01}$, $\hat{t}_{12}$, $\hat{t}_{02}$) and outputs (O_1, O_2) of changing the demands (D_1, D_2) and the point $\hat{t}_1$, under the model mentioned above.

The analysis method is comparative statics.

L_1 in (39) is a function of w_1, P_1 and O_1 from (42). O_1 is a function of O_2 from (47) (49), O_2 that of P_1 and P_2 from (48) (50), P_1 that of w_1 from (43), P_2 that of w_2 from (46), w_1 that of p_{10} from (7), and w_2 that of p_{20} from (8). Therefore L_1 is a function of p_{10} and p_{20}. Q_1 in (39) is a function of N_{10}, $\hat{t}_{01}$ and $\hat{t}_{12}$ from (37). $\hat{t}_{12}$ is a function of r_{10} and r_{20} from (24), $\hat{t}_{01}$ that of r_{10} from (22), r_{10} that of p_{10} from (16), r_{20} that of p_{20} from (20), and N_{10} that of p_{10} from (29). Therefore Q_1 is a function of p_{10} and p_{20}. As a result, (39) can be regarded as an equation in p_{10} and p_{20}.

Considering (40) similarly, we will easily find that (40) is an equation in p_{10} and p_{20}, too. Consequently (39) and (40) can be regarded as simultaneous equations in p_{10} and p_{20}.

Differentiating (39) and (40), and calculating the effects on p_{10} and p_{20} of changing the exogenous variables of the problem, we can find the effects on $\hat{t}_{01}$, $\hat{t}_{12}$, $\hat{t}_{02}$, O_1 and O_2 by means of these results.

Shift in the Demand for Good 1

First, we will examine the case of a shift in D_1. Differentiating (39) and (40) with respect to D_1 *,[9)]

$$E_{11}\frac{\partial p_{10}^*}{\partial D_1^*} + E_{12}\frac{\partial p_{20}^*}{\partial D_1^*} = \frac{D_1}{O_1}, \tag{51}$$

$$E_{21}\frac{\partial p_{10}^*}{\partial D_1^*} + E_{22}\frac{\partial p_{20}^*}{\partial D_1^*} = 0, \tag{52}$$

where $\quad E_{11} = \dfrac{gO_2}{O_1}\dfrac{\eta gP_1}{P_2+gP_1+\theta}\dfrac{\delta p_{10}\bar{q}}{w_1} + \dfrac{\gamma p_{10}\bar{q}}{w_1} + \dfrac{\alpha}{\beta} + \dfrac{\alpha}{\beta X}e^{\frac{\alpha\lambda}{\beta}\hat{t}_{01}}$

$\qquad\qquad + \dfrac{\alpha}{2\beta X}e^{-\frac{\alpha\lambda}{\beta}\hat{t}_{12}} > 0,$

$\qquad E_{12} = \dfrac{gO_2}{O_1}\dfrac{\eta P_2}{P_2+gP_1+\theta}\dfrac{\zeta p_{20}\bar{q}}{w_2} - \dfrac{\alpha}{2\beta X}e^{-\frac{\alpha\lambda}{\beta}\hat{t}_{12}},$

---

9)   In the following, we shall analyse with the logarithm values except at the boundaries.

$$E_{21} = \frac{\eta g P_1}{P_2 + g P_1 + \theta} \cdot \frac{\delta p_{10} \bar{q}}{w_1} - \frac{\alpha}{2\beta Y} e^{\frac{\alpha\lambda}{\beta}(\hat{t}_{12} - \hat{t}_1)},$$

$$E_{22} = \frac{\eta P_2}{P_2 + g P_1 + \theta} \cdot \frac{\zeta p_{20} \bar{q}}{w_2} + \frac{\epsilon p_{20} \bar{q}}{w_2} + \frac{\alpha}{\beta} + \frac{\alpha}{\beta Y} e^{\frac{\alpha\lambda}{\beta}(\hat{t}_1 - \hat{t}_{02})}$$
$$+ \frac{\alpha}{2\beta Y} e^{\frac{\alpha\lambda}{\beta}(\hat{t}_{12} - \hat{t}_1)} > 0,$$

$$X = 2 - e^{\frac{\alpha\lambda}{\beta}\hat{t}_{01}} - e^{-\frac{\alpha\lambda}{\beta}\hat{t}_{12}} > 0,$$

$$Y = 2 - e^{\frac{\alpha\lambda}{\beta}(\hat{t}_1 - \hat{t}_{02})} - e^{\frac{\alpha\lambda}{\beta}(\hat{t}_{12} - \hat{t}_1)} > 0.$$

Hence from (51) (52),

$$\frac{\partial p_{10}^*}{\partial D^*} = \frac{E_{22} D_1}{E O_1}, \tag{53}$$

$$\frac{\partial p_{20}^*}{\partial D_1^*} = \frac{D_1}{E O_1} \left(\frac{\alpha}{2\beta Y} e^{\frac{\alpha\lambda}{\beta}(\hat{t}_{12} - \hat{t}_1)} - \frac{\eta g P_1}{P_2 + g P_1 + \theta} \cdot \frac{\delta p_{10} \bar{q}}{w_1} \right), \tag{54}$$

where
$$E = \det \begin{vmatrix} E_{11} & E_{12} \\ E_{21} & E_{22} \end{vmatrix} = E_{11} E_{22} - E_{12} E_{21} > 0.$$

Differentiating (16) and (22), we will have the following equation;

$$\frac{\partial |\hat{t}_{01}|}{\partial D_1^*} = \frac{1}{\lambda} \cdot \frac{\partial p_{10}^*}{\partial D_1^*}. \quad 10)$$

And from (16), (20) and (24),

$$\frac{\partial \hat{t}_{12}}{\partial D_1^*} = \frac{1}{2\lambda} \left(\frac{\partial p_{10}^*}{\partial D_1^*} - \frac{\partial p_{20}^*}{\partial D_1^*} \right).$$

Further from (20) and (26),

$$\frac{\partial \hat{t}_{02}}{\partial D_1^*} = \frac{1}{\lambda} \cdot \frac{\partial p_{20}^*}{\partial D_1^*}.$$

On the other hand, we will have the following relationships between O_1, O_2 and D_1:

$$\frac{\partial O_1^*}{\partial D_1^*} = \frac{D_1}{O_1} - \frac{g O_2}{O_1} \cdot \frac{\eta g P_1}{P_2 + g P_1 + \theta} \cdot \frac{\delta p_{10} \bar{q}}{w_1} \cdot \frac{\partial p_{10}^*}{\partial D_1^*}$$
$$- \frac{g O_2}{O_1} \cdot \frac{\eta P_2}{P_2 + g P_1 + \theta} \cdot \frac{\zeta p_{20} \bar{q}}{w_2} \cdot \frac{\partial p_{20}^*}{\partial D_1^*},$$

$$\frac{\partial O_2^*}{\partial D_1^*} = - \frac{\eta g P_1}{P_2 + g P + \theta} \cdot \frac{\delta p_{10} \bar{q}}{w_1} \cdot \frac{\partial p_{10}^*}{\partial D^*} - \frac{\eta P_2}{P_2 + g P_1 + \theta} \cdot \frac{\zeta p_{20} \bar{q}}{w_2} \cdot \frac{\partial p_{20}^*}{\partial D_1^*}.$$

As a result,

$$\frac{\partial |\hat{t}_{01}|}{\partial D_1^*} = \frac{D_1 E_{22}}{E \lambda O_1} > 0, \tag{55}$$

---

10) As $\hat{t}_{01}$ is negative, we consider the change of $\hat{t}_{01}$'s absolute value.

$$\frac{\partial \hat{t}_{12}}{\partial D_1^*} = \frac{D_1}{2E\lambda O_1}\left(\frac{\eta P_2}{P_2+gP_1+\theta}\frac{\zeta p_{20}\bar{q}}{w_2} + \frac{\eta gP_1}{P_2+gP_1+\theta}\frac{\delta p_{10}\bar{q}}{w_1}\right.$$

$$\left. + \frac{\alpha}{\beta} + \frac{\alpha}{\beta Y}e^{\frac{\alpha\lambda}{\beta}(\hat{t}_1-\hat{t}_{02})}\right) > 0, \tag{56}$$

$$\frac{\partial \hat{t}_{02}}{\partial D_1^*} = \frac{D_1}{E\lambda O_1}\left(\frac{\alpha}{2\beta Y}e^{\frac{\alpha\lambda}{\beta}(\hat{t}_{12}-\hat{t}_1)}\right.$$

$$\left. - \frac{\eta gP_1}{P_2+gP_1+\theta}\frac{\delta p_{10}\bar{q}}{w_1}\right), \tag{57}$$

$$\frac{\partial O_1^*}{\partial D_1^*} = \frac{D_1}{EO_1}\left\{E_{22}\left(\frac{\gamma p_{10}\bar{q}}{w_1} + \frac{\alpha}{\beta} + \frac{\alpha}{\beta X}e^{\frac{\alpha\lambda}{\beta}\hat{t}_{01}}\right) + \frac{\alpha}{2\beta X}e^{-\frac{\alpha\lambda}{\beta}\hat{t}_{12}}\right.$$

$$\cdot \left(\frac{\eta P_2}{P_2+gP_1+\theta}\frac{\zeta p_{20}\bar{q}}{w_2} + \frac{\epsilon p_{20}\bar{q}}{w_2} + \frac{\alpha}{\beta} + \frac{\alpha}{\beta Y}e^{\frac{\alpha\lambda}{\beta}(\hat{t}_1-\hat{t}_{02})}\right.$$

$$\left.\left. + \frac{\eta gP_1}{P_2+gP_1+\theta}\frac{\delta p_{10}\bar{q}}{w_1}\right)\right\} > 0, \tag{58}$$

$$\frac{\partial O_2^*}{\partial D_1^*} = -\frac{D_1}{EO_1}\frac{\eta}{P_2+gP_1+\theta}[gP_1\frac{\delta p_{10}\bar{q}}{w_1}$$

$$\cdot \left\{\frac{\epsilon p_{20}\bar{q}}{w_2} + \frac{\alpha}{\beta Y}\left(2-\frac{1}{2}e^{\frac{\alpha\lambda}{\beta}(\hat{t}_{12}-\hat{t}_1)}\right)\right\}$$

$$+ P_2\frac{\zeta p_{20}\bar{q}}{w_2}\frac{\alpha}{2\beta Y}e^{\frac{\alpha\lambda}{\beta}(\hat{t}_{12}-\hat{t}_1)}] < 0. \tag{59}$$

The increase in D_1^* leads to increases in $|\hat{t}_{01}|$ and $\hat{t}_{12}$. Therefore region 1 expands. Region 2 contracts because $\dfrac{\partial(\hat{t}_{02}-\hat{t}_{12})}{\partial D_1^*} < 0$ from (56) and (57), though the sign of $\dfrac{\partial \hat{t}_{02}}{\partial D_1^*}$ is undecided. Besides, O_1 increases but O_2 decreases. That is, the increase in D_1 brings about not only the expansion of region 1 and the increase in the production of good 1, but also the contraction of region 2 and the decrease in the production of good 2. The reason why the sign of $\dfrac{\partial \hat{t}_{02}}{\partial D_1^*}$ is undecided will be supposed as follows. $\hat{t}_{02}$, on the one hand, increases in order to supplement the decrease in housing-service supply in region 2 with the increase in $\hat{t}_{12}$, but on the other, decreases on account of the effect of the good 2 market, that is, the decrease in the demand for good 2 with the rise of the price of good 2 due to the rise of the wage rate. If the effect of the good 2 market is neglected, namely, $\eta = 0$, we shall find $\hat{t}_{02}$ increases from (57).

Shift on the Demand for Good 2

Likewise, the effects of D_2's change is as follows:

$$\frac{\partial |\hat{t}_{01}|}{\partial D_2^*} = \frac{1}{E\lambda}[\frac{gO_2}{O_1}\left\{\frac{\epsilon p_{20}\bar{q}}{w_2} + \frac{\alpha}{\beta Y}\left(2-\frac{1}{2}e^{\frac{\alpha\lambda}{\beta}(\hat{t}_{12}-\hat{t}_1)}\right)\right\}$$

$$+ \frac{\alpha}{2\beta X} e^{-\frac{\alpha\lambda}{\beta} \hat{t}_{12}}] > 0 , \qquad (60)$$

$$\frac{\partial \hat{t}_{12}}{\partial D_2^*} = \frac{1}{2E\lambda} [\frac{gO_2}{O_1} \{ \frac{\epsilon p_{20} \bar{q}}{w_2} + \frac{\alpha}{\beta Y} (2 - e^{\frac{\alpha\lambda}{\beta}(\hat{t}_{12} - \hat{t}_1)}) \}$$
$$- \{ \frac{\gamma p_{10} \bar{q}}{w_1} + \frac{\alpha}{\beta Y} (2 - e^{-\frac{\alpha\lambda}{\beta} \hat{t}_{12}}) \}] \qquad (61)$$

$$\frac{\partial \hat{t}_{02}}{\partial D_2^*} = \frac{1}{E\lambda} \{ \frac{\gamma p_{10} \bar{q}}{w_1} + \frac{\alpha}{\beta X} (2 - \frac{1}{2} e^{-\frac{\alpha\lambda}{\beta} \hat{t}_{12}})$$
$$+ \frac{gO_2}{O_1} \frac{\alpha}{2\beta Y} e^{\frac{\alpha\lambda}{\beta}(\hat{t}_{12} - \hat{t}_1)} \} > 0 , \qquad (62)$$

$$\frac{\partial O_2^*}{\partial D_2^*} = \frac{1}{E} [\{ \frac{\gamma p_{10} \bar{q}}{w_1} + \frac{\alpha}{\beta X} (2 - \frac{1}{2} e^{-\frac{\alpha\lambda}{\beta} \hat{t}_{12}}) \}$$
$$\cdot \{ \frac{\epsilon p_{20} \bar{q}}{w_2} + \frac{\alpha}{\beta Y} (2 - \frac{1}{2} e^{\frac{\alpha\lambda}{\beta}(\hat{t}_{12} - \hat{t}_1)}) \}$$
$$- \frac{\alpha^2}{4\beta^2 XY} e^{-\frac{\alpha\lambda}{\beta} \hat{t}_1}] > 0 , \qquad (63)$$

$$\frac{\partial O_1^*}{\partial D_2^*} = \frac{gO_2}{O_1} \frac{\partial O_2^*}{\partial D_2^*} > 0 . \qquad (64)$$

The increase in D_2^* leads to increases in $|\hat{t}_{01}|$ and $\hat{t}_{02}$. Namely the urban space expands. Further both O_1 and O_2 tend to increase. But changes of region 1, region 2 and $\hat{t}_{12}$ are undecided. Supposedly, the increase in D_2^* leads to an increase in O_2 directly, and brings about the increase in the derived demand for good 1, too. If the effect of the good 1 market is neglected, that is, $g = 0$, we shall find that $\hat{t}_{12}$ decreases from (61), region 2 expands and region 1 contracts, while O_1 is unchanged. But there is the reaction of the expansion of region 1 so long as the effect of the good 1 market is taken into consideration.

Shift on Industry 2's Location Point

It is conceivable that it is difficult for industry 1 to change its location because of necessity for acquisition of information from public agencies etc. But the case of industry 2 is not so difficult as that of industry 1 because it has possibility of becoming foot-loose.[11] Though the point $\hat{t}_1$ is exogenous in this model, industry 2 will change its own location toward the suburbs when traffic facilities are well arranged and the pressure from the region 1 is strengthened, such as the case of shift on the demand for good 1 mentioned above. What changes are brought about when the point $\hat{t}_1$ is shifted? In the following, we analyse the effects of $\hat{t}_1$'s change.

$$\frac{\partial |\hat{t}_{01}|}{\partial \hat{t}_1} = - \frac{\alpha}{2E\beta} \{ (\frac{\eta P_2}{P_2 + gP_1 + \theta} \frac{\zeta p_{20} \bar{q}}{w_1} + \frac{\epsilon p_{20} \bar{q}}{w_2} + \frac{2\alpha}{\beta Y}) e^{-\frac{\alpha\lambda}{\beta} \hat{t}_{12}}$$

---

11) Kojima [2].

$$-\frac{gO_2}{O_1}\frac{\eta P_2}{P_2+gP_1+\theta}-\frac{\zeta p_{20}\bar q}{w_2}\frac{1}{Y}e^{\frac{\alpha\lambda}{\beta}(\hat t_{12}-\hat t_1)}\}\,,\qquad(65)$$

$$-\frac{\partial \hat t_{12}}{\partial \hat t_1}=\frac{1}{2E}\{(P_2\frac{\zeta p_{20}\bar q}{w_2}+gP_1\frac{\delta p_{10}\bar q}{w_1})\frac{gO_2}{O_1}\frac{\eta}{P_2+gP_1+\theta}$$

$$\cdot\frac{\alpha}{\beta Y}e^{\frac{\alpha\lambda}{\beta}(\hat t_{12}-\hat t_1)}+(\frac{\gamma p_{10}\bar q}{w_1}+\frac{\alpha}{\beta}+\frac{\alpha}{\beta X}e^{\frac{\alpha\lambda}{\beta}\hat t_{01}})$$

$$\cdot(\frac{\eta P_2}{P_2+gP_1+\theta}\frac{\zeta p_{20}q}{w_2}+\frac{\epsilon p_{20}q}{w_2}+\frac{2\alpha}{\beta Y})\}>0\,,\qquad(66)$$

$$\frac{\partial \hat t_{02}}{\partial \hat t_1}=\frac{1}{E}[\,(-\frac{gO_2}{O_1}\frac{\eta gP_1}{P_2+gP_1+\theta}\frac{\delta p_{10}\bar q}{w_1}+\frac{\gamma p_{10}\bar q}{w_1})\{\frac{\epsilon p_{20}q}{w_2}+\frac{\alpha}{\beta Y}$$

$$\cdot(2-e^{\frac{\alpha\lambda}{\beta}(\hat t_{12}-\hat t_1)})\}+(\frac{\eta P_2}{P_2+gP_1+\theta}\frac{\zeta p_{20}q}{w_2}+\frac{\epsilon p_{20}q}{w_2})\{\frac{\gamma p_{10}q}{w_1}+\frac{\alpha}{\beta X}$$

$$\cdot(2-\frac{1}{2}e^{\frac{\alpha\lambda}{\beta}\hat t_{12}})\}-\frac{\gamma\epsilon p_{10}p_{20}\bar q^2}{w_1 w_2}+\frac{\eta}{P_2+gP_1+\theta}\frac{\alpha}{\beta}(\frac{gP_1}{X}\frac{\delta p_{10}\bar q}{w_1}$$

$$\cdot e^{-\frac{\alpha\lambda}{\beta}\hat t_{12}}+\frac{gO_2}{O_1}\frac{P_2}{2Y}\frac{\zeta p_{20}\bar q}{w_2}e^{\frac{\alpha\lambda}{\beta}(\hat t_{12}-\hat t_1)})$$

$$+\frac{\alpha^2}{\beta^2 XY}(4-2e^{\frac{\alpha\lambda}{\beta}(\hat t_{12}-\hat t_1)}-e^{-\frac{\alpha\lambda}{\beta}\hat t_{12}})\,]>0\,,\qquad(67)$$

$$\frac{\partial O_2^*}{\partial \hat t_1}=\frac{\alpha\lambda}{2E\beta}\frac{\eta}{P_2+gP_1+\theta}\{\frac{gP_1}{X}\frac{\delta p_{10}\bar q}{w_1}e^{-\frac{\alpha\lambda}{\beta}\hat t_{12}}(\frac{\epsilon p_{20}q}{w_2}+\frac{2\alpha}{\beta Y})$$

$$+\frac{P_2}{Y}\frac{\delta p_{20}\bar q}{w_1}e^{\frac{\alpha\lambda}{\beta}(\hat t_{12}-\hat t_1)}(\frac{\gamma p_{10}q}{w_1}+\frac{2\alpha}{\beta X})\}>0\,,\qquad(68)$$

$$\frac{\partial O^*}{\partial \hat t_1}=\frac{gO_2^*}{O_1}\frac{\partial O_2^*}{\partial \hat t_1}>0\,.\qquad(69)$$

The increase in $\hat t_1$ leads to increases in O_1 and O_2. Besides, region 1, region 2 and the urban space expand because $\dfrac{\partial(|\hat t_{01}|+\hat t_{12})}{\partial \hat t_1}>0$, $\dfrac{\partial(\hat t_{02}-\hat t_{12})}{\partial \hat t_1}>0$, and $\dfrac{\partial(|\hat t_{01}|+\hat t_{02})}{\partial \hat t_1}>0$, though the sign of $\dfrac{\partial|\hat t_{01}|}{\partial \hat t_1}$ is undecided. Further, we can say that region 2 is shifted to the suburbs because $\hat t_{12}$ and $\hat t_{02}$ increase.

IV. Concluding Remarks

The following table summarizes above results.

	increase of D_1	increase of D_2	increase of $\hat{t}_1$
$|\hat{t}_{01}|$	increase	increase	?
$\hat{t}_{12}$	increase	?	increase
$\hat{t}_{02}$	?	increase	increase
region 1	expansion	?	expansion
region 2	contraction	?	expansion
production of good 1	increase	increase	increase
production of good 2	decrease	increase	increase
the urban space	?	expansion	expansion

Now we seem to be able to say the following.

It is well known that today management-service demand is increasing day after day. Especially the management-service in a metropolitan area is demanded not only by adjacent manufacturing regions (the 2nd region in this paper), but also by many regions across the nation. When this demand increases, the management-service output tends to increase and the management region (the 1st region) tends to expand, while it follows that the adjacent manufacturing region contracts and its output decreases.

An increase in the demand for the manufacturing product has two forces; one is to increase the manufacturing output, another is to increase the derived demand for the management-service. Consequently it leads to the expansion of the urban space. But this is not to say that the manufacturing region expands on the boundary between two regions.

When the manufacturing activity (physical-production activity) shifts its location point towards the suburbs on account of the development of traffic facilities and the pressure of the management region, then the two regions and the urban space expand, while the two outputs increase. Consequently, spatial urbanization will make progress.

References

[1] Fujii, T., "Daitoshi Keisei no Keizai Riron (Economic Growth Theory in Formation of Big Cities)," in *Gendai Daitoshi no Shomondai (Various Problems of Modern Big Cities)*, Chapter 3, Japan Center for Area Development Research, 1964, pp. 39-151.

[2] Kojima, K., "Kukan Bungyo Ron no Kenkyu (Theories on Division of Space)," *Keizai Kagaku (Economic Science)*, Vol. 22, No. 3, Nagoya University, 1975, pp. 25-47.

[3] Muth, R.F., "Economic Change and Rural Urban Land Conversions," *Econometrica*, Vol. 29, No. 1, 1961, pp. 1-23.

[4] Muth, R.F., *Cities and Housing*, Chicago Univ. Pr., 1969.

[5] Sakashita, N., "Toshi Keizaigaku no Keiryoteki Shuho ni tsuite (On Econometric Methods in Urban Economics)," *Kikan Gendaikeizai (Contemporary Economics)*, No. 5, 1972, pp. 152-165.

[6] Solow, R.M. and W.S. Vickrey, "Land Use in a Long Narrow City," *Journal of Economic Theory*, Vol. 3, 1971, pp. 430-447.

The Double-Ring Structure Model of

Metropolitan Area

Takao Fukuchi

1.   Introduction

The purpose of this paper is to present a theoretical model to operationally define main urban problems in the context of general equilibrium and to clarify the stability condition of increase of urban land price and related urban sprawl. We present two models: Model No. 1. treats the distributions of income and firm, and also interregional movement of population and business exogenously, and is utilized to induce the stability condition; Model No. 2. treats these exogenous factors endogenously and is utilized to various simulation studies. The Tokyo Metropolitan Area in Japan faces with several important urban problems such as double ring structure of office town and bed town, dense utilization of urban land and its' sprawl to farming area, growth of subcentres, wavelike population dispersion, transport congestion and various public nuisances, rapid increase of urban land price and related inflation, etc. The two models are expected to describe these urban issues qualitatively and also to serve as the basis for the future similation studies to deduce the comprehensive urban policies quantitatively.

The past studies of large urban area in Japan included several different approaches : (a) Regional econometric models (Fukuchi-Nobuyuki [7] , [10] , Fukuchi-Yamane [12] , Ohkawa [18] , Kaneko [17] , Ogata-Shimofusa [27] , etc.) handled the main urban economic aggregate variables, but did not consider the distancial distribution; (b) Partial Equilibrium Analysis about Land Price Formation (Orishimo [28] , Fukuchi-Nobukuni [9] , Kumada [23] , etc.) were also partial; (c) Mathematical Model (Yamada [38] , [39] , Sakashita [30] , etc.) concentrated on specific topics; (d) Some interesting conceptual studies (Fujii [5] , Ihara [14] , etc.) needed the rigorous theoretical formulations. One of the weakness was the lack of prototype model with the context of general equilibrium.

As the preceeding studies, Mills [24] treated the allocation of manufactures, housings, and transportations, and Muth [26] treated the rural-urban conversion. Our prototype model (i) explains business, houshold and farmers and does not treat the transportation sector,[1] (ii) and puts an emphasis on strong urban sprawl and increase of urban land price and seeks the stability condition, and (iii) incorporates the special household preference pattern which reflects the severe shortage of housing assets. Thus we tried to incorporate some important features of urban problems in Japan.[2]

2. Construction of the theoretical model

We write a variable (x), which is a function of time (T) and distance (D) as $X_T(D)$, and its derivatives by T and D as X' and $\dot{X}$, and it's rate of change by T and D as $\hat{X}$ and R_X.

(a) Determination of radiator of urban area (D)

We assume that the prices of land for urban use (P_A) and for farming (P_F) are exponential functions of distance from the centre or urban area (D).

$$P_A[D] = \gamma_0 \cdot exp\,[-\gamma_1 D] \tag{2-1}$$

$$P_F[D] = P_F[0] \cdot exp\,[-\epsilon_1 D] \tag{2-2}$$

and postulate

$$\gamma_1 > \epsilon_1 , \quad \gamma_0 > P_F[0] \tag{2-3}$$

The radiator of urban area (D) is determined by their equivalence, thus

$$\tilde{D} = [\frac{1}{\gamma_1 - \epsilon_1}] \cdot \log\,(\frac{\gamma_0}{P_F[0]}) \tag{2-4}$$

and max (P_A, P_F) prevails at any distance.

(b) Location of each firm

Each firm purchases the services of capital, labor, and land (K, L, A) by corresponding prices (r, w, P_A), and pays the transportation cost $(n \cdot D \cdot O)$ parallel to the product of output (O) and distance, as the output is assumed to be traded at the centre, and maximizes the output under the cost (G) constraint.

$$MAX \; O + \lambda(r \cdot K + w \cdot L + P_A[D] \cdot A + n \cdot D \cdot O - G) \tag{2-5}$$

Here the output function is assumed to have the economy of scale, the neutral technical progress, and the decreasing management efficiency by distance as the access to informations is

1) National Railway Corporation stresses on matching budget only nationwide, and admits the transport congestion increase through under-investment in Tokyo Metropolitan Area. So it is difficult to specify the behavior of transport sector as a rational maximizing firm.
2) Our Model 2 includes 36 Variables, and (i) explains the doubled distribution of firms and households, and (ii) treate the influences of distributions of firms and incomes on dynamics of city, and (iii) considers urban inflation related with sprawl, and (iv) projects NCW considering travelling loss and public nuisance.

lessened when located in the distant site.[3],[4]

$$O = \alpha_0^* \cdot K^{\alpha_1} \cdot L^{\alpha_2} \cdot A^{\alpha_3} \cdot exp[-\alpha_4 D] \cdot exp[\alpha_5 T] \tag{2-6}$$

$$1 < h(\equiv \alpha_1 + \alpha_2 + \alpha_3) < 2, \quad \alpha_1 + \alpha_2 < 1 \tag{2-7}$$

$$\alpha_0 \equiv \alpha_0^* \cdot exp[\alpha_5 T] \tag{2-8}$$

Assuming the significance condition,

$$a \equiv -\alpha_3 \cdot \hat{P}_A - \alpha_4 = \alpha_3 \cdot \gamma_1 - \alpha_4 > 0 \tag{2-9}$$

we get the following optimum solutions,

$$A = g_A \cdot r^{\frac{\alpha_1}{h-1}} \cdot w^{\frac{\alpha_2}{h-1}} \cdot n^{\frac{-1}{h-1}} \gamma_0^{\frac{1-\alpha_1-\alpha_2}{h-1}} \cdot exp(\frac{\alpha_4 - \gamma_1[1-\alpha_1-\alpha_2]}{h-1} \cdot D) \tag{2-10}$$

$$K = g_K \cdot r^{\frac{1-\alpha_1-\alpha_2}{h-1}} \cdot w^{\frac{\alpha_2}{h-1}} \cdot n^{\frac{-1}{h-1}} \cdot \gamma_0^{\frac{\alpha_3}{h-1}} \cdot exp(\frac{-a}{h-1} \cdot D) \tag{2-11}$$

$$L = g_L \cdot r^{\frac{\alpha_1}{h-1}} w^{\frac{1-\alpha_1-\alpha_3}{h-1}} \cdot n^{\frac{-1}{h-1}} \cdot \gamma_0^{\frac{\alpha_3}{h-1}} \cdot exp(\frac{-a}{h-1} \cdot D) \tag{2-12}$$

$$O = g_O \cdot r^{\frac{\alpha_1}{h-1}} \cdot w^{\frac{\alpha_2}{h-1}} \cdot n^{\frac{-h}{h-1}} \cdot \gamma_0^{\frac{\alpha_3}{h-1}} \cdot exp(\frac{-a}{h-1} \cdot D) \tag{2-13}$$

$$G = g_G \cdot r^{\frac{\alpha_1}{h-1}} \cdot w^{\frac{\alpha_2}{h-1}} \cdot n^{\frac{-1}{h-1}} \cdot [h + a \cdot D] \cdot \gamma_0^{\frac{\alpha_3}{h-1}} \cdot exp(\frac{-a}{h-1} \cdot D) \tag{2-14}$$

where,
$$g_A \equiv [\alpha_0 \cdot \alpha_1^{\alpha_2} \cdot \alpha_2^{\alpha_2} \cdot \alpha_3^{1-\alpha_1-\alpha_2} \cdot a^{-1}]^{\frac{-1}{h-1}} \tag{2-15}$$

$$g_K \equiv [\alpha_0 \cdot \alpha_1^{1-\alpha_2-\alpha_3} \cdot \alpha_2^{\alpha_2} \cdot \alpha_3^{\alpha_3} \cdot a^{-1}]^{\frac{-1}{h-1}} \tag{2-16}$$

$$g_L \equiv [\alpha_0 \cdot \alpha_1^{\alpha_1} \cdot \alpha_2^{1-\alpha_1-\alpha_3} \cdot \alpha_3^{\alpha_3} \cdot a^{-1}]^{\frac{-1}{h-1}} \tag{2-17}$$

$$g_O \equiv [\alpha_0 \cdot \alpha_1^{\alpha_1} \cdot \alpha_2^{\alpha_2} \cdot \alpha_3^{\alpha_3} \cdot a^{-h}]^{\frac{-1}{h-1}} \tag{2-18}$$

$$g_O \equiv [\alpha_0 \cdot \alpha_1^{\alpha_1} \cdot \alpha_2^{\alpha_2} \cdot \alpha_3^{\alpha_3} \cdot a^{-1}]^{\frac{-1}{h-1}} \tag{2-19}$$

The cost-output ratio (G/O) is an increasing function of distance. Based upon the postulate of going concern we assume that this ratio does not exceed unity. The net profit $(O-G)$ will be imputed to resources. Perhaps the remuneration may be differed by scale, but this difference is not explicity analyzed here.

The size of Central Business District (CBD) or the marginal distance of firm location is deter-

---

3) Fujii [5] preassumed a special function with kinks between output and capital to explain the benefit of accumulation. We want to explain this by the whole model.
4) Cost component ($n.D.O.$ for firms and $m.D.$ for households) is our special assumption, for example, compared with Alonso [1].

mined by $MIN(D^*, D)$, where

$$D^* \equiv \frac{1}{n} - \frac{h}{a}, \quad G[D^*]/O[D^*] = 1 \tag{2-20}$$

Postulating $\qquad n < (a/h)$ \hfill (2-21)

within CBD, we have

$$\text{sign}(A') = \text{sign}\left(\gamma_1 - \frac{a}{h-1}\right) = \text{sign}\left(\gamma_1 - \frac{\alpha_4}{1-\alpha_1-\alpha_2}\right), \quad L'<0, O'<0, G'<0 \tag{2-22}$$

So $G(MIN (D^*, D))$ gives the minimum size cost of CBD firm. The firm of smaller size will adopt the another technology with smaller economy of scale and depend upon the local demand by daytime and nighttime population, and be distributed widely in the city. So it's distribution will not influence greatly to the distribution of population and other firms, so it is not explicitly analyzed here.[5)]

(c) Distancial distribution of firms

Once the distribution of firm size and the total number of firms (M) are given, the ratio of firm space to total space (H) can be explicitly calculated. We write the size distribution by employment as F_L and the available angle of the city as θ (radian). We assume an exponential distribution for F_L[6)]

$$F_L(L) = \frac{1}{\sigma} \cdot \exp\left(-\frac{L}{\sigma}\right) \tag{2-23}$$

then the ratio is expressed as follows.

$$H[D] = M \cdot A \cdot F_L \cdot |L'|/\theta \cdot D \quad (0 < D \leqq MIN [D^*, \widetilde{D}])$$

$$= \frac{g_H}{D} \cdot \exp\left\{ \left[\gamma_1 - \frac{2a}{h-1}\right] \cdot D - \frac{g_L}{\sigma}(r^{\alpha_1} \cdot w^{[1-\alpha_1-\alpha_3]} n^{-1} \cdot \gamma_0^{\alpha_3})^{\frac{1}{h-1}} \cdot \exp\left[\frac{-aD}{h-1}\right] \right\} \tag{2-24}$$

where, $\qquad g_H \equiv \dfrac{M \cdot a \cdot g_A \cdot g_L}{\theta \cdot \sigma \cdot (h-1)} (r^{2\alpha_1} \cdot w^{[1-\alpha_1+\alpha_2-\alpha_3]} \cdot n^{-2} \cdot \gamma_0^{[1-\alpha_1-\alpha_2+\alpha_3]})^{\frac{1}{h-1}}$

Writing the exponential part of (2-24) as X^*,

$$\frac{H'[D]}{g^H} = \frac{1}{D^2} [X^{*'} \cdot D - 1] \cdot \exp [X^*] = \frac{\exp[X^*]}{D^2} \left\{ -1 + \left(\gamma_1 - \frac{2a}{h-1} + \Omega \cdot \exp[\frac{-aD}{h-1}]\right) D \right\}. \tag{2-25}$$

where, $\qquad \Omega \equiv \dfrac{g_L \cdot a}{\theta (h-1)} (r^{\alpha_1} w^{1-\alpha_1-\alpha_3} n^{-1} \gamma_0^{\alpha_3})^{\frac{1}{h-1}} \qquad (>0)$ \hfill (2-26)

We limit ourselves for the case, $A' < 0$ or $\gamma_1 < a/(h-1)$, and classify the two cases:

---

5) This may relate to the separation of Basic and Non-Basic Sectors (for example, see Yasuda [40]).
6) Data [9] revealed that the percent distribution of all firms at Tokyo (1963) of firms (number of employees) was as follows -0.1827(1), 0.1448 (2-4), 0.0396 (5-9), 0.0095 (10-19), 0.0032 (20-29), 0.0014 (30-49), 0.0004 (50-99), 0.0001 (100-199), and showed a good fit except very small firms.

$H-1$ and $H-2$.

$H-1$ type if $H'[D] < 0$ for $0 < D \leqq MIN\ (D^*,\ D)$

$H-2$ type if there exists the root (D) for $H'[D] = 0$

for $0 < D \leqq MIN\ (D^*,\ D)$

Ω is an increasing function of r, w and γ_0. So $H-1$ type may be observed at the beginning stage of urban development, and will gradually shift to $H-2$ type, and the gravity centre of

Fig. 2-1   Distancial Distribution of Firm Space Density

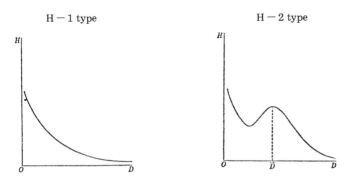

business activity will remove from the centre.[7]

(d)   Location of each household

Each household purchase the consumption good, land service and food (C, B, S) by corresponding prices $(P_C,\ P_A,\ P_S)$, and pays the transportation cost $(m \cdot D,\ m > 0,\ m' < 0)$ as the family members necessarily visit to the centre for business, cultural contact, entertainment, and other purposes, and maximizes the utility under the income (Y) constraint.

$$\underset{C,B,S,D}{MAX} \quad U + \eta (P_C \cdot C + P_A [D] B + P_S [D] \cdot S[D] + m \cdot D - Y) \qquad (2\text{-}27)$$

Here the utility function is assumed to be increasing for C, B, and S, and also decreasing for distance.[8]

$$U = \beta_0 \cdot C^{\beta_1} \cdot B^{\beta_2} \cdot S^{\beta_3} \cdot \exp[-\beta_1 D] \qquad (2\text{-}28)$$

$$k \equiv \beta_1 + \beta_2 + \beta_3 > 1, \quad 0 < \beta_1 + \beta_3 < 1 \qquad (2\text{-}29)$$

We specify that the food price (P_S) is parallel to the farm product price at the margin of urban area, which is assumed to be parallel to the land price, and increasing for the distance from the margin and the wage rate.

7)   This corresponds to a wave-like dispersion as for the firm space ratio (see Korcelli [22]). A sufficient condition
for H-1 type is $\quad \Omega > [1 + \dfrac{2a}{h-1} - \gamma_1]\ exp\ [\dfrac{a}{h-1}]$.

8)   Based upon the decrease of disposable time and also decrease of available facilities and informations. In the allocation
model with $\beta_4 = 0$, it is assumed that the travel cost is increasing with distance (see Yamada [38]).

$$P_S[D] = \delta_0 \cdot P_F[\tilde{D}] \cdot \exp(\delta_1 [\tilde{D} - D]) \cdot w^{\delta_2} \tag{2-30}$$

We assume the significance conditions,[9]

$$b \equiv -\beta_2 \cdot \hat{P}_A - \beta_4 = \beta_2 \cdot \gamma_1 - \beta_4 > 0 \tag{2-31}$$

$$\beta_2 \cdot \gamma_1 - \beta_4 - \delta_1 \cdot \beta_3 > 0 \tag{2-32}$$

and also assume

$$\eta = -1 \tag{2-33}$$

then we get the following optimum solutions,[10]

$$C = g_C \cdot P_C^{\frac{1-\beta_2-\beta_3}{k-1}} \cdot P_S^{\frac{\beta_3}{k-1}} \cdot \gamma_0^{\frac{\beta_2}{k-1}} \cdot \exp\left[\frac{-b \cdot D}{k-1}\right] \tag{2-34}$$

$$B = g_B \cdot P_C^{\frac{\beta_1}{k-1}} \cdot P_S^{\frac{\beta_3}{k-1}} \cdot \gamma_0^{\frac{1-\beta_1-\beta_3}{k-1}} \cdot \exp\left(\frac{\beta_4 - \gamma_1[1-\beta_1-\beta_3]}{k-1} \cdot D\right) \tag{2-35}$$

$$S = g_S \cdot P_C^{\frac{\beta_1}{k-1}} \cdot P_S^{\frac{1-\beta_1-\beta_2}{k-1}} \cdot \gamma_0^{\frac{\beta_2}{k-1}} \cdot \exp\left[\frac{-b \cdot D}{k-1}\right] \tag{2-36}$$

$$Y = g_Y \cdot P_C^{\frac{\beta_1}{k-1}} P_S^{\frac{\beta_3}{k-1}} \gamma_0^{\frac{\beta_2}{k-1}} (k + [b + \delta_1 \cdot \beta_3]D) \cdot \exp\left[\frac{-b \cdot D}{k-1}\right] \tag{2-37}$$

where

$$g_C \equiv [\beta_0 \cdot \beta_1^{1-\beta_2-\beta_3} \cdot \beta_2^{\beta_2} \cdot \beta_3^{\beta_3}]^{\frac{1}{1-k}} \tag{2-38}$$

$$g_B \equiv [\beta_0 \cdot \beta_1^{\beta_1} \cdot \beta_2^{1-\beta_1-\beta_3} \beta_3^{\beta_3}]^{\frac{1}{1-k}} \tag{2-39}$$

$$g_S \equiv [\beta_0 \cdot \beta_1^{\beta_1} \cdot \beta_2^{\beta_2} \cdot \beta_3^{1-\beta_1-\beta_2}]^{\frac{1}{1-k}} \tag{2-40}$$

$$g_Y \equiv [\beta_0 \beta_1^{\beta_1} \beta_2^{\beta_2} \beta_3^{\beta_3}]^{\frac{1}{1-k}} \tag{2-41}$$

In this model the Schwäbe's Law is not held as

$$[P_A \cdot B/Y]' = -\beta_2 \cdot [b + \delta_1 \cdot \beta_3]/(k + [b + \delta_1 \cdot \beta_3] \cdot D)^2 < 0 \tag{2-42}$$

Also we have[11]

$$\text{sign}(B') = \text{sign}\left[\gamma_1 - \frac{b}{k-1}\right] = \text{sign}\left[\frac{\beta_4}{1-\beta_1-\beta_3} - \gamma_1\right], \quad C' < 0, \quad S' < 0, \quad Y' < 0 \tag{2-43}$$

---

9) (2-32) Corresponds with $m > 0$. (2-31) is neccessary to have (2-32). When we specify that $m' < 0$, we must have $(P_A \cdot B)' < 0$. But this is automatically satisfied.

10) The constant rations of $P_C \cdot C$, $P_A \cdot B$, and $P_S \cdot S$ for $(Y - m \cdot D)$ is the result of long-linear utility function. $P_A \cdot B$ includes the reserve demand (see Komiya [20], Iwata [16]) as Y is understood to include wage and other rental income through the relation between μ and w (4-4).

11) Ogata-Shimofusa [27] gave the result that the household space (B) is positive function of (land price)/(construction price index) (P_L/P_H) and (GNP)/(number of household) (V/F):

$B = 0.154 \left(\frac{P_L}{P_H}\right) + 0.0217 \left(\frac{V}{F}\right) + 55.3 \ (R^2 = 0.946)$. In our model, $B = (g_B/g_Y) \cdot Y \cdot \exp[\gamma_1 \cdot D]/\gamma_0 \cdot (k + [b + \delta_1 \cdot \beta_3] \cdot D)$,

$\partial B/\partial Y > 0$ and $\partial B/\partial \gamma_0 < 0$.

Therefore $Y[\tilde{D}]$ gives the minimum household income in the urban area. The household with lower income cannot purchase the sufficient land service and are not explicitly analyzed here, and may reside in the low-rent houses subsidized by autohority or in the shabby small apartments, forming up slams.[12]

(e) Distancial distribution of households

Once the distribution of household income (F_Y) and the total number of households (N) are given, the ratio of household space to total space (I) can be explicitly calculated. We assume a log-normal distribution fo r F_Y[13]

$$F_Y[\log Y] = \frac{1}{\sqrt{2\pi} \cdot \Sigma} \cdot \exp\left(-\frac{1}{2\Sigma^2}[\log Y - \mu]^2\right) \tag{2-44}$$

then the ratio is expressed as

$$I[D] = N \cdot B \cdot F_Y \cdot |Y'| / \theta \cdot D \quad (0 < D \leqq \tilde{D})$$

$$= N \cdot B \cdot F_Y[\log Y] \cdot |(\log Y)'| / \theta \cdot D$$

$$= \frac{g_I}{D} \cdot \frac{b[b + \delta_1 \cdot \beta_3] \cdot D + b - \delta_1 \cdot \beta_3 (k-1)}{k + [b + \delta_1 \cdot \beta_3] \cdot D}$$

$$\cdot \exp\left\{\left[\gamma_1 - \frac{b + \delta_1 \cdot \beta_3}{k-1}\right] \cdot D - \frac{1}{2\Sigma^2}(\log Y[D] - \mu)^2\right\} \tag{2-45}$$

where

$$g_I \equiv \frac{N \cdot g_B}{\sqrt{2\pi} \cdot (k-1) \cdot \theta \cdot \Sigma} \left\{ P_C^{\beta_1} \cdot \gamma_0^{1 - \beta_1 - \beta_3} \delta_0^{\beta_3} \cdot P_F[0]^{\beta_3} \cdot w^{\delta_2} \right.$$

$$\left. \cdot \exp\left(\beta_3[\delta_1 - \epsilon_1]\tilde{D}\right)\right\}^{\frac{1}{k-1}} \tag{2-46}$$

Writing the exponential part of (2-45) as X, we have

$$\frac{[k-1] \cdot [k + u \cdot D]^2 D^2}{g_I \cdot \exp[X]} \cdot I'[D] = q \cdot b \cdot u^2 \cdot D^3 + u \cdot \left\{ b(u + \gamma_1 \cdot k \cdot [k-1] - v \cdot q \right\} \cdot D^2$$

$$- v \cdot (2u \cdot [k-1] - k \cdot q) \cdot D - k \cdot v \cdot (k-1) + D \cdot [b \cdot u \cdot D + v]^2$$

$$\cdot \frac{[\log Y - \mu]}{\Sigma^2} \tag{2-47}$$

$$u \equiv b + \delta_1 \cdot \beta_3 \tag{2-48}$$

$$v \equiv u - \delta_1 \cdot \beta_3 \cdot k = b - (k-1) \cdot \delta_1 \cdot \beta_3 \tag{2-49}$$

$$q \equiv \gamma_1 (k-1) - u \tag{2-50}$$

---

12) At 1968, 774,000 persons or 242,000 household (7 percent of total population) live in the public low-rent houses (see [36], pp.12-13, 170-1). About 60 percent of these houses are in kubu or usual concept of Tokyo city.
13) An empirical support is given in Ichikawa-Sengoku [15].

$$\text{sign } (\lim_{D \to 0} I'[D]) = \text{sign } [-v] \tag{2-51}$$

In (2-47) the last term prevails as $D \to +\infty$, and $\lim_{D \to +\infty} I'[D] \to 0^-$. The sign of I' may change depending the combination of parameters. For example, when $\delta_1 = 0$, $u = v = b$, $q = \gamma_1 (k-1) - b$, and (i) if $\overline{D} > (k/2)$ and $\log Y [\overline{D}] = \mu$, I' changes from negative to positive and then negative, and (ii) if $\overline{D} << (k/2)$ and Σ^2 is sufficiently large, I' is always negative. Therefore we classify three cases: $I-1, I-2$ and $I-3$ (see Fig. 2-2).

$I-1$ type if $v < 0$

$I-2$ type if $v > 0$, and $I'[D] \leqq 0$

$I-3$ type if $v > 0$, and $I'[D] > 0$ for some D

Fig. 2-2 Distancial Distribution of Household Space Density

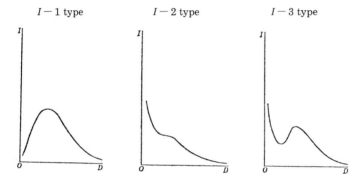

$I-1$ type $I-2$ type $I-3$ type

If $\delta_1 = 0$, and q is small, the distribution shifts from $I-2$ to $I-3$ type as μ increases.
If we loose the assumption $k > 1$, and define t as

$$t \equiv \delta_1 \cdot (k-1) - u \tag{2-52}$$

we can classify the next cases considering

$$\text{sign } (Y'[D]) = \text{sign } (\frac{u \cdot [1 + u \cdot D]}{1-k}) \tag{2-53}$$

		sign[C']	sign[S']	sign[B']	sign[Y']	$I[D]$
$b > \delta_1 \cdot \beta_3 > 0$	$k > 1$	$-$	sign[t]	sign[q]	$-$	undefined
$[u > 0]$	$k < 1$	$+$	sign[$-t$]	sign[$-q$]	$+$	$I-2$ or $I-3$ $(v > 0)$

If $1 < k < 2$, the type of $I[D]$ is $I-2$ or $I-3$. In the special case of $\beta_4 = \delta_1 = 0$, the signs above are as follows

$$b > 0 \; \left\{ \begin{array}{l} k > 1 \\ [u > 0] \quad k < 1 \end{array} \right. \quad \begin{array}{cccc} - & - & - & - \\ + & + & + & + \end{array} \left.\begin{array}{c} \\ \end{array}\right\} \quad I-2 \text{ or } I-3 \; (v > 0)$$

The sign$[q]$ is positive, for example, if $\gamma_1 > \beta_1$, $\beta_4 > \gamma_1 (1-\beta_1)$, and, when $k > 1$, the household income will decrease, but the household purchases a larger site as the distance increases. When β_4 and δ_1 are not zero, and δ_1 is large as the distribution system is badly organized, v is probably nagative. In this case the type of $I[D]$ is $I-1$, and shifts to $I-2$ or $I-3$ as δ_1 decreases.

We write the density of population or household as J,

$$J[D] = N \cdot F_Y(\log Y[D]) \cdot |(\log Y[D])'|/\theta \cdot D \tag{2-54}$$

Then
$$\hat{J}[D] = \hat{I}[D] - \hat{B}[D] = \hat{I}[D] - \frac{q}{k-1} \tag{2-55}$$

The maximum point of J appears to the right (left) of one of I if $B' < 0$ $(B' > 0)$. The distance of maximum point of I in $I-1$ and $I-3$ ($\check{D}$) increases with μ, $\partial \check{D}/\partial \mu > 0$. Therefore the mountain of density removes from the centre with income growth, and the wavelike dispersion will be observed.

The residence preference parameter (β_2) generally decreases historically as the residential stock increases, so we induce that in Japan β_2 is relatively large and $k > 1$, but in U.S.A and european countries β_2 is relatively small and $k < 1$. As the result, in American large cities where the distribution system is well organized and δ_1 is small and t is probably nagative, $Y'[D]$ and $B'[D]$ are positive and the rich people resides in the big house at the suburn area, and the poor people concentrates in the centre and forms the slum residing in the shabby apartment. To the contrary, in Japanese large cities, $k > 1$ and δ_1 is probably large and q is negative with small absolute value, therefore the poor people will purchase the minimum land service to build a house at suburb area. In U.S.A. the distribution of household space will be $I-2$ or $I-3$ with skyscrapers at the centre, and a hump (or subcentre) apart from the centre. In Japan, at the beginning stage of the city, δ_1 is large and $I-1$ type is observed, and the residential density is high around the centre and decreasing to the suburb area with small skyscrapers at the centre and without big subcentres. But this type will gradually shift to $I-2$ or $I-3$ type historically. A bold generalization of urban development stages is as follows; (1) premature stage with underseparation of production and living revealing the firm and household space distribution $H-1$ and $I-1$ types, (2) transition stage with growing centre and with $H-1$ and $I-2$ types, and (3) matured stage with skyscrapers at the centre and growing subcenters reveraling $H-2$ and $I-3$ types. At the final stage the office town and the bedtown will be cleary separated, and a large scale sprawl to farming area will be observed. Figure 2—3 shows the vertical cutting of a city of matured stage assuming $D^* < \tilde{D}$, which is very similar to the current shape of Tokyo metropolitan area in Japan.[14]

Fig. 2-3   Double-Ring-Structure of Large Urban Area

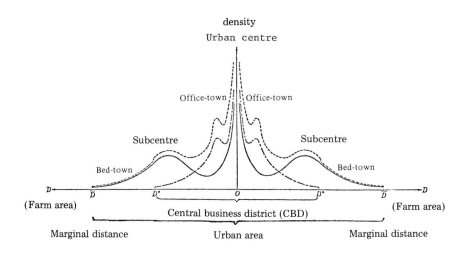

(f)   Determination of travelling structure from residences to offices

From (2-12) and (2-23), the employment at distance D and the total employment of the city $(E[D]$ and $E)$ are given as

$$E[D] = M \cdot L \cdot F_L\,(L[D]) \tag{2-56}$$

$$E = \int_{D*}^{0} M \cdot L[D] \cdot F_L\,(L[D]) \cdot |L[D]'| \cdot dD \tag{2-57}$$

We assume that each household supplies the labor force of average units (E/N). Then the labor supply at distance D and the excess demand of labor $(LA$ and $ED)$ are given as

$$LA[D] = E \cdot F_Y\,(\log Y[D]) \cdot |(\log Y[D])'| \tag{2-58}$$

$$ED[D] \equiv E[D] - LA[D] \tag{2-59}$$

We define "office town" ("bedtown") as the area where $ED > 0$ $(ED < 0)$ and the net social inflow in the daytime is positive (negative). We postulate the monotonous direction of travelling structure such as

$$\int_0^D ED[p]dp \; = \int_0^D E\,[p]dp - \int_0^D LA\,[p]dp \; > 0 \tag{2-60}$$

---

14)   As for an actual form, see [14] (Fig. 16-1, p.174).

Then the travelling distance (R) of the resident at distance D is given as

$$R[D] = D - (E^{-1}[D]) \cdot LA[D] \tag{2-61}$$

where E^{-1} expresses the inverse function of E, and $E^{-1} \cdot LA$ is defined as

$$E^{-1}[D] \cdot LA[D] \equiv D^+ \Big|_0^{D^+} E[p] dp = \int_0^D LA[p] dp \tag{2-62}$$

Thus we can explain the "successive travelling structure" such as the residents in the far suburb work in the near suburb and the residents in the near suburb work in CBD. We assume that s transportation lines to the centre are equally distributed in θ radian, and the capacity of each line is l persons per hour. Then the congestion at distance $Q[D]$ is defined as the ratio of the travelling persons to the transportation capacity.

$$Q[D] \equiv \frac{1}{s \cdot l} \int_0^D (E[p] - LA[p]) dp \tag{2-63}$$

We define the total loss of travel (LO) as the excess loss by fatigue of total workers by roundtrips assuming the loss at each distance as an increasing function of $Q(\xi_1 > 1)$ following Vickery-Mills-Ferranti [25].

$$LO = 2 \int_0^{\tilde{D}} \cdot \Big\{ \int_D^{D-R[D]} \xi_0 \, (Q[p])^{\xi_1} \cdot dp \Big\} \cdot LA[D] dD \tag{2-64}$$

(g) Determination of GCP and NCW

The Gross City Product (GCP, V) is the total output of total firms in the city, and is specified as

$$V \equiv M \cdot \int_{D^*}^{0'} O[D] \cdot F_L (L[D]) \cdot (L[D])' \cdot dD \tag{2-65}$$

We assume that the amount of neccessary compensation for the public nuisance (air pollution, noises, decrease of land level, vibration etc.) (Z) is given as a function of firm density, household density, and transport congestion such as

$$Z[D] = \nu_0 \cdot (H[D])^{\nu_1} \cdot (I[D])^{\nu_2} \cdot (Q[D])^{\nu_3} \tag{2-66}$$

The total value of public nuisance in the city (Z) is given as [15]

$$Z = \int_D^0 N \cdot F_Y (\log Y[D]) \cdot (\log Y[D])' \cdot Z[D] \cdot dD \tag{2-67}$$

---

15) (i) Rothenberg [29] suggested to conceptually integrate the congestion and pollution, but we interpret Z as the social cost accompanied with agglomeration and separated from travel loss (see Ezawa [3], p.89).
(ii) Fukuchi-Yamane [12] estimated the trash as the function of household income and industrial activities quantitatively. Some empirical models incorporated the simple "congestion index" which is defined as a weighted sum of various external diseconomies (shortage of house, transport congestion, public nuisance, deterioration of environment, etc.); for example, Fukuchi-Nobukuni [7] [8] [10], Ohkawa [18], Fukuchi-Matsuyuki [4], Maysuyuki [32] [33].

We define the net welfare of each household as the sum of consumption good, land service, and food purchased minus the travel loss and the public nuisance, and the "Net City Welfare" (NCW) as the sum by total households. [16]

$$NCW \equiv \int_0^{\widetilde{D}} \{ P_C \cdot C[D] + P_A[D] \cdot B[D] + P_S[D] \cdot S[D] - 2 \int_D^{D-R[D]} \xi_0$$

$$\cdot (Q[P])^{\xi_1} \cdot dp - Z[D]\} J[D] \cdot \theta \cdot D \cdot dD = \int_0^{\widetilde{D}} Y[D] \cdot J[D] \cdot \theta \cdot D \cdot dD$$

$$- \{ m \int_0^{\widetilde{D}} \theta \cdot D^2 \cdot J[D] \cdot dD + LO + Z \} \tag{2-68}$$

(h)   Determination of urban land price

We assume that the price of urban land and the marginal distance of urban area are determined through the demand and supply equality of marginal urban land. The demand by the developer who purchases the land and sells to the household the bandle of land and constructed house (D^D) is assumed as an increasing function of utilizing density at the previous year at the previous marginal distance ($\widetilde{D}_{-1}$)   and an decreasing function of land price at the new marginal distance ($\widetilde{D}$).

$$\widetilde{D}^D = \kappa_0 \cdot (H[\widetilde{D}_{-1}]_{-1} + I[\widetilde{D}_{-1}]_{-1})^{\kappa_1} \cdot (P_A[\widetilde{D}])^{-\kappa_2} \tag{2-69}$$

The supply of farmers is specified as an increasing function of the parity of urban land price to farm land price, the rate of change of urban land price, and the urban land price itself.

$$\widetilde{D}^S = \tau_0 \cdot (\frac{P_A[D_{-1}]}{P_F[D_{-1}]})^{\gamma_1} \cdot (\frac{P_A[\widetilde{D}]}{P_A[D_{-1}]})^{\tau_8} (P_A[\widetilde{D}])^{\tau_8} \tag{2-70}$$

The demand and supply equality

$$\widetilde{D}^D = \widetilde{D}^S = D$$

and (2-1), (2-2), (2-4), (2-69) and (2-70) give us [17]

$$\gamma_0 = [\frac{\kappa_0}{\tau_0}]^{\frac{1}{q}} \cdot (H[\widetilde{D}_{-1}]_{-1} + I[\widetilde{D}_{-1}]_{-1})^{\frac{1}{q}} \cdot [\gamma_{0,-1}]^{\frac{\kappa_1}{q}} \cdot (P_F[0])^{\frac{1}{q}(\tau_1 - \frac{\gamma_1[\tau_3+\kappa_2]}{\gamma_1-\epsilon_1})}$$

$$\cdot \exp (\frac{[\gamma_1-\epsilon_1] \cdot \tau_1 \cdot \widetilde{D}_{-1}}{q}) \tag{2-71}$$

where $q \equiv \tau_1 + \tau_2 - \frac{\epsilon_1[\kappa_2+\tau_3]}{\gamma_1-\epsilon_1}$ \tag{2-72}

(i)   Construction of urban model

Thus we constructed an urban model with 29 endogenous and 11 exogenous variables as

---

16)   As for the definition of NNW, see [19]. NCW does not includes the governmental activity and leisure activity.
17)   Fukuchi-Nobukni's four regions model of Japanese economy [7] determined the land price and the land space for housing by demand and supply equality. As for the dispute about the determination of urban land price, see [34] [35] [21].

follows. This model depends upon two distribution function F_L (2-23) and F_Y (2-44) and accompanies the assumptions about parameters such as (2-3), (2-7), (2-9), (2-21), (2-31), (2-32), (2-33), and about variables such as (2-60). We call this model as the double ring structure model No. 1 as it suggests the double ring distribution of officetown and bedtown.

$$
\text{MODEL No. 1} \left\{
\begin{array}{l}
\text{Endogenous variables: } P_A\,(2\text{-}1),\, P_F\,(2\text{-}2),\, P_S\,(2\text{-}30),\, A\,(2\text{-}10),\, K\,(2\text{-}11),\, L\,(2\text{-}12),\, O\,(2\text{-}13), \\[4pt]
G\,(2\text{-}14),\, C\,(2\text{-}34),\, B\,(2\text{-}35),\, S\,(2\text{-}36),\, Y\,(2\text{-}37),\, H\,(2\text{-}24),\, I\,(2\text{-}45),\, J\,(2\text{-}54),\, E\,(2\text{-}56),\, LA\,(2\text{-}58), \\[4pt]
R\,(2\text{-}61),\, ED\,(2\text{-}59),\, Q\,(2\text{-}63),\, Z\,(2\text{-}66) \text{ (as functions of distance } D),\, \widetilde{D}\,(2\text{-}4),\, D^*\,(2\text{-}20), \\[4pt]
\gamma_0\,(2\text{-}71),\, E\,(2\text{-}57),\, LO\,(2\text{-}64),\, V\,(2\text{-}65),\, Z\,(2\text{-}67),\, NCW\,(2\text{-}68) \text{ (as scalars)} \\[4pt]
\text{Exogenous variables: } M,\, N,\, \delta,\, \mu,\, \Sigma,\, P_F[0],\, r,\, w,\, P_C,\, n,\, T
\end{array}
\right.
$$

We summarize the distribution of land utilization in the following theorems:

Theorem I (Density distribution of office space)

In the business allocation model (2-1), (2-5) $\sim$ (2-8), (2-20), (2-21) and (2-23), the density of office space decreases from the centre monotonously ($H-1$ type) or accompanied with maximum point ($H-2$ type).

Theorem II (Density distribution of household space)

In the household allocation model (2-1), (2-4), (2-27) $\sim$ (2-30), and (2-44), the density of household space increases when $v < 0$ ($I-1$ type) or decreases when $v > 0$ ($I-2$ and $I-3$ types) from the centre, and approaches to zero as distance increases ($D \to +\infty$).

3.   Stability condition of urban sprawl

We discuss whether the sprawl and the land price increase persists when every exogenous variable (including the number of firms or households) is held constant. First we assume

$$
\gamma_0 > P_F[0] \cdot \exp \left([\gamma_1 - \epsilon_1] \cdot \left[\frac{1}{n} - \frac{\alpha_1 + \alpha_2 + \alpha_3}{\alpha_3 \cdot \gamma_1 - \alpha_4} \right] \right) \tag{3-1}
$$

therefore $\widetilde{D} > D^*$. Then eight endogenous variables (γ_0, P_F, P_A, $\widetilde{D}$, Y, P_S, B, I) depend on the six exogenous variables ($P_F[0]$, P_C, w, N, Σ, μ), and constitute a closed dynamic submodel. Then, from (2-4) (2-71), we have[18]

$$
\gamma_0 = \left\{ \left[\frac{\kappa_0}{\tau_0} \right] \cdot \delta_0^{\frac{\beta_3 \cdot \kappa_1}{k-1}} \cdot \left[\frac{g_B}{\sqrt{2\pi} \cdot (k-1) \cdot \ell} \right]^{\kappa_1} \right\}^{\frac{1}{q}}
$$
$$
\cdot \left[\frac{N_{-1}}{\Sigma_{-1}} \right]^{\frac{\kappa_1}{q}} \cdot [P_{C,-1}]^{\frac{\beta_1 \cdot \kappa_1}{(k-1) \cdot q}} \cdot w^{\frac{\beta_3 \cdot \kappa_1 \cdot \delta_2}{(k-1) \cdot q}}
$$

---

18) Of course the land price of T and D is expressed as γ_0 $[T]$ $\cdot \exp[-\gamma_1 D]$. The past empirical studies of land price such as Orishimo [28], Fukuchi-Nobukuni [9], Fukuch-Yamane [12] mainly concentrated in the estimation of γ_1 and influences of N and μ. As for a socail engineering approach, see Kumada [23].

$$\cdot (P_F[0]_{-1}) \frac{1}{(k-1)\cdot q} \{\beta_3 \cdot \kappa_1 - \tau_1 (k-1) - \frac{(\epsilon_1 \cdot \beta_3 - \gamma_1 \cdot [k-1] + b) \cdot \kappa_1}{\gamma_1 - \epsilon_1}\}$$

$$\cdot (P_F[0])^{\frac{1}{q}(\tau_1 - \frac{\tau_1 [\tau_3 + \kappa_2]}{\gamma_1 - \epsilon_1})}$$

$$\cdot \{\frac{b \cdot [b + \delta_1 \cdot \beta_3] \tilde{D}_{-1} + b - \delta_1 \cdot \beta_3 \cdot [k-1]}{(k + [b + \delta_1 \cdot \beta_3] \cdot \tilde{D}_{-1}) \cdot \tilde{D}_{-1}}\}^{\frac{\kappa_1}{q}}$$

$$\cdot [\gamma_{0,-1}]^{\frac{1}{(k-1)\cdot q}} \{\kappa_1 \cdot [1 - \beta_1 - \beta_3] + [\tau_1 + \tau_2] \cdot [k-1] + \frac{\kappa_1 (\gamma_1 [k-1] - b - \epsilon_1 \cdot \beta_3)}{\gamma_1 - \epsilon_1}\}$$

$$\cdot \exp\{\frac{-\kappa_1}{2 \cdot \Sigma_{-1}^2 \cdot q} (\log Y[\tilde{D}_{-1}]_{-1} - \mu_{-1})^2\} \qquad (3\text{-}2)$$

$$\text{sign}[\frac{\partial \gamma_0}{\partial N_{-1}}] = \text{sign} [\frac{\partial \gamma_0}{\partial Pc_{,-1}}] = \text{sign} [\frac{\partial \gamma_0}{\partial w}] = \text{sign} [q] ,$$

$$\text{sign} (\frac{\partial \gamma_0}{\partial P_F[0]}) = \text{sign} [1 - \frac{\tau_2}{q}] \qquad (3\text{-}3)$$

When the exogenous variables are held constant, we have (exponential part of (3-2) as l)

$$\tilde{D} = l \cdot \tilde{D}_{-1} + \frac{\kappa_1}{(\gamma_1 - \epsilon_1) \cdot q} \cdot \log \frac{b \cdot [b + \delta_1 \cdot \beta_3] \cdot \tilde{D}_{-1} + b - \delta_1 \cdot \beta_3 \cdot (k-1)}{(k + [b + \delta_1 \cdot \beta_3] \cdot \tilde{D}_{-1}) \tilde{D}_{-1}}$$

$$+ (\text{const.}) - \frac{\kappa_1}{2 \Sigma^2 \cdot q \cdot (\gamma_1 - \epsilon_1)} (\log Y[\tilde{D}_{-1}]_{-1} - \mu_{-1})^2 \qquad (3\text{-}4)$$

where

$$Y[\tilde{D}] = g_Y * \cdot [k + u \cdot \tilde{D}] \cdot \exp[\frac{p \cdot \tilde{D}}{k-1}] \qquad (3\text{-}5)$$

$$g_Y * \equiv g_Y \cdot P_C^{\frac{\beta_1}{k-1}} \cdot [\delta_0 w^{\delta_2}]^{\frac{\beta_3}{k-1}} \cdot (P_F[0])^{\frac{\beta_2 + \beta_3}{k-1}} \qquad (3\text{-}6)$$

$$p \equiv (\gamma_1 - \epsilon_1) \cdot \beta_2 - (b + \epsilon_1 \cdot \beta_3) = \beta_4 - \epsilon_1 \cdot (\beta_2 + \beta_3) \qquad (3\text{-}7)$$

$$\text{sign} (\frac{\partial Y[\tilde{D}]}{\partial D}) = \text{sign} (p \cdot u \cdot \tilde{D} + p \cdot k + u \cdot [k-1]) \qquad (3\text{-}8)$$

If $p > 0$, then $\partial Y[\tilde{D}]/\partial \tilde{D} > 0$, and if $P < 0$, $\text{sign} (\partial Y[\tilde{D}]/\partial \tilde{D}) = - \text{sign} (\tilde{D} - |\frac{u \cdot (k-1) + p \cdot k}{(-)p \cdot u}|)$. Dividing the both side of (3-4) by $\tilde{D}_{-1}$ and taking $\tilde{D}_{-1}$ as infinite, the last term at right-hand side prevails and will be positive (negative) according to $q < 0$ (> 0). So, even if $\log Y$ increases (decreses) when $p > 0$ (< 0), when $q < 0$, $\tilde{D}$ diverges, and when $q > 0$, there exists $\tilde{D}$ such as $\lim_{T \to \infty} \tilde{D} < \hat{D}$. We call a city stable when $\tilde{D}$ exists and unstable when $\tilde{D}$ diverges overtime. In the unstable city, the price of land also diverges overtime.[19]

Theorem III (Stability condition of city size)

In the submodel of eight variables, the stability condition of city size is $q > 0$. In the unstable city, $\log Y[\tilde{D}] \to \pm \infty$ according to $p \gtrless 0$.

In a stable city, the increases of exogenous variables N, P_C, and w result in the increase of $\tilde{D}$, and the actual increasing trends of $\tilde{D}$ and γ_0 can be interpreted as the sum of the dynamic converging process

---

19) There may exist a bang-bang solution.

to $\hat{D}$ and the comparative dynamic process caused by the shift of $\hat{D}$. The successive increases of N, P_C and w may convert a stable city to unstable type at her outlook.

When we interpret the right-hand side of (3-2) as a function of Σ_{-1} and μ_{-1}, we have

$$R_{\gamma_0} = [\frac{\kappa_1}{q}]\{(\frac{[\log Y_{-1}-\mu_{-1}]^2}{\Sigma^2}-1)R_{\Sigma_{-1}} + \frac{[\log Y_{-1}-\mu_{-1}]}{\Sigma_{-1}}\cdot\frac{\mu_{-1}}{\Sigma_{-1}}\cdot R_{\mu_{-1}}\} \qquad (3\text{-}9)$$

If $p > 0$, $\log Y_{-1} > \mu_{-1}$ and $[\log Y_{-1}-\mu_{-1}]/\Sigma_{-1} > 1$, then the increases of Σ_{-1} and μ_{-1} will increase $\hat{D}$, and the increases of $R_{\Sigma_{-1}}$ and $R_{\mu_{-1}}$ will increase R_{γ_0} and $\hat{D}$. If $p < 0$ and $R_{\mu_{-1}} > 0$, then R_{γ_0} decreases, and an unbalanced income growth such as $R_{\Sigma_{-1}} > 0$ and $R_{\mu_{-1}} < 0$ resulting in the increase of variation coefficient will result in the acceleration of increase of land price.

4. Urban structural inflation

In the following two sections we treat some exogenous variables as endogenous and explain the urban inflation and the social movement of population. We define the consumer's price index at distance D ($P_{CON}[D]$) and average index of the city (P_{con}) as [20]

$$P_{con}[D] = \frac{P_C\cdot C[D]+P_S[D]\cdot S[D]+P_A[D]\cdot B[D]}{C[D]+S[D]+B[D]} \qquad (4\text{-}1)$$

$$P_{con} \equiv \int_0^{\tilde{D}}\theta\cdot D\cdot J[D]\cdot P_{con}[D]\cdot dD \qquad (4\text{-}2)$$

We specify that the changing rate of nominal wage (R_w) is a positive function of Philips-Lipsey type with the previous changing rate of consumer's price and the demand to supply ratio at the labor market (represented by E/N).

$$R_w = \xi_0[P_{con,-1}]^{\xi_1}\cdot\exp(\xi_2[E/N]_{-1}) \qquad (4\text{-}3)$$

We also specify

$$\mu = f(w, T), \quad [\partial f/\partial w] > 0 \qquad (4\text{-}4)$$

$$\Sigma = f(\mu, T) \qquad (4\text{-}5)$$

and the consumer's price as a function of factor prices (r, w, γ_0) and technological progress (T in (2-6))

$$P_C = f(r, w, \gamma_0, T) \qquad (4\text{-}6)$$

and the average firm size (σ in (2-23)) as a function of product price and time trend,

$$\qquad (4\text{-}7)$$

---

20) C,S and B are measured by the constant price.

$$\sigma = f(P_C, T) \tag{4-7}$$

Then we give two definitions about the price system $(P_{con}, P_S, \gamma_0, P_C, w)$,[21]

Definition of price stability in wide sense: The price system is stable in wide sense if

$$\lim_{T \to \infty} \vec{R}(P_{con} \cdot P_S[\tilde{D}] \cdot \gamma_0 \cdot P_C \cdot w) \to \vec{0} \quad \text{when the exogenous variables } (P_F[0], r, T, N, M, n)) \text{ are held}$$

constant.

Definition of price stability in narrow sense: The price system is stable in narrow sense if

$$\lim_{T \to \infty} \vec{R}(P_{con} \cdot \vec{P}_S[\tilde{D}] \cdot \gamma_0 \cdot P_C \cdot w) \to \vec{0} \quad \text{when } q > 0 \text{ and the exogenous variables } (P_F[0], r, T, N, M, n)$$

are held constant.

We may say that the former stability is the stability condition of urban inflation, and the latter is the one of wage-consumer's price spiral. If the former stability is not held, the price system will diverge because (a) the stability condition for sprawl and land price increase is not met or (b) there exists a sprial mechanism of wage and consumer's price, or (c) both. We say "the urban inflation" because this inflation is tightly connected with a regional phenomena such a surban sprawl.[22] When $q > 0$ is not held, the urban inflation cannot be eliminated through the elimination of costpush inflation mechanism. We need further quantitative simulation studies as the stability condition depends upon the initial conditions. But thus we successfully clarified the interraction between inflation , sprawl, and poverty in the urban policy issues.

5.   Enlargement of the theoretical model

We add the two equations to explain the mass movement of firms and households and to enlarge our model.

We specify that the number of firms (M) depends upon the ratio of average productivity to the national average ($V_J \div M_J$; V_J implies GDP and M_J is the number of firms in Japan) as the indicator of interregional movement, and upon the number of previous period as the indicator of aggloremating trend.

$$M = f([V/M]_{-1} \div [V_J/M_J]_{-1}, M_{-1}) \tag{5-1}$$

The social increase of household depends upon the ratio of per-household NCW to real GDP per-household, and the employment as the indicator of mobility speed. Adding the number at previous year as the trend variable we specify

---

21)   The constancy of an exozenous variable T implies the constancy in (4-4), (4-5), (4-6), (4-7), and (2-6).
22)   Actually the national consumer's price index is the weighted sum of urban and rural indices by relative weight 7 and 3. Thus we cannot explain the global inflation precisely without the analysis of urban inflation.

$$N= f([\frac{NCW}{P_{con} \cdot N}]_{-1} \div [\frac{V_J}{P_{con,J} N_J}]_{-1}, E_{-1}, N_{-1}) \tag{5-2}$$

Thus we treat the seven exogenous variables in Model No. 1 endogenously, and add four exogenous and one endogenous variables, and construct next Model. No. 2 with 37 endogenous and 8 exogenous variables (see Fig. 5-1).[23]

MODEL No. 2 $\{$

Endogenous variables: 29 variables of Model No. 1 and P_{con} (4-2), w (4-3), μ(4-4), Σ(4-5), P_C (4-6), σ(4-7), M(5-1), N(5-2)

Exogenous variables: $P_F[0]$, r, n, T, V_J, M_J, N_J, $P_{con,J}$

In this model, once (i) the global variables (V_J, M_J, N_J, $P_{con,J}$), (ii) the surrounding farm area variable ($P_F[0]$), (iii) trend (T), (iv) the monetary policy variable (r), and (v) the transportation SOC variables (n, θ, s, l) are given, the main urban variables and problems are explained as postulated in the introduction. We summarize here some operational definitions.

Intensive Land Utilization at the Centre: $\lim (H[D] + I[D])' \to -\infty$

in $H-1, H-2, I-2$, and $I-3$ type distribution

Existence of Subcentre: $I'[\overline{D}] = 0, 0 < \overline{D} < +\infty$ in $I-3$ type

Separation of Office- town and Bed-town: $ED[D] \gtrless 0$

Urban Sprawl: $\tilde{D} > 0$

Wave-like Population Dispersion[24] : $\frac{\partial \tilde{D}}{\partial \gamma_0} > 0, \frac{\partial \check{D}}{\partial \mu} > 0, I[\check{D}] = 0$

Successive Traveling Structure: $\exists : D^\Delta |R[D^\Delta] > 0, \int_p^{D^\Delta} E(p)dp = \int_0^{D^\Delta + \epsilon} LA(p)dp, \epsilon > 0$

---

23) Some regional econometric models (Fukuchi [6], Fukuchi-Nobukuni [7], Fukuchi-Yamane [12]) incorporated the interraction of population increase and variation of land price.
24) See korcelli [22]. We may define based on $J[D]$ also.

Fig. 5-1. Causal Order Map of Urban Model No. 2

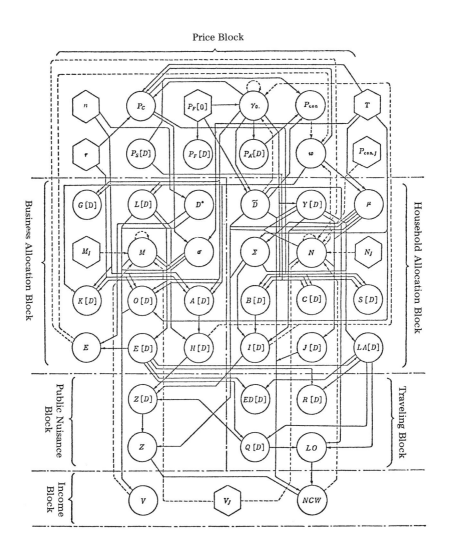

(Remark) ⬡, endogenous variable; ◯, exogenous variable; →, current relation; · · · · · · →, lagged relation; [D] means the function of distance, and others are scalars.

6.   Urban policies

In the previous Model 2, each firm or household was formulated as profit or utility maximizer. The growth of urban activities increases the external diseconomies, which in turn affect to the population movement. But we dis not introduce the control of public sector. Therefore the result of simulations reveal the image of capitalistic or privated-sector-oriented city. But if the external dis-economic s suppress the people's living, the welfare state must interfere with some means, based upon the postulated political targets of growth, equality and welfare. We want to suggest some different types of the city, which in principle consists of different two sectors: private and public, and may be understood as the immage of city under the regime of dual economies.[25]

We define the social welfare of the city(W) as a function of the vector of net welfare of house-holds ($\vec{W}[D]$).[26]

$$W = f*(\vec{W}[D]), \quad \partial W / \partial \vec{W}[D] > \vec{0} \tag{6-1}$$

$\vec{W}$ is a N-dimension vector, and it's component is defined as

$$W[D] = \frac{1}{P_{con}[D]} \{ Y[D] - m \cdot D - LO[D] - Z[D] \} \tag{6-2}$$

where $$LO[D] = 2 \int_D^{D-R[D]} \xi_0 \cdot (Q[p])^{\xi_1} \cdot dp \cdot [\frac{E}{N}] \tag{6-3}$$

In the course of urban growth and income increase, each household on the average can enjoy the internal economy through the increases of w, μ, and $Y[D]$. On the other hand she will suffer from three external diseconomies: (i) If the price system is not stable in wide sense, the consumer's price index will diverge. If the real income cannot grow as the nominal wage pursues the price increase with time-lags, and the land price increase prevails or the price of foods is large, these tendencies will decrease $W[D]$. (ii) The merit of agglomaration (high efficiency coefficient α_0) pulls the firms and households, which increases the travel loss (L_0) and also the damage by the public nuisance (Z). Therefore, the behavior of local government is specified as[27]

$$\underset{I_n\{P_{con}[D], LO[D], Z[D]\}}{\text{MAX}} \cdot f*(\vec{W}[D]) \Big| \underset{K,L,A,D}{\text{MAX}} \{O + \lambda \cdot (r \cdot K + w \cdot L + P_A \cdot A + n \cdot D \cdot O - G)\},$$

$$\underset{C,B,S,D,}{\text{MAX}} \{V + \eta \cdot (P_C \cdot C + P_A \cdot B + P_S \cdot S + m \cdot D - Y)\} \tag{6-4}$$

where $I_n \{x\}$ means the political instruments (fiscal or monetary measures) to control x.

As an example the authority wants to decrease those external diseconomies by increasing the

---

25)   First discussed in [11].
26)   As an example of aggregative function, refer Henderson [13]. As an example of living utility function, see Ishihara-Kaji [37].
27)   As a trial to reveal the people's demand through voting, refer Borcherding-Deacon [2].

land tax (γ_0 will shift to γ_0 [1 + t] ; t as tax rate). Then firstly (a) [L[D*], G[D*] increase, and
H[D*], E decrease, (b) Y[$\widetilde{D}$], B[$\widetilde{D}$] increase and I[$\widetilde{D}$], L_A decrease, (c) P_{con}[D] increases. At the
next stage the trends of land price and inflation are determined based upon the controlling factors
like the decreases o fnumbers of firms and populations, and the accelerating factors like the increses
of w, μ and P_C. The social inflow of population depends upon the trend of NCW. So the long-term
effects of increasing land tax depend upon the stability, the initial conditions, and the trends of
exogenous variables.[28]

As the other example the authority wants to levy the income tax to firms and households (f_M
and f_N) and to increase the public investment into three fields (G_R to transport and communication,
G_I to industries, G_W to direct welfare). Then, considering the shift of goods price (P_C), the optimiz-
ing behavior will be written as

$$\underset{\Delta G_R, \Delta G_I, \Delta G_W}{MAX} f^*(W[D]) \left| P_g (\Delta G_R + \Delta G_I + \Delta G_W) = \sum_{i=1}^{M} f_M (O_i) + \sum_{i=1}^{N} f_N (Y_j), \right.$$

$$\widetilde{P}_C = \widetilde{f}(r, w, \gamma_0, T, \sum_{i=1}^{M} f_M (O_i)/\sum_{i=1}^{N} O_i) \qquad (6\text{-}5)$$

where P_g stands for the deflator for public investment. The optimum public investment will be
positive if the welfare increasing effects by the elimination of public nuisance offsets the welfare
decreasing effects through the price increase and the income tax. Practically (6-5) will be solved
comparing the results of dynamic simulations based upon the specification of (6-5) and the suitable
time-lags.[29]

Of course from the long-term point of view , the planning of Tokyo Metropolitan Area must
be established considering the strong social inflow of population endogenously by applying a nation-
wide multi-regional model, which handles the main variables like employment, income, agglomeration
and public nuisance of each region endogenously.[30]

7.   Additional remarks

We state some important open questions to the future.

(1)   Explicit treetment of urban agglomeration: we implicitly include this by introducing the
distance into (2-6) and (2-28). But it is desirable to explicitly construct an index to express the
political, cultural, social and economic agglomeration and to introduce into the model.[31]

---

28)   Therefore the effects of land tax on price must be clarified through adequate simulations, refer [16], [9].
29)   The studies of optimum form of city to minimize the congestion loss (or the sum with the land value) such as
      Mills-Ferranti [25], Sheshinski [31], Sakashita [30] can be interpreted as a partial solution for this problem
      specifying ΔG_R as an instrument.
30)   See the nine regions model of Japan [7] as an example.
31)   As some examples to incorporate a simple indicator of agglomeration, see Fukuchi-Nobukuni [10] [7] [8] for
      Tokyo, Ohkawa [18] for Osaka, and also Fukuchi-Matsuyuki [4], Shibuyaku [32] and Shinagawaku [33].

(2)   Subdivision of business activities: it is desirable to divide the business secotr to descrive the historical development and structural features of the city?[32]

(3)   Construction of multi-city chain model: in the actual world, the cities are linked together and and accelerating each other their agglomeration.

These problems as well as the integration with other type model such as urban dynamics or system models[33]   are open to the future study.

---

32)   For the subdivision, see Hoover, Alonso, Sakashita [30], Ihara [14]. The Metropolitan Model which introduced an agglomeration index into the production function [10] can be interpreted as an aggregative expression of these product-mix.

33)   See Yasuda [40] for a survey.

[*References*]

[1] Alonso, W., *Location and Land Use*, Harvard University Press, 1964.

[2] Borcherding, T.E. and R.T. Deacon, The Demand for the Services of Non-Federal Governments," *American Economic Review*, December, 1972.

[3] Ezawa, J, "Partial Equilibrium Analysis of Allocation," in *New Development of Economic Allocation Theories* (ed. by Ezawa , J. and Kaneko, Y), Keisoshobo, 1973 (in Japanese).

[4] Fuchu City, *Comprehensive Development Plan of Fuchu City, 1967-71* (guided by Fukuchi, Tand Matsuyuki, Y), April, 1967 (in Japanese).

[5] Fujii, T, "Accumulation of Population and Capital — Conditions for Sustained Growth of Industry and City —," *Keizaikenkyu*, October, 1966 (in Japanese).

[6] Fukuchi, T, "Econometric Analysis of Mitaka City," *Shakaikagakukenkyu*, No. 10, International Christian University, 1964 (in Japanese).

[7] Fukuchi, T and M. Nobuyuki,"Econometric Model of Japanese Economy with Regional Decomposition — I.C.U. Model No. 5," *Economic Studies Quarterly*, Vol. 19, No. 2, 1968 (in Japanese).

[8] Fukuchi, T. and M. Nobukuni, "Economic Analysis of Population Movement," *Kodokagakukenkyu*, Tokai University, Vol. 3, No. 1, 1967 (in Japanese).

[9] Fukuchi, T. and M. Nobukuni, "Analysis of Increasing Urban Land Price, " *Oriental Economist*, May, 1971 (in Japanese).

[10] Fukuchi, T. and M. Nobukuni, "Econometric Analysis of Tokyo Metropolitan Area," in *Survey of Economic Growth theories* (ed. by Tsukui, J. and Murakami, T.), Iwanamishoten, 1968 (in Japanese).

[11] Fukuchi, T. and M. Nobukuni, "Pattern of Cities," in *Johoshakaikagakukoza 10*, Gakushukenkyusha, 1972 (in Japanese).

[12] Fukuchi, T. and K. Yamane, "Econometric Regional Planning — Case Study of Mitaka City *Chiikikeizaigakutaikei 3* (ed. by Ezawa, J. and Kaneko, Y), Keisoshobo, 1974 (in Japanese).

[13] Henderson, J.H., "Local Government Expenditures: A Social Welfare Analysis,'' *Review of Economics and Statistics*, May, 1968.

[14] Ihara, T., *Giant City and Population Distribution — it's Energy for Concentration*, Mainichi Newspaper, 1973 (in Japanese).

[15] Ichikawa, Y. and T. Sengoku, "Social Insurance and Income Distribution," *Keizaibunseki*, November, 1972 (in Japanese).

[16] Iwata, K., "Theory of Land Price and Land Tax System (1) (2)," *Keizaihyoron*, August - September, 1973 (in Japanese).

[17] Kaneko, Y., *Regional Econometric Model of Japanese Economy*, Nihonkeizai Newspaper,

1972 (in Japanese).

[18] Kansaijoho Centre, *"Simulation & Projection by Econometric Model of Osaka City"* (guided by T. Ohkawa), September, 1972 (in Japanese).

[19] Economic Advisory Council N N W Committee, *NNW Committee Report — New Welfare Index NNW —*, 1971 (in Japanese).

[20] Komiya, R., "Land Price," in *Regional Economy and Transportation* (ed. by Ohtsuka H., Kom Komiya, R. and Okano, H.) Tokyo University Press, 1971 (in Japanese).

[21] Komiya, R. and K. Iwata, "To Correct the Confusion in Land Price Theory," *Oriental Economist*, October, 1973 (in Japanese).

[22] Korcelli, P., " A Wave-like Model of Metropolitan Spatial Growth," *Regional Science Association Papers*, Vol. 24, 1970.

[23] Kumada, Y., "Mechanism of Land Price Formation," in *Control of Cities* (ed. by Ishihara, S., Itoh, S. and Kumada, Y.), Nihonhosokyokai, 1971 (in Japanese).

[24] Mills, E., "An Aggregative Model of Resource Allocation in Metropolitan Area," *American Economic Review*, 1967.

[25] Mills, E.S. and D.M. de Ferranti, "Market Choices and Optimum City Size, *American Economic Review*, 1971.

[26] Muth, R.F., "Economic Changes and Rural-Urban Land Conversions," *Econometrica*, 1961.

[27] Ogata, M. and K. Shimofusa,"Simulation of Housing Investment," in *Economics of Housing* (ed. by Honjo, K and K. Shimofusa), Japan economic Research Centre, June, 1968 (in Japanese).

[28] Orishimo, K.,"Urban Land Price Slope and It's Variation Factors," *Annual Report of Japan Regional Science Association*, 1972 (in Japanese).

[29] Rothenberg, J., "The Economics of Congestion and Pollution: An Integrated View," *American Economic Review*, 1970.

[30] Sakashita, N., "On the Econometric Method of Economic Analysis of Cities," *Gendaikeizai*, 5, 1972 (in Japanese).

[31] Sheshinski, E., "Congestion and the Optimum City Size, *American Economic Review*, 1973.

[32] Shibuyaku, *Shibuyaku Long-term Development Planning Study Report*, March, 1970 (in Japanese).

[33] Shinagawaku, *Shinagawaku Long-term Development Planning Study Report*, March, 1969 (in Japanese).

[34] Shinzawa, K. and K. Hanayama, *Land Price and Land Policy*, Iwanamishoten, 1970 (in Japanese).

[35] Shinzawa, K., "Price Formation Mechanism of Residential Area, *"Keizaihyoron*, September,

1972 (in Japanese).

[36] Tokyohyakunenshi Editorial Committe, *Trend of Tokyo Seen From Post-war Data*, Kokon-shoin, 1971 (in Japanese).

[37] Ishihara Study Group, *Report on Living Environment of Kyoto City* (ed. by Ishihara, S. and Kaji, H.) March, 1972 (in Japanese).

[38] Yamada, H., "Urban Structure and Urban Environment, *Gendaikeizai*, 7, 1972 (in Japanese).

[39] Yamada, H., "Basic Theory of Housing Allocation," *Annual Report of Japan Regional Science Association*, 1972 (in Japanese).

[40] Yasuda, I., "System Analysis of Urban Society — Pursuing & Control System of Variation of Urban Society —, *Mathematical Sociology* (ed. by Fukutake, T. and Yasuda, S.), Tokyo University Press, 1973 (in Japanese).

A THEORY OF SPACE AND ORGANIZATION

Takashi Fujii

Introduction

In spite of the common awareness that industrialization depends upon the productivity of capital, it seems to me, the fact that capital is a movable factor of production among spaces and organizations has not been paid any proper attention in the hisotry of economic analyses.

There are two types of movement of capital among spaces and organizations: capital accumulation and capital concentration (or dispartion). Not only macro economics but also micro economics has treated the accumulation of capital as one of the core issures, while the concentration of capital was left the neoclassical assumptions behind.

This is a brief explanation and some expansions for new field of the theory of concentrated accumulation of capital which was presented at "Pacific Conference on Urban Growth" at Honolulu, May 1-12, 1967. Because the basic ideas of this theory is important not only in case of urban growth but also in case of industrial organization. Here I would like to reconsider this ideas as a theory which will explain the development of human settlement or the development of scale and structure for economic circulation system.

This theory is constructed at first in terms of the movement of capital as a stock, then introduced another stock: a knowledge which is concentrated and accumulated in the course of development. This is rather a dynamics of stocks, not a mere growth theory. This is also the third theory which treats a spacial development of human society as an autonomous subject, in relation to its organization, against macro and micro theories.

1. Notations and Assumptions

A: Notations

ys: Production scale of unit management: Product level per unit management (Product means tangible and intangible value added.)

yb: Production density: Production level per unit space.

ks: Scale of unit management in terms of capital.

kb: Capital density of unit space.

ns:　Number of unit management.

nb:　Number of unit space.

B:　Assumptions*

1)　Narrow, high densely populated country of industry like Japan.

2)　High rate of chnage in technology. This means high speed obsolessence of capital and knowledge.

3)　Marginal productivity (efficiency) principle is dominant in the investment priority. This is an observation in rapid growth of Japan. (As like as that in case of vintage model, only the efficiency in last period is effective for investment decision.)

4)　Close location in supply and demand is preferable in every decision.

5)　Simmetry in the movement of capital and labor (or population).

6)　Production function are assumed as depicted in Fig. 1)

Fig. 1

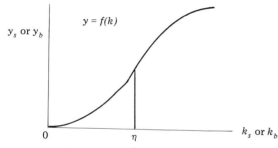

(1)　$0 \to \eta$　:　$\dfrac{dy}{dk} > 0,$　$\dfrac{d^2y}{dk^2} > 0$

(2)　η　:　$0 < \dfrac{dy}{dk} < \infty$

(3)　$\eta \to$　:　$\dfrac{dy}{dk} > 0,$　$\dfrac{dy^2}{dk} < 0$

(4)　Over *ks* or *kb* where $\dfrac{dy}{dk} = 0$ is neglected.

7)　Total numbers of unit management and unit space are fixed.

*Notes

1)　Unit of management consists of one entreprenur and certain numbers of dependant. (Unit of sovereiginity, irrespective of one independant person or family, or tribe, or co-operative or company.)

2)　Entreprenur confronts uncertain economic situation which should be overcome by his creative activities.

2. Concentrated Accumulation of Capital (the simplest model)

　　1)　Two spaces or two managements case*

Fig. 2

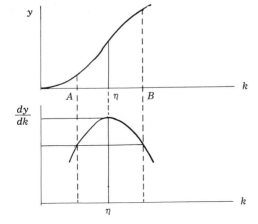

In Fig. 2, A space (management) and B space locates both sides of η (density or scale at turning point of function).

　　First equilibrium comes at $(\frac{dy}{dk})^A = (\frac{dy}{dk})^B$ point, but this is not stable. New investment concentrates A from A and B. B's capital will be obsolated. This means net investment A is positive, B is nagative.

　　Then A shifts right hand for η, B shifts left hand for η. When A and B comes to η, the productivity of A and B is equal at the same scale or the same density of A and B. The marginal productivity is at the highest. We can say η is optimum density or scale.

———————

*Notes (Continued)

3)　Dependants are such that whose incertainity of income etc. will be solved by belonging
　　to his boss entreprenur.

4)　Unit of space is a wideness of space(km^2) in which at least one unit of management could
　　be located. (unit of regional sovereignity)

5)　Organization (organic combination of unit of management) could be located in space
　　which consists of over two units of space.

*Note　This case coresponds the two countries case of Umeshita's paper and Okuguchi's.
　　But I would like to add the fact that this mechanism is also valid in case of two units of
　　management. Company B used to realize this mechanism when amalgamates him with company A.

There are two movements in capital up to here, one is accumulation and another is concentration. After this point(η), only accumulation carrys on as like as the case of neoclasical theory. In this case, the accumulation will be nagative if obsolessence overcomes net investment.

To keep the productivity level, new entry should appear in $0 \to \eta$ density or scale. This supply of new space or new factory (management) is basic condition for development.

2) Multi space or multi management case

We can imagin the case number of space or management distributed on the axis of k. (assuming normal distribution)

Fig. 3

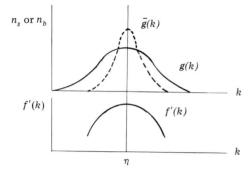

The distribution function $g(k)$ is depicted in Fig. 3 assumingly.

$$N = \int_0^\infty g(k)\, dk = \sum_i n_s^i = constant$$

The mechanism above mentioned works in this case, too. And $g(k)$ will increse the hight at η as $\bar{g}(k)$.

We have assumed that demand and supply should be located closely each other.

This change in distribution means an increase in number of space or management which has the density level or the scale level η(optimum level). These spaces should be located closely. The meaning in reality is a growth of urban area. Urban growth is an expansion of the area with this optimum density(η). When these area's periferies are overlaped, we can say megalopolis formation. These management should be related closely. This meaning in reality is the formation of the huge group of functions which has optimum scale(η). This is a giant enterprise or a group formation of enterprise.

Here,

$$Y_{g(k)} = \int_0^\infty g(k) \cdot f'(k)\, dk$$

Then, if the saving ratio is constant, because $Y_{g(k)} < Y_{\bar{g}(k)}$, we can conclud that in the movement of

capital the concentration accelelats the accumulation and the accumulation accelelates the concentration. We can define this functional concept of capital movement as the concentrated acuumulation
of capital. Economic development proceeds through this concentrated accumulation of capital. This
is not only the economic growth but also the change of structure in space and in organization.

Regarding growth, it is notable that the concentration of nation-wide capital is cohesive in the urban
area, but this means at the same time the expansion of optimum area in density. Some times we call
it the dispartion of urban function. But it does not mean the dispartion beyond this expansion scale.
Concentration and dispartion will balance at this line of η. If this scale covers several cities, we can say
megalopolis formation.* In case of EC-Central, it covers wider area beyond national boundaries.

Regarding organization, a big enterprise divides their business scale to several section or makes
a group with the related companies. This type activity in management is aimed to establish the group
of this optimum scale management unit. Such a group is also able to spread out as a multi-national
enterprise.

These two type movements in space or in organization have no relation each other except only
macro aggregate identity.** This is the problem between national sovereign and multinational enterprise.

---

*Note

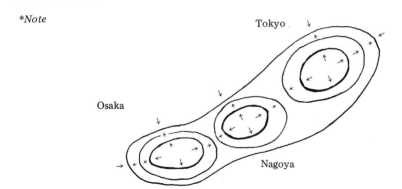

Tokaido Megalopolis (Tokyo-Nagoya-Osaka) is forming through this mechanism. Concentrated
accumulation of capital was proceeded, one way was concentration from other of Japan, another
way was expansion (dispartion) from inside of cities. Density of η covers Tokyo Nagoya Osaka,
then Central Japan Concentrated Accumulations of capital (Megalopolis) expands east and west.
Almost of the same reasons and ways we can see in case of the amalgamation of Yahata with Fuji
Iron and Steel Company for making New Japan Iron and Steel Co. Ltd.

**Note

$$\int_0^\infty g(k_s) \cdot f'(k_s)dk \equiv \int_0^\infty g(k_b) \cdot f'(k_b)dk \qquad \text{though} \qquad f'(k_s) \neq f'(k_b)$$

3) Two sectors case*

Suppose sector A and sector B have their own functions denoted in Fig. 4.

Fig. 4

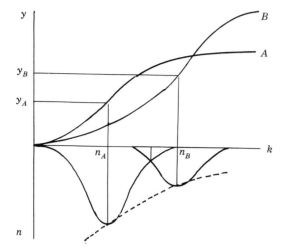

In this case sector B concentrates with density η_B, and sector A concentrates with density η_A. But sector A can not enter in the area of sector B, and if a part of sector A were in the area of sector B it should be out from that area. This means the rule that the same functions come together each other and different functions separate each other. (specialization and separation rule)

We have assumed demand and supply should be located closely. Then sector A and sector B are located as shown in Fig. 5^a. This mechanism, without saying, is true in case of organization. Group B should be a inner group of industrial organization. In due course of time, technological changes are so rapid to exchange the function A and B in its own position. We can say it as the substitution of functions in space or in organization. This is a structural change in spacial order or organization. This

---

* Note

    This corresponds the two sector case of Hori in this book, but here I also add the distribution of unit of management in each sector. The total distribution of k is decreasing function of k (dotted line). This coresponds a problem of Kurabayashi's in this book: distribution of assets.

means an other rule that an industry which has comperatively high value added productivity locates innercircle in space and in organization. When sector A, sector B and sector C, for instance office (management and administration), housing (consumption) and factory (production) have the same productivity, they may locate as Fig. 5^b.

These space structure will be decided through the balance between scale of management and scale of space. This means the type of human settlement (town or city) is a shadow of the organization

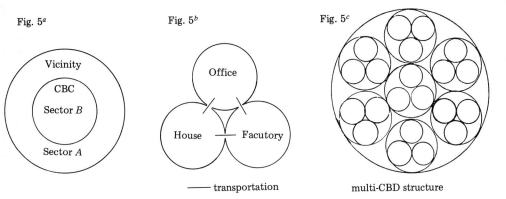

Fig. 5^a Fig. 5^b Fig. 5^c

——— transportation   multi-CBD structure

in the economic society. The difference between London and Tokyo is the difference between English and Japanese economic society.*

3. Supply of Space

Space has been treated as a neutral pure space without any charactor in section 1)-3). Space is dimension like time in ordinary economic theory. But space has its special charactors in ecological sence or in natural circulation. Some of these charactors sustain economic activities in case of industrized society in which natural productivity is not important different from agriculture. Then we can treat the space which sustains economic activities as a resource.

Economic activity will consume this resource indue course of time. In addition that, changing location will deteriolate the value of space, even in case of unchanged comparative location in the system of economy, distinguishing it from consumption of the space.

———————

* Note

Fukuchi's and Kozima's contributions are in this field. I would like to emphasize the mutual influences between space structure and structure of society.

Against this consumption of space, we can define excess production or excess supply of space, if social overhead capital $(SOC)^*$ invested to the space it will make upward and right hand shift of the function offseting obsolessence and consumption. This shift increases the optimum density level to the right hand.

In this way we can get another function between yb, k and z, if we devide yb and z by k, we obtain

$$y_b/k_b = f(z_b/k_b)$$

Here z is a density of social overhead capital.

Again we can assum function as shown in Fig. 6.

Fig. 6

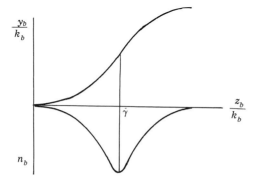

According to the same logic in section 1)-3), γ is the optimum ratio balancing the supply of space and demand for space. If $z/k > \gamma$, we can say advanced SOC, in this case private producing investment

Notes*

    (1) SOC means not only infrastructure investment like transportation and urban renewals but also investment to support the ecological balance and thermal balance etc.

    (2)   In spite of this SOC controll, when we can not induce private capital, we have an other policy measure. That is a redistribution of effective demand to that space, e.g. : redistribution income in space and organization. The former is the policy to transfer supply power, and the latter is the policy to transfer effective demand. These are two major policy instruments in spacial development.

    (3)   We can use this ratio for public share of capital formation. This two types of transfer are important issue for the problems retated to obtimum share of government in national economy.

should be induced to such space. And z/k will decrease. If $z/k < \gamma$, we can say delayed SOC, in this case private capital should be shifted to the other space from this area. And z/k will increase. Or we can say we have a demand for policy to invest SOC.

When the distribution pattern of space comes to the shape depicted in Fig. 6, k which coresponds to γ is the optimum k. So that $z/k = \gamma$ is the optimum density of SOC.

At this balance γ is the ratio by which the total capital formation divides SOC investment and private producing investment. Because our assumption shows that marginal principle works here, too.

Narrow country like Japan can only sustain her development shairing the capital formation to SOC investment to keep the ratio γ. This ratio z/k is an important policy measure in the field of regional development.

4. Addition New Factor of Production

In this high densely populated area, the communications of people are tremendously increased not only through the sociocultural activities but also through the economic activities.

This is a situation as such that people can accumulate their knowledges rapidly. Knowledge is a new factor of production which obsolessence may be much more rapid comparing in capital case. We can treat a knowledge problem which is embodied in capital itself. But that type of knowledge is a knowledge which consumed in capital goods production process.

What we are treating here is a knowledge which embodied in human himself different from neoclassical convension.* If we denote

    ws: scale of knowledge embodies in unit management,

    wb: density of knowledge accumulated in unit space,

we can reach the same conclusions in section 1)-3) through the same logic. We can say the law of concentrated accumulation of knowledge. This is of cource much more important than the concentrated accumulation of labor or population to the cities and groups of enterprises.

5. Conbination of Capital and Knowledge

Knowledges are embodied in human himself, this means the ownership of knowledge belongs to human individuals.

We have assumed L/K is constant, but w/k is possible to change industry by industry different from in the case of z. So that we can find some rules as like as section 3).

You can find in Fig. 7, high level of w in industry promises high level of marginal productivity comparing with k level.

---

*Note

    There are several ways to realize the knowledge variable. Cummulative index of experience period and education among people is one of them.

Fig. 7

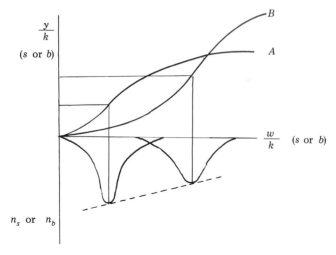

As like as in Fig. 4, inner circle corresponds to the industry which has higher level of w. Substitution of functions above mentioned works here between inner circle and outer circle. This means at same time the substitution between capital and knowledge. This is the mechanism in transition from the age of industiralization to the age of knowledge. Urban area will become much more knowledge oriented, and industrial organization will become much more knowledge oriented.

This means that in the city soft structure of society or community is more important than hard structure, and that in industry technological links and market links as a social contract is more important than capital ownership controll. The change from economic absolutism to economic constitutionalism is the fact in rationalism.

In this context the fact that the ownership of knowledge is individual person is very important. Everybody has its own right to keep his knowledge for himself, and he can bot lost it except in case of obsolessence.

6.   Supply of New Organization

To sustain the mechanism of concentrated accumulation of capital, the condition needed is the supply of new space which has the capital density level to promise increasing return of value added. This supply of new space becomes possible to use social overhead capital. The condition needed to sustain the mechanism for making optimum group organization is a new entry of the management which is small but with increasing return of value added.

Such a new entry is only possible in case that he is equiped with new technology which is new knowledge. We can say it information when knowledge can be conveted to the form of conveyable.

Organization needs the system to organize its own participants. This means organization needs a certain level common knowledge which is conveying from each other in the form of informations. Common knowledge is also a basis of production of knowledge.

We can take about knowledge consumption and production now using the concept of common knowledge as like as social overhead capital. Expansion of knowledge by using the knoledge is a kind of consumption of knowledge, but it is produced through all activities with common knowledge. If the level of common knoeledge, denoted here vs or vb, comparing with private knowledge ws or wb, are possible to shift the functions to upward and right hand, we can say excess supply of new entry which has increasing patern of value added.

Then we can obtain the same conclusions as in case of z. If $v/w > \delta$, we can say advanced common knowledge. This is a situation such that the education advanced beyond the level to sustain the system of social and economic organization. If $v/w < \delta$, we need much more education to sustain the system of society. Here δ is the optimum ratio of v/w corresponding the turning point of the function.

The supply of new entry equiped new technology will balance at δ with the demand which sustains the mechanism of concentrated accumulation of knowledge, if the level of optimum in the sence of knowledge keeps at η. Here it is notable that the policy of education is a great measure for development as like as a social overhead capital formation. New entry supplied by this measure is a basic condition to renewal industrial organization.

7.   Stability of the Society

Above mentioned theory clearly denied the case ultimated concentration of capital and of knowledge.

Expostly capital density and capital scale, and knowledge dencity and knowledge scale are distributed in the time to time. This distribution pattern is not decided clearly, sometime it will be disparsed and sometime it will be contracted arround the optimum level.

This is a result of concentrated accumulation of capital and of knowledge with appropriate policy for social overhead capital and of education.

We can say the system of this order, as the division of space and the division of organization. The cordination between spacial order of many regions or nations and organizational order of many groups of economic subject especially enterprise is world wide crucial problem now we are confronting.

The theory presented in this paper is so simple to solve the real problem but it can explain the major context of this matter. These models and analytical devices are sometimes such that certain new results are induced very carefully and sometimes such that new ideas are audaciously prompted.

References

[1] Fujii, T., "Economic Space of Japanese Archipelago", *Pacific Conference on Urban Growth,* Honolulu: May, 1967. The title of original paper is "Jinko Shihon no Shuseki to Keizai Seicho (Concentrated-accumulations of Population and Capital and Economic Growth)" in *Keizaiken-kyu (The Economic Review)* Vol. 17, No. 4, 1966.

[2] Fujii, T., "An Economic Space Theory of Urban Growth," Above-mentioned Conference: May, 1967.

[3] Fujii, T., "On Development Policy of the Chubu Region." Three Lectures on Regional Development at Nagoya published UN Center for Regional Development, 1969.

[4] Fujii, T., "A Theory of Urban Growth and Economic Progress — The Aim and Theory of Regional Development in Organized Society," *International Conference: The World in 2000,* Tokyo: Sept., 1967.

[5] Fujii, T., "Metropolitan Development in Japan," *The 3rd International Symposium on Regional Development:* Sept., 1969, Tokyo.

[6] Report on Pacific Conference on Urban Growth, Honolulu, May, 1967, *The New Urban Detate,* Agency for International Development, Washington, D.C., Feb., 1968.

Authors List

1. Ryuzo Sato

   Professor of Economics, Brown University, Providence, R.I. 02912, U.S.A.

2. Yoshio Kimura

   Professor of Economics, Nagoya City University, Mizufo-cho, Mizufo-ku, Nagoya, Japan.

3. Takashi Negishi

   Professor of Economics, Tokyo University, Hongo, Bunkyo-ku, Tokyo, Japan.

4. Tadashi Minagawa

   Lecturer of Economics, Nagoya University, Furoh-cho, Chikusa-ku, Nagoya, Japan.

5. Yoshimasa Kurabayashi

   Professor of Economics, Hitotsubashi University.

   Atsuo Yatsuka

   Graduate Student, Hitotsubashi University, Kunitachi, Tokyo, Japan.

6. Hajime Hori

   Associate Professor of Economics, Tohoku University, Katahira, Sendai-shi, Miyagi-ken, Japan.

7. Koji Okuguchi

   Associate Professor of Economics, Tokyo Metropolitan University, Yagumo, Meguro-ku, Tokyo, Japan.

8. Akira Takayama

   Professor of Economics, Purdue University, West Lafayette, Indiana, 47907, U.S.A.

9. Takayoshi Umeshita

   Associate Professor of Economics, Aichi University of Education, Hirosawa, Igaya-cho, Kariya-shi, Aichi-ken, Japan.

10. Martin J. Beckmann

    Professor of Economics, Brown University, Providence, R.I. 02912, U.S.A.

11. Kenji Kojima

    Lecturer of Economics, Oita University, Tannohara, Oita-shi, Oita-ken, Japan.

12. Takao Fukuchi

    Professor of Economics, Tsukuba University, Sakura-mura, Niiharu-gun, Ibaragi-ken. Japan.

13. Takashi Fujii

    Professor of Economics, Nagoya University, Furoh-cho, Chikusa-ku, Nagoya, Japan.

Vol. 59: J. A. Hanson, Growth in Open Economies. V, 128 pages. 1971.

Vol. 60: H. Hauptmann, Schätz- und Kontrolltheorie in stetigen dynamischen Wirtschaftsmodellen. V, 104 Seiten. 1971.

Vol. 61: K. H. F. Meyer, Wartesysteme mit variabler Bearbeitungsrate. VII, 314 Seiten. 1971.

Vol. 62: W. Krelle u. G. Gabisch unter Mitarbeit von J. Burgermeister, Wachstumstheorie. VII, 223 Seiten. 1972.

Vol. 63: J. Kohlas, Monte Carlo Simulation im Operations Research. VI, 162 Seiten. 1972.

Vol. 64: P. Gessner u. K. Spremann, Optimierung in Funktionenräumen. IV, 120 Seiten. 1972.

Vol. 65: W. Everling, Exercises in Computer Systems Analysis. VIII, 184 pages. 1972.

Vol. 66: F. Bauer, P. Garabedian and D. Korn, Supercritical Wing Sections. V, 211 pages. 1972.

Vol. 67: I. V. Girsanov, Lectures on Mathematical Theory of Extremum Problems. V, 136 pages. 1972.

Vol. 68: J. Loeckx, Computability and Decidability. An Introduction for Students of Computer Science. VI, 76 pages. 1972.

Vol. 69: S. Ashour, Sequencing Theory. V, 133 pages. 1972.

Vol. 70: J. P. Brown, The Economic Effects of Floods. Investigations of a Stochastic Model of Rational Investment. Behavior in the Face of Floods. V, 87 pages. 1972.

Vol. 71: R. Henn und O. Opitz, Konsum- und Produktionstheorie II. V, 134 Seiten. 1972.

Vol. 72: T. P. Bagchi and J. G. C. Templeton, Numerical Methods in Markov Chains and Bulk Queues. XI, 89 pages. 1972.

Vol. 73: H. Kiendl, Suboptimale Regler mit abschnittweise linearer Struktur. VI, 146 Seiten. 1972.

Vol. 74: F. Pokropp, Aggregation von Produktionsfunktionen. VI, 107 Seiten. 1972.

Vol. 75: GI-Gesellschaft für Informatik e.V. Bericht Nr. 3. 1. Fachtagung über Programmiersprachen · München, 9.–11. März 1971. Herausgegeben im Auftrag der Gesellschaft für Informatik von H. Langmaack und M. Paul. VII, 280 Seiten. 1972.

Vol. 76: G. Fandel, Optimale Entscheidung bei mehrfacher Zielsetzung. II, 121 Seiten. 1972.

Vol. 77: A. Auslender, Problèmes de Minimax via l'Analyse Convexe et les Inégalités Variationelles: Théorie et Algorithmes. VII, 132 pages. 1972.

Vol. 78: GI-Gesellschaft für Informatik e.V. 2. Jahrestagung, Karlsruhe, 2.–4. Oktober 1972. Herausgegeben im Auftrag der Gesellschaft für Informatik von P. Deussen. XI, 576 Seiten. 1973.

Vol. 79: A. Berman, Cones, Matrices and Mathematical Programming. V, 96 pages. 1973.

Vol. 80: International Seminar on Trends in Mathematical Modelling, Venice, 13–18 December 1971. Edited by N. Hawkes. VI, 288 pages. 1973.

Vol. 81: Advanced Course on Software Engineering. Edited by F. L. Bauer. XII, 545 pages. 1973.

Vol. 82: R. Saeks, Resolution Space, Operators and Systems. X, 267 pages. 1973.

Vol. 83: NTG/GI-Gesellschaft für Informatik, Nachrichtentechnische Gesellschaft. Fachtagung „Cognitive Verfahren und Systeme", Hamburg, 11.–13. April 1973. Herausgegeben im Auftrag der NTG/GI von Th. Einsele, W. Giloi und H.-H. Nagel. VIII, 373 Seiten. 1973.

Vol. 84: A. V. Balakrishnan, Stochastic Differential Systems I. Filtering and Control. A Function Space Approach. V, 252 pages. 1973.

Vol. 85: T. Page, Economics of Involuntary Transfers: A Unified Approach to Pollution and Congestion Externalities. XI, 159 pages. 1973.

Vol. 86: Symposium on the Theory of Scheduling and its Applications. Edited by S. E. Elmaghraby. VIII, 437 pages. 1973.

Vol. 87: G. F. Newell, Approximate Stochastic Behavior of n-Server Service Systems with Large n. VII, 118 pages. 1973.

Vol. 88: H. Steckhan, Güterströme in Netzen. VII, 134 Seiten. 1973.

Vol. 89: J. P. Wallace and A. Sherret, Estimation of Product. Attributes and Their Importances. V, 94 pages. 1973.

Vol. 90: J.-F. Richard, Posterior and Predictive Densities for Simultaneous Equation Models. VI, 226 pages. 1973.

Vol. 91: Th. Marschak and R. Selten, General Equilibrium with Price-Making Firms. XI, 246 pages. 1974.

Vol. 92: E. Dierker, Topological Methods in Walrasian Economics. IV, 130 pages. 1974.

Vol. 93: 4th IFAC/IFIP International Conference on Digital Computer Applications to Process Control, Part I. Zürich/Switzerland, March 19–22, 1974. Edited by M. Mansour and W. Schaufelberger. XVIII, 544 pages. 1974.

Vol. 94: 4th IFAC/IFIP International Conference on Digital Computer Applications to Process Control, Part II. Zürich/Switzerland, March 19–22, 1974. Edited by M. Mansour and W. Schaufelberger. XVIII, 546 pages. 1974.

Vol. 95: M. Zeleny, Linear Multiobjective Programming. X, 220 pages. 1974.

Vol. 96: O. Moeschlin, Zur Theorie von Neumannscher Wachstumsmodelle. XI, 115 Seiten. 1974.

Vol. 97: G. Schmidt, Über die Stabilität des einfachen Bedienungskanals. VII, 147 Seiten. 1974.

Vol. 98: Mathematical Methods in Queueing Theory. Proceedings 1973. Edited by A. B. Clarke. VII, 374 pages. 1974.

Vol. 99: Production Theory. Edited by W. Eichhorn, R. Henn, O. Opitz, and R. W. Shephard. VIII, 386 pages. 1974.

Vol. 100: B. S. Duran and P. L. Odell, Cluster Analysis. A Survey. VI, 137 pages. 1974.

Vol. 101: W. M. Wonham, Linear Multivariable Control. A Geometric Approach. X, 344 pages. 1974.

Vol. 102: Analyse Convexe et Ses Applications. Comptes Rendus, Janvier 1974. Edited by J.-P. Aubin. IV, 244 pages. 1974.

Vol. 103: D. E. Boyce, A. Farhi, R. Weischedel, Optimal Subset Selection. Multiple Regression, Interdependence and Optimal Network Algorithms. XIII, 187 pages. 1974.

Vol. 104: S. Fujino, A Neo-Keynesian Theory of Inflation and Economic Growth. V, 96 pages. 1974.

Vol. 105: Optimal Control Theory and its Applications. Part I. Proceedings 1973. Edited by B. J. Kirby. VI, 425 pages. 1974.

Vol. 106: Optimal Control Theory and its Applications. Part II. Proceedings 1973. Edited by B. J. Kirby. VI, 403 pages. 1974.

Vol. 107: Control Theory, Numerical Methods and Computer Systems Modeling. International Symposium, Rocquencourt, June 17–21, 1974. Edited by A. Bensoussan and J. L. Lions. VIII, 757 pages. 1975.

Vol. 108: F. Bauer et al., Supercritical Wing Sections II. A Handbook. V, 296 pages. 1975.

Vol. 109: R. von Randow, Introduction to the Theory of Matroids. IX, 102 pages. 1975.

Vol. 110: C. Striebel, Optimal Control of Discrete Time Stochastic Systems. III. 208 pages. 1975.

Vol. 111: Variable Structure Systems with Application to Economics and Biology. Proceedings 1974. Edited by A. Ruberti and R. R. Mohler. VI, 321 pages. 1975.

Vol. 112: J. Wilhlem, Objectives and Multi-Objective Decision Making Under Uncertainty. IV, 111 pages. 1975.

Vol. 113: G. A. Aschinger, Stabilitätsaussagen über Klassen von Matrizen mit verschwindenden Zeilensummen. V, 102 Seiten. 1975.

Vol. 114: G. Uebe, Produktionstheorie. XVII, 301 Seiten. 1976.